THE INSTITUTE OF ASIAN ECONOMIC AFFAIRS

THE CURRENCY AND FINANCIAL SYSTEM OF MAINLAND CHINA

BY TADAO MIYASHITA

UNIVERSITY OF WASHINGTON PRESS

Translated by J. R. McEwan
from the Japanese text

Printed in Japan by the
Daini Insatsu Printing Co., Ltd.

The People's Bank of China
(Head Office)

People's Currency

Five *yüan* note (obverse)

ALL PHOTOGRAPHS ARE NATURAL SIZE.

People's Currency

Five *yüan* note (reverse)

People's Currency

Two *yüan* note (obverse)

People's Currency

One *yüan* note (obverse)

Subsidiary Paper Currency

People's Currency

Five *chiao* note (obverse)

People's Currency

Two *chiao* note (obverse)

Two *chiao* note (obverse)

One *chiao* note (obverse)

One *fen* note (obverse)

Subsidiary Coin Currency

Five *fen*

Two *fen*

One *fen*

(obverse on left)

FOREWORD

Since its inauguration in 1958 the Institute of Asian Economic Affairs has produced a large number of research publications. These are concerned not only with the Asian region but also with all the so-called " developing countries," including those in Africa and Latin America. In the process of producing these results we have enjoyed the co-operation of many scholars and specialists from outside the Institute, as well as relying upon the members of our own staff, the training of whom is one of the missions with which the Institute is charged, and in which field notable successes are also being achieved.

The present work represents the results of research carried out for the Institute by Professor Tadao Miyashita of Kōbe University as a part of the Institute's research programme for the year 1963. We have already published this work in Japanese in March, 1965, under the title *Chūgoku no Tsūka Kinyū Seido* 中國の通貨・金融制度, Asian Economic Research Studies Series, No. 115, and we are now publishing an English version in order to make it available to foreign research workers and industrialists.

The aim of this study is to elucidate the nature of the Chinese currency system, centred on the People's Currency, and the Chinese financial system, centred on the People's Bank of China. In the running of socialist economy the currency and the organs of finance perform special functions which differ from those performed under a capitalist system, and, as need hardly be said, they are much subject to influence from current economic development and economic policy. These facts necessitate the following two demands on the student. First, he must continually bear in mind the economic development and economic policies under the Communist system which form the basis of the currency and financial systems, and he must make clear the connexions between them at each point in time. Such a mode of working may also produce the result of being of great assistance in achieving a deeper understanding of economic development and economic policies under the Communist system. Second, he must not merely treat the currency and financial systems as static entities at different points in time, but must grasp the long-term as well as the short-term processes through which they change. This method will also be of assistance in making more precise the point of view adopted under the first head.

From this point of view the present work faithfully traces the history of the currency and financial systems under Communist rule, from November, 1931, when the Chinese Communist Party got its first currency policy, down to the present day. In this matter one of the special characteristics of this work which we may mention is the fact that original sources in the Chinese language have been employed. Further, we know of no other work on these questions in which the subject is treated as systematically as in the present study.

The author, Professor Tadao Miyashita, is a specialist who has been engaged in the study of the Chinese currency and financial systems for many years, and who has published many works dealing with this field. The present work is the product of studies of new objects of research, based on the results of the author's earlier work and the vast body of source material accumulated in the course of it. The author has also had the opportunity to confirm the results of his many years of study on the spot by his recent visit to China, which is fully made use of in the present work. It is a great pleasure for us to add this work to the Institute's *English Research Report Series,* and we are confident that it will be fully appreciated by those who use it.

December, 1965.

SEIICHI TŌBATA

President

PREFACE

This book is a study of the currency system of China, centred on the People's Currency, and of the mechanisms of the Chinese financial system, centred on the People's Bank of China.

In carrying out this study, particular attention has been paid to the following three points.

1. The main emphasis has been placed on an examination of the currency and financial system of the People's Republic of China, but efforts have also been made to make clear its historical background. This is why the author has gone back to the period of the Chinese Soviets and the period of the Border Areas to give an account of the historical development of the currency and financial system of the Chinese Communist Party.

2. Although this study is concerned with currency and financial systems, the policies which set the keynote for the operation of this system have also been subjected to examination and efforts have been made to elucidate these matters in relation to the development of the Chinese economy in general.

3. As far as possible efforts have been made to go back to primary sources, and references to the sources used have been given.

The book consists of eight chapters. In Chapter I the currencies and currency policies in the Chinese Soviet set up at Juichin by the Chinese Communist Party in November, 1931, and in the Shanpei Soviet after the arrival of the Chinese Communist armies at Yenan in October, 1935, are examined. In Chapter II an examination is made of the Border Currencies issued in the Border Areas by the Chinese Communist Party and the currencies issued by them in the Liberated Areas during the period of the war between China and Japan and the period following it. In particular, a detailed examination has been made of the economy and Border Currency of the Shan-Kan-Ning Border Area. In Chapter III the following two questions are dealt with. The first is the process of the unification of the Chinese currency system under the People's Currency. The second is the question of the value of the People's Currency and its stabilization. Chapter IV contains an examination of the price question which became marked between 1956 and 1957, in the latter period of the First Five-Year Plan. In Chapter V, after giving a general account of the various types of financial organ, the cash control and currency control systems are analysed. In Chapter VI an examination is made of the process by which 60 Shanghai banks, native banks and trust companies were eventually organized into a single joint state-private bank. In Chapter VII an examination is made of a number of questions which have recently arisen in Chinese financial policy. Among them the following three questions have been given particular attention. The first is the strengthening of the banks' credit loan policy. The second is the supply of agricultural credit funds by the state. The third is the supply of liquid funds to state enterprises by the state. In Chapter VIII, after giving a general account of the meaning, types and functions of the Chinese rural credit co-operative organizations, an examination is made of the historical development of these organizations, going back to the period of the Shan-Kan-Ning Border Area.

I began work on the study of the currency and financial system of China in 1932, when I took up a teaching post at Tung Wen College, Shanghai, on graduating from university. Since then more than thirty years have passed. During this period I have published seven volumes in Japanese on the subject of the currency and financial system of China. However, these books were concerned with a historical examination of the currency and financial system of China in the period between the end of the Ch'ing dynasty and the war between China and Japan. This is my first book which includes studies of the currency and financial system of the People's Republic of China.

In December, 1964, I travelled in China for the first time in 19 years, and was able to make observations of the state of currency and finance in that country. The new knowledge which I obtained on this occasion has been added in the Postscript at the end of this book.

I hope that the publication of this book will provide an opportunity for developing my studies one stage further. I earnestly look forward to criticism of the book.

The publication of this book is due to the special good offices of the Institute of Asian Economic Affairs. In translating the text into English, Dr. J. R. McEwan and the staff members of the English Editorial Section of the Institute have given their unstinted co-operation. To them, and to the Institute of Asian Economic Affairs, I wish to express my most profound thanks.

Kōbe University.
August, 1965.

T. MIYASHITA

CONTENTS

CHINESE MEASUREMENTS
(Conversion Table)

LENGTH

Li （里）:   1 *li* = 0.5 kilometres = 0.3107 miles
Ch'ih （尺）:   1 *ch'ih* = 0.3333 metres = 1.0936 feet

WEIGHT

Tan （擔） = Picul: 1 picul = 50 kilogrammes = 0.984 hundred-weights = 0.05 metric tons = 0.0492 long tons = 0.0551 short tons
Chin （斤） = Catty: 1 catty = 0.5 kilogrammes = 1.1023 pounds
Liang （兩） = Tael: 1 tael = 31.25 grammes = 1.1023 ounces

CAPACITY

Sheng （升）:   1 *sheng* = 1 litre
Mu （畝）:   1 *mu* = 0.0666 hectares = 0.1647 acres

THE CURRENCY AND FINANCIAL SYSTEM
OF MAINLAND CHINA

CHAPTER I

THE CURRENCIES AND CURRENCY POLICIES
OF THE CHINESE SOVIETS

INTRODUCTION

THE CHINESE Communist Party's issue of its own currency
and the effecting of its own currency policies date from the time
of the Party's establishment of the Provisional Government of
the Chinese Soviet Republic at Juichin in Kiangsi Province in
November, 1931. However, the Chinese Communist Party had
some previous experience of carrying out currency policies of its
own. These were the policy for the concentration of cash silver
enforced by the Chinese Communist Party at Wuhan on the 17th
of April, 1927, and the currency policies which followed this
measure in the succeeding three months. (All Chinese Communist
Party members had withdrawn from the Wuhan Government by
the 15th of July, 1927.)[1] At that time, however, the Chinese
Communist Party did not have a currency of its own. For this
reason we may say that the history of currency and currency
policies among the Chinese Communists begins in 1931.[2] It is

---

[1] See Yü Chieh-ch'iung, "The Monetary Crisis Connected with the Concentration
of Silver in Wuhan in the 16th year of the Chinese Republic," *Shehui K'ohsüeh Tsachih*,
Vol. VI, No. 4 (Dec., 1936). For an account of the influence exercised on the silver
tael system of Hank'ou by this policy of the Chinese Communists, see Tadao
Miyashita, *A Specialized Study of the Chinese Currency System—A Study of the Silver Tael
System in Modern China* (Tokyo, 1952), pp. 271–272.

[2] Shang Ming has said, "In April, 1928, shortly after the engagement at Ching-
kangshan, the P'ing Min Bank issued 'currency of the people' for the first time at
Tungku, and later such currency was also issued by the Minhsi Revolutionary Base
in western Fukien. The currency system made especially notable progress from its
previous condition after the establishment of the Central Workers' and Peasants'

also for this reason that before examining the currency and financial systems associated with the People's Currency (人民幣), the present currency of Communist China, we propose first to look at the currency and currency policies of the Chinese Soviets.

I. The Aims of the Currency Policies of the Chinese Soviets

The Soviet Areas in China did not come into being as a single entity from the beginning, but were established at various places over a wide range of territory and developed along individual lines. In this point they were different from those in Soviet Russia. The first Soviet Area is taken to be the so-called Hai-Lu-Feng Soviet Area established by the remnants of Ho Lung's army in November, 1927, when they entered the Haifeng and Lufeng areas of Kwangtung Province. The army of Ho Lung and Yeh T'ing, which had raised a rebellion in Nanch'ang in August of the same year, had been pursued into Fukien Province by the Kuomintang army led by Chang Fa-kuei and Chu P'ei-te, and, having by-passed Swatow and headed for Canton, had been defeated by the army of Li Chi-shen. Shortly afterwards, on the 11th of December, the workers and peasants of Canton rose and proclaimed the establishment of a Soviet régime, and maintained that régime during their three-days' resistance to the forces of the Kuomintang army. By the establishment of these two Soviet régimes in the Hai-Lu-Feng Area and in Canton the Chinese Revolution entered the new stage of a Soviet Revolution. However, in the early years of the Chinese Soviet movement, from 1928 to about 1930, the Chinese Soviets were not yet firmly constituted, nor did they control large areas of territory, and consequently the Chinese Soviets did not have any established

Democratic Government at Juichin in Kiangsi Province in 1931." [Shang Ming, "The Achievement of the Chinese Currency Policy," in *The Significance and Functioning of the New People's Currency* (Peking, 1955), p. 45.] Apart from the above, there are a number of scholars on the side of New China who mention the issue of currency by the Chinese Communist Party before the establishment of the Juichin government. On this question, the present writer feels that he would like to press his examination further.

economic policy. In response to the needs of partisan warfare the economic policies of the Chinese Soviets at this period were · directed towards the expropriation of counter-revolutionaries and the utilization of existing accumulations of capital. However, while the Chinese Soviet Areas developed and became stronger and more stable after 1931, the direction of the efforts of the now mature Red Army into the fields of large-scale operations, mechanized warfare, and warfare from fixed positions made the questions of positive economic construction in the Chinese Soviets increasingly urgent.

On the 7th of November, 1931, the First National Congress of the Chinese Soviets was opened at Juichin in Kiangsi Province, and on the basis of the resolutions passed at this Congress the Provisional Government of the Chinese Soviet Republic was set up on the same day. For the following three years the Chinese Soviets, with their centre at Juichin, set themselves in opposition to the government of the Kuomintang. On several occasions after 1930 Chiang Kai-shek carried out " wei chao " (圍剿), or encircling attacks, against the Chinese Soviets, both on the military and economic fronts. In November, 1934, the Chinese Communists abandoned Juichin, and between that time and October of the following year they made the "long march of 25,000 li " to Yenan in Shensi Province, where they undertook the expansion and strengthening of the Shanpei Soviet.

The Chinese Soviets came into possession of a programme governing a unified and established economic policy for the first time after the First National Congress of the Chinese Soviets which we have mentioned above. The Congress passed "Resolutions concerning Economic Policy," and these were nothing other than a programme for the Chinese Soviets in economic policy. The Resolutions were drawn up by the Central Committee of the Chinese Communist Party. The Resolutions are headed by the statement, " For the development of anti-imperialism and agrarian revolution and for the strengthening of the revolutionary alliance of workers and peasants, the First National Congress of the Chinese Soviets has laid down the following articles as the basis of economic policy in the Soviets." After this preamble, the articles are set out under four heads, (1) Industry, (2) Commerce, (3) Financial Administration and Taxation, and (4) Municipal

Administration.[3]

At present we do not propose to go into the details of these Resolutions, but it may be necessary for us to note briefly that by this time the Li Li-san line, which had been the revolutionary line of the Chinese Communist Party between 1929 and 1930, had been buried, and that the tone was now set by the Mao Tse-tung line. In connexion with this point, we will do well to listen to G. Kara Murza's opinion, that the economic policy of the period of the Chinese Soviet Republic was established on the basis of the following three principal elements.[4]

(1) The fact that the nature of the Chinese Revolution is such that at the present stage it is a bourgeois democratic revolution, the tasks of which are those of pursuing the struggle against imperialism and survivals of feudalism, and of raising the standard of living of the whole of the labouring masses.

(2) The fact that at present the Soviet Areas are on the whole located in agricultural regions, require military funds because they are in a state of incessant civil war, and possess no great industrial centres.

(3) The fact that at the present stage the future of the Chinese Revolution requires not only the creation of political preconditions but also the creation of economic preconditions for the development of the Chinese people's economy along noncapitalist lines.

We may pick out the following from the regulations governing currency, banks and finance in the Resolutions concerning economic policy which we have mentioned above.

(1) All differences in the market value of old currencies within the Soviet Areas are declared void, and all currencies will circulate within these Areas on an equal footing. To this is added the provision that the Soviet governments shall carry out inspection in regard to such currencies, and shall stamp

---

3 The complete text of the Resolutions concerning Economic Policy of the Chinese Soviets is given in Tōa Keizai Chōsa Kyoku, *A Study of the Chinese Soviet Movement* (Tokyo, 1934), pp. 259–262, and in Torao Himori, " The Chinese Red Army and the State of the Development of the Soviet Areas -II-," *MCG*, Vol. XII, No. 9 (Sept., 1932), pp. 93–97.

4 G. Kara Murza, " The Economic Policies of the Chinese Soviet Areas," *MCG*, Vol. XVI, No. 5 (May, 1936), pp. 178–179 (translated into Japanese by Shichirō Homma).

or mark them in order to facilitate efficiency of supervision. The Soviet governments are empowered to issue their own currencies and to exchange them for old currencies and to exchange currencies stamped or marked by the Soviets, or issued by the Soviets, for the currencies from outside areas, and are required to ensure that it shall be possible for such currencies to circulate within their Soviets. (Section 3, Financial Administration and Taxation, sub-section 3.)

(2)   In order to put into effect a unified currency system and to assist the whole of the labouring masses, the Soviet government must set up a Workers' and Peasants' Bank, and establish its branches in each Soviet Area. This Bank is to have the right to issue currency. The Workers' and Peasants' Bank is required to lend money to peasants, handicraftsmen, small merchants, and co-operatives, in such a manner as to promote the development of their economies. The Bank will exchange currency, and its branches will carry out the collection of taxes in addition to their functions as banks. (Section 3, sub-section 4.)

(3)   In regard to the locally established private large banks and native banks (*ch'ien chuang*: 錢莊), the organs of the Soviets must send representatives to supervise their activities. These banks are absolutely forbidden to issue currency of whatever kind, and the organs of the Soviets must decisively forbid all attempts on the part of bankers to use their banks for counter-revolutionary purposes. (Section 3, sub-section 5.)

(4)   Trade and commerce with areas outside the Soviets are permitted, but it is absolutely forbidden for external trade to be caused to be monopolized. At the same time, the Soviet governments must carry out supervision of these forms of trade, in such a manner as to assure the supply of the commodities urgently required by the Soviet Areas. Again, the permission of the local Soviet government is required for the export of silver currency. (Section 2, Commerce, sub-section 2.)

We are not able to make sure whether the Chinese Communist Party's issue of its own currency and the effecting of its own currency policy started from the above Resolutions or not, but at least it will become clear as our discussion proceeds that they started about the time when these Resolutions were made in 1931.

The Chinese Soviet Areas extended over a number of Provinces, and their boundaries were fluid, depending on the state of military operations. In the report made to the Shanghai Party Centre from the First National Congress of the Chinese Soviets which was held on the 7th of November, 1931, it is stated that at that time there were seven Soviet Areas, (1) the Central Area (the Juichin Area in Kiangsi Province), (2) the North-Western Area of Fukien Province, (3) the Hunan-Anhui Border Area, (4) Hunan-Kiangsi Border Area, (5) the Hunan-Hupei-North-Eastern Kiangsi Area, (6) the Hunan-Hupei-Western Border Area, and (7) the Hainan Area (Kwangtung Province). At the time of the Second National Congress of the Chinese Soviets held in January, 1934, it was announced that the Red Army comprised 200,000 personnel, the Communist Party 300,000, and the population of the Soviet Areas more than 50,000,000. In October, 1934, immediately before the abandonment of Juichin, the Chinese Soviet Areas consisted of the following seven great Soviet Areas. (1) The Central Area (This was the site of the central government. It was centred on the capital, Juichin, and extended over the three Provinces of Kiangsi, Fukien and Kwangtung. It was the largest of the Soviet Areas), (2) The North-Eastern Kan Area (also called the Min-Che-Kan Area, this extended over the three Provinces of Kiangsi, Fukien, and Chekiang), (3) The Hsiang-O-Kan Area (an area extending along the boundaries of the Provinces of Hunan, Hupei and Kiangsi), (4) The Hsiang-Kan Area (an area extending along the boundaries of the Provinces of Hunan and Kiangsi), (5) The O-Yü-Wan Area (This extended over the three Provinces of Hupei, Honan, and Anhui), (6) The Hsiang-O-Hsi Area (This extended from the boundaries of Hunan and Hupei to the boundaries of Szechuan), and (7) The Ch'uan-Shan Area (This was the most recent Soviet Area, and extended from the northern parts of Szechuan to the boundary area of Shensi Province). That is to say, it appeared that at this time the Chinese Soviet Areas extended over an area mainly in the seven Provinces of Kiangsi, Hunan, Hupei, Anhui, Honan, Fukien and Szechuan, and ruled about one-sixth of the area and population of these provinces. Accordingly, it was estimated that the Chinese Soviets ruled an area of 100,000 square miles and a population of approximately

36,000,000.[5]   Further, the Chinese Soviet Areas were based on an agricultural economy, and in such industry as they possessed handicrafts and domestic industry were overwhelmingly predominant.

II. The Currencies of the Chinese Soviets

The following is an account of the currencies of the Chinese Soviets, as far as can be known from the written sources.[6]

1. Coins

The one *yüan* silver coin which must clearly be taken as having been minted in Hunan Province in 1931 has, on the obverse, the vertical inscription "One Yüan" (壹圓) enclosed in a laurel wreath or ears of corn, and on the reverse a star-shaped design enclosed in a small circle, with an axe and sickle in the centre of the star, and the inscription "The Hunan Soviet Government" (湖南省蘇維埃政府) round the upper circumference and the inscription "Made in 1931" (一九三一年製) round the lower circumference, written from right to left.

The following one *yüan* silver coins appear to have been minted in 1932.

One of these was issued in the Central Soviet Area, and bears a portrait of Lenin.   An inscription of twelve characters, " Made By the Chinese Central Soviet Provisional Government " (中華中央蘇維埃臨時政府造) is engraved round the upper circum-

---

5 Tōa Keizai Chōsa Kyoku, pp. 239–250; Shigezō Yoshikawa, *A Guide to Chinese Communism* (Tokyo, 1950), p. 6.

6 The sources for this section are as follows:

Eduard Kann, *History of Minting in China* (Shanghai, 1939), p. 46, or *The Central Bank of China Bulletin*, Vol. III, No. 1 (March, 1939), pp. 26–27; E. Kann, "Modern Banknotes of China," *Finance & Commerce*, Vol. XXX, No. 12 (Oct., 1937), pp. 268–269; Duncan Raeburn, "Chinese Soviet Coins and Notes," *China Journal of Science and Arts,* Vol. XXVI, No. 3 (March, 1937); Chiang Chung-ch'uan, *Illustrated Account of Chinese Gold, Silver and Nickel Coins* (Shanghai, 1939), pp. 237–241; Ch'i Ch'i-sheng, " Financial Policy in the Red Areas of China," *MCG,* Vol. XV, No. 12 (Dec., 1935), pp. 149–151. And also refer to illustrations at the beginning of *A Study of the Chinese Soviet Movement.*

ference, and a design of ears of corn round the lower circumference. On the back there are the two characters "One Yüan" (壹圓) in the centre, surmounted by the crossed axe and sickle. At the top of the upper circumference there is a star, and round the lower circumference the inscription "Minted A. D. 1932" (公曆 一九三二年鑄造). The others were issued for use in the Soviet Area in Hupei, Honan and Anhui, and there are two varieties of them. One of them has a central inscription "One Yüan" (壹圓), surrounded by a small circle, with the inscription "The Soviet Government of the O-Yü-Wan Provinces" (鄂豫皖省蘇維埃政府) round the upper circumference and "Made by the Workers' and Peasants' Bank, 1932" (工農銀行一九三二年造), written from left to right round the lower circumference. On the back there is a representation of a globe of the world, surrounded by a small circle, with the emblem of the axe and sickle in the centre of the figure. Round the circumference, surrounding the globe, there is the inscription, "Workers of the World, Unite!" (全世界無產階級聯 合起來啊) written from left to right. The obverse of the second variety of this coin has the central inscription "One Yüan" (壹圓), written from left to right, surrounded by a small circle, with the inscription "Made in 1932" round the upper circumference, and "CORETG HИSHKB IPEB" (meaning "The Chinese Soviet Republic") round the lower circumference. The reverse shows the globe in the centre, with the axe and sickle in a slightly different position, and it also differs in that the inscription "Workers of the World, Unite!" (全世界無產階級聯合起來啊) is written from the top of the circumference towards the right (whereas in the first variety of the coin the inscription runs from the left side towards the right). This coin bears no inscription referring specifically to the Soviet government which issued it, but since Eduard Kann considers it to have been issued by the Hunan-Hupei-Honan Soviet and Chiang Chung-ch'uan's illustration of the coin is accompanied by a note to the effect that the piece was collected in Chingfu *Hsien*, Honan, Province, we will probably not be mistaken if we assume it to have been issued by the O-Yü-Wan Soviet government.

As a coin minted in 1933 we may mention a piece issued in the Central Soviet Area. The obverse shows a profile head of Marx, with the inscription "State Currency of the Chinese Soviet

Republic" (中華蘇維埃共和國國幣) round the upper circumference, and "Made in A. D. 1933" (公曆一九三三年造) round the lower circumference. Two stars are set at the sides of the coin. On the reverse there is the inscription "One Yüan" (壹圓) in the centre, with the axe and sickle below. A star appears above the centre of the coin and the lower part is surrounded by a design of ears of corn.

It appears that a considerable quantity of one *yüan* silver coins was issued in Szechuan Province in 1934. One of these coins has the vertical inscription "One Yüan" (壹圓) enclosed in a dotted circle on the obverse, with the inscription "The Chinese Soviet Republic" (中華蘇維埃共和国) round the upper circumference and "Made at the Mint of the Ch'uan-Shan Provinces" (川陝省造幣廠造) round the lower circumference, written from right to left. The reverse shows the globe of the world, enclosed in a circle, with the design of the axe and sickle. The inscription "Workers of the World, Unite!" (全世界無産階級聯合起來) runs round the upper circumference and "1934" (一九三四年) is written from right to left round the lower circumference. However, it appears that there were many varieties of one *yüan* silver coins issued in Szechuan Province. E. Kann says, "The writer had, by the end of 1938, 15 differing coins of the Szechuan one silver piece in his collection, but undoubtedly many more exist, possibly 25 varieties, all of which are dated 1934."

We may now describe some coins which have no date inscription. One of these shows a full-face head of Lenin, while another shows a profile head of Lenin. The former has the inscription "State Currency of the Chinese Soviet Republic" (中國蘇維埃共和國國幣) above, and a design of corn ears below. The latter has the inscription "Made by the Chinese Soviets" (中國蘇維埃造) above, and a design of corn ears below. On the reverse sides of both coins there are the two characters "One Yüan" (壹圓) in the centre, with the axe and sickle below. The star appears in the centre of the upper circumference, while round the lower circumference there are two tendril designs. Ch'i Ch'i-sheng considers both of these to have been issued by the Hupei Central Soviet. E. Kann considers the latter coin to have been issued for the first time in Hunan Province in 1931 by the Chinese Soviets, but there is doubt about this testimony. This type of silver coin is illustrated in Chiang Chung-ch'uan's book, but with an annotation stating that the piece was acquired in Enshih *Hsien*, Hupei Province.

In Kiangsi Province, the location of the Central Soviet Area, one *yüan* silver coins were issued in the manner which we have described above, but the most widely used form of currency in this area was paper money, supplemented by issues of two *chiao* silver coins and five *fen* and one *fen* copper coins. On the obverse of the two *chiao* silver coins there is a central inscription "Two Chiao" (貳角), with "The Chinese Soviet Republic" (中華蘇維埃共和國) above, and "A. D. 1932" (公曆一九三二年) or "A. D. 1933" (公曆一九三三年) below, written from right to left. On the reverse there is a design embodying the axe and sickle situated in the lower part of the coin and enclosed in a small circle surrounded by ears of corn, with the inscription "Five of These Coins Equivalent to One Yüan" (每五枚當一圓) above, written from right to left. The two *chiao* silver coins were of the same size as the *shuang hao* (雙毫) of Kwangtung Province. The fineness of silver in both the one *yüan* and two *chiao* coins was extremely low. In the case of the former it was less than 50% and the coin had a brownish appearance, while the latter contained only 4 or 5% of silver. On the obverse of the five *fen* copper coins there was the central inscription "Five Fen" (五分), with the inscription "The Chinese Soviet Republic" (中華蘇維埃共和國) round the circumference above it and "Twenty of These Coins Equivalent to One Yüan of State Currency" (每二十枚當國幣一圓) below. The reverse was decorated with the star and a design of ears of corn. The five *fen* copper coins were slightly smaller than the *tang shih t'ung yüan* (當拾銅元) coins which were then in circulation, while the one *fen* coin was one-fifth of the size of the five *fen* coin and was decorated with a design similar to that of the five *fen* coin. We may add that in Szechuan Province copper coins of the value of two hundred *wen* and five hundred *wen* were also issued.

In the above we have covered the range of coins issued by the Chinese Soviets, and we may learn from it, first, that although there were several varieties of silver coins they all bore the emblem of the axe and sickle, second, that the Western calendar was always used in the date inscriptions, and third, that some of the horizontal inscriptions in the Chinese script were written from left to right. (The second and third points differed from the general practice in China at the time.)

2. *Paper Currency*

It appears that many kinds of paper currency were issued by the Chinese Soviets, among which we may describe the following.

First, the notes with the inscriptions " Made in 1931" (一九三一年造) and " Issued by the State Bank of the Chinese Soviet Republic, Hsiang-O-Hsi Special Area Branch" (中華蘇維埃共和國國家銀行湘鄂西特區分行發行). There were one *yüan*, two *chiao*, and one *chiao* notes of this kind. The back of the one *yüan* note bore the inscription "Workers of the World, Unite!" (全世界無產階級聯合起來). On these notes there was no inscription promising conversion into coined currency.

According to E. Kann, the following kinds of notes were issued in Kiangsi Province. All of them bore the inscription " Issued by the State Bank of the Chinese Soviet Republic" (中華蘇維埃共和國國家銀行發行), as well as a promise of conversion into silver coins.

(1)   One *yüan* notes, issued in 1932. The front of the note bears a full-face head of Lenin in the centre. Its design is red, but the design of the back is light green.

(2)   Five *chiao* notes, issued in 1933. The design is printed in purple.

(3)   One *chiao* notes, issued in 1932. The design is printed in red.

(4)   Five *fen* notes, issued in 1932. The design is printed in green.

In addition to the above, in Kiangsi Province, that is, in the Central Soviet Area, there was also a note of the same design as the one *yüan* note described above, printed in pale purple in 1933. The five *chiao* note described above was also printed in red.

The following notes were issued with the inscription " The Bank of the Soviet of the Min-Che-Kan Provinces" (閩浙贛省蘇維埃銀行). These notes bear no inscription promising conversion into coined currency.

(1)   One *yüan* notes, printed in red and light green. On the front of the note the red flag is printed in the centre, with a red star in the centre of the flag. Within the

star is the emblem of the axe and sickle. The note is inscribed " Printed in 1932 " (一九三二年印).

(2) " Copper Yüan " (銅圓) notes. These are inscribed " Equivalent to Ten Copper Yüan " (銅元拾枚). Some of these notes are printed in blue, and some in red and green.

In the Min-Che-Kan Soviet Area no coinage was issued, and only paper currency was employed.

In addition to the above there were also the following.

(1) A one *yüan* note bearing "Printed by the Bank of the O-Yü-Wan Soviet " (鄂豫皖蘇維埃銀行印). On the front of this note the words " The Workers' and Peasants' Bank of Kiangsi" (江西工農銀行) are printed along the top from right to left. On the right side there is a full-face head of Marx, and on the left a full-face head of Lenin. Down the right side of the note there is a vertical inscription " Increase Industrial and Agricultural Production" (增加工農生産) and down the left side " Develop the Social Economy " (發展社會經濟). On the back of the note, "Workers of the World, Unite ! " (全世界無産階級聯合起來) is written along the top from right to left, and in the centre there is a seal reading " Printed by the Bank of the O-Yü-Wan Soviet" (鄂豫皖蘇維埃銀行印). The note also has an inscription in Russian characters. The date of printing does not appear, but it would seem, by its relation to the silver coins, to have been issued in 1932. We may note that there is no inscription promising conversion into coined currency.

(2) A one *chiao* note issued by the Bank of the Soviet of the Hsiang-Kan Provinces in 1933. This is printed in red and blue.

(3) The " Copper Cash Notes" (制錢票) issued by the Workers' and Peasants' Bank of the Soviet Government of the Provinces of Szechuan and Shensi. These are printed in black on cotton cloth which is either white, or of light or dark blue colour. On the front of the note a clenched fist is printed in the centre, surrounded by a star superimposed on the emblem of the crossed axe and sickle. Immediately beneath this design there is the

inscription " Three Strings of Cash " (參串). (One 'string' contains 1,000 copper cash (*wen*).)   At the top there is "Workers of the World, Unite ! " (全世界無產階級聯合起來), and underneath it the words " The Soviet Government of the Provinces of Szechuan and Shensi " (川陝省蘇維埃 政府) written in a semi-circle shape. Beneath this, in turn, there are the words "The Workers' and Peasants' Bank" (工農銀行).   All these inscriptions are written from right to left.   At the very bottom there is the inscription " 1933 " (一九三三年).   There was also a one *yüan* note issued in 1933 which was printed on cotton in green, as well as a "one string note " (printed in blue and green) and a " three string note " (printed in blue, green and red), issued in 1934.

We have no detailed information about the currency after the move to the Shanpei Soviet.   According to Edgar Snow, the greater part of the metallic currency in the southern Soviet Areas was transported to the north-western parts of China, and after the issue of the order for the nationalization of silver by the Kuomintang government in 1935 and the consequent rise in the price of silver the Shanpei Soviet government called in its silver and held it in preparation for the issue of paper currency. If this is true, paper currency has been in exclusive use among the Chinese Communists since that time.   E. Snow also gives the following account of the paper currency of the Shanpei Soviet. "Paper currency in the South, bearing the signature of the 'Chinese Workers' and Peasants' Soviet Government State Bank,' was excellently printed, on good bank paper.   In the North-west, technical deficiencies resulted in a much cruder issue on poor paper, and sometimes on cloth.   Their slogans appeared on all money. Notes issued in Shensi bore such exhortations as these : ' Stop civil war ! ' ' Unite to resist Japan ! ' ' Long live the Chinese revolution ! ' "[7]

---

[7] Edgar Snow, *Red Star Over China* (London, 1937), p. 223.

III. The Currency Policies of the Chinese Soviets

The procedure among the Chinese Soviets was for hard currency to be issued by the Central Government of the Chinese Soviets and the Financial Departments of the provincial Soviet governments, these bodies giving instructions to the mints for the minting of coins. Paper currency was to be issued either from the Chinese Soviet State Bank or from the provincial banks. The issue of paper currency in these ways had to receive the permission of the Central Government of the Chinese Soviets and the Financial Department of the provincial Soviets, and detailed regulations governing this matter were provided in the Regulations for Soviet Banks. However, in practice, it seems that the mints were established as appendages to the Soviet State Bank or to the provincial banks.[8] For example, according to a report by the Workers' and Peasants' Bank of the Hsiang-Kan Soviet in 1932, the above bank established a mint in October of that year, and minted a large quantity of silver coin with the labour of 30 employees.

It is clear that there was decentralization of mints and issuing banks among the Chinese Soviets, and consequently a regional system in currency issues, and although the creation of a unified currency was looked up to as an ideal it was not realized in practice. This situation arose as a result of the fact that the Soviets did not occupy a continuous expanse of territory but were located in separate blocks. This was accompanied by the advantage that confusion in the currency of one area did not affect other areas.

The State Bank was first established at T'ungku, with branches at Hsingkuo and Yunghsin, and later branches were opened at Lungyen and in many other areas. According to the Report of the Lytton Commission the cash held in November, 1932, by nine banks located in T'ungku and Lungyen amounted to 12,000,000 *yüan*. Among the Workers' and Peasants' Banks there were some which were of a joint state-private character. An example is the

---

[8] The sources for this section are as follows:
Ch'i Ch'i-sheng, pp. 151–158; G. Kara Murza, pp. 182–191; Tōa Keizai Chōsa Kyoku, pp. 418–419.

Workers' and Peasants' Bank of the Hsiang-Kan Soviet. When first established, the bank, in order to make up a proposed capital fund of 100,000 *yüan*, screwed 40,000 *yüan* out of the provincial Soviet government, and put shares to the value of 60,000 *yüan* before the public. Only 20,000 *yüan*, however, was subscribed, and the bank thus started with a capital of 60,000 *yüan*.

The Chinese Soviets at first adopted the policy of not permitting the circulation of currency issued by the Kuomintang government in their own areas. That is to say, they withdrew all such currency, together with other older currencies, for re-minting into Soviet currencies. However, since this merely resulted in a currency scarcity, a change was made in this policy at a later date. Hereafter the circulation of such currency was permitted, with the sole addition of a stamped inscription of " The Chinese Soviets " on the face of the notes. Consequently, when merchants entered the Soviet Areas they exchanged the Kuomintang government currency which they brought with them for Soviet currency, and if there was no Soviet currency available in the particular Soviet Area in question the Soviet government stamped the Kuomintang notes and returned them to circulation. However, it became apparent that this measure was inappropriate, since the Kuomintang government forbade under the severest penalties the use of Kuomintang notes stamped by the Chinese Soviets, as well as the use of currency issued by the Soviets. The measure made normal trade relations between the Soviet Areas and the non-Soviet Areas impossible, and resulted in the increased economic isolation of the Soviet Areas. As a consequence of this, it came about that permission was given for the currency issued by the Kuomintang government to circulate in the Soviet Areas alongside the currency issued by the Soviet governments. On the whole, however, the following policy was adopted after the Spring of 1933. When merchants entered the Soviet Areas with Kuomintang currency this currency was changed into Soviet currency, and the Kuomintang currency was handed over to the Soviet government banks, external trade organs, etc., for use by these institutions when they went to the Kuomintang areas to make purchases of goods. The circulation of Kuomintang currency in the Soviet Areas was not permitted, and the Soviets went on to forbid the withdrawal from circulation or melting-down of such currency. For the Chinese Soviets the currency of the Kuomintang government was a foreign currency, to be safeguarded along with gold, silver, and other treasures, and efforts were made to utilize these resources in the most efficient manner possible.

As we have noted above, the paper currency issued by the Chinese Soviets was not necessarily subject to a promise of conversion into silver. Even if silver conversion of paper currency were carried out, the silver coins given in exchange would have been of very low quality, and such conversion could not have been expected to contribute to the promotion of confidence in the paper currency and the maintenance of its value. The quality of the paper on which these notes were printed was poor, and some of them were lithographed. What is more, in the early years notes were over-issued on a grand scale as a measure for coping with financial deficits and balancing income and expenditure. For example, the paper currency of the Hsiang-O-Hsi Soviet Area was the object of absolute confidence, not only within the Soviet Areas, but also in the adjacent Kuomintang areas, so that all the merchants who came from the Kuomintang areas to trade in the Soviet Areas collected Soviet currency with easy minds and made large purchases of goods in the Soviet Areas. Later, however, as a result of unrestricted issues of paper currency by the Soviet (inconvertible paper currency to the value of 500,000 *yüan* is said to have been issued within a short period) confidence in its currency declined greatly. Again, inconvertible paper currency to the value of 200,000 *yüan* was issued in the southwestern part of Kiangsi in 1930. There are also instances of military forces issuing their own currency on their own initiative. Furthermore, the currency of the Chinese Soviets was the object of plot and propaganda from the Kuomintang side, and it was found difficult to establish confidence in it. There were trade union representatives in the Chinese Soviet Areas who demanded that factory managers should pay wages in silver and not in Soviet paper currency, and organs of the Chinese Soviets in some provinces demanded that taxes should be paid in silver. Such things ruined confidence in the Soviet paper currency, and were remedied at a later date. Among the paper currencies issued by the Chinese Soviets, that issued by the Workers' and Peasants' Bank in the Central Soviet Area inspired a comparatively high degree of confidence and maintained stable values, but it would seem that this was due to the political supremacy of the Chinese Communists in these areas and to the successful management of the quantities of notes issued.   One *yüan* silver coins were issued in the Central Soviet Area, but paper money was the principal form of currency used, supplemented, as we have already pointed out, by other forms of currency.

The Chinese Soviets had a large unfavourable balance of trade against the areas subject to the Kuomintang government. Besides being due to the economic weakness of the Soviet Areas, this was also due to the fact that the Chinese Soviets, based as they were on an agricultural economy, had fallen into an unfavourable position in external economic relations as a result of the general worsening of the barter terms of trade between the Chinese agricultural villages and the towns (an increase in the " price-scissors" difference between town and country) which took place in the years following the world agricultural depression of 1929, as well as being due to the Kuomintang government's economic blockade.   In this situation, the State External Trade Commission, the Food Control Bureau and the co-operatives played important parts in breaking the economic blockade and achieving a favourable balance of trade.   No monopolistic foreign trade took place in the Chinese Soviet Areas.   However, foreign trade was carried on under the supervision of the Chinese Soviet governments, their aim being that of securing the supply of necessary material resources.   The State Foreign Trade Commission was the body which exercised this supervision, and was a powerful factor in normalizing external trade relations and in assisting the development of state commerce.   Mao Tse-tung said, "Carrying on planned foreign trade means, at present, importing certain necessary articles, such as salt, and exporting wolfram and agricultural and food products.   At present, this is very necessary.   The Min-Che-Kan Area has been carrying out this type of work for a much longer time than any other area.   In the Central Soviet Area this type of work commenced in the spring of 1933, and thanks to the establishment of the Foreign Trade Bureau the Soviets have achieved great successes in this field."   The duties of the Food Control Bureau were (1) the accumulation of reserved food stocks, (2) the provision of rations for the army, (3) the adjustment of prices, and (4) the organization of the export trade. In connexion with the fourth point, the organization of the export trade, the Food Control Bureau came into administrative contact with the External Trade Commission. It is said that at the end of 1933 the members of co-operatives in all the Chinese Soviet Areas numbered more than a million. The consumers' co-operatives, in particular, developed to a large extent. One of the important duties of the consumers' co-operatives was that of exporting agricultural produce to the non-Soviet areas as a counterpart of the importation of industrial goods from these areas. This trade was carried on in two forms, cash trading and barter. The Resolutions of the Second National Congress of the Chinese Soviets held in January, 1934, contain the following. "The establishment of the Food Control Bureau and the External Trade Commission, together with close co-operation between these bodies and co-operatives of every kind, has played a decisive part in supplying food to the Red Army and in improving the living-conditions of the masses. Further, as a result of the establishment of the Bureau for the Management of the National Economy within the Soviet government, it has become possible to direct economic construction in the Soviet Areas in a unified and planned manner."

Viewed from the other side, this development of planned foreign trade control may be regarded as having been an important factor contributing to the maintenance of the value of the currency of the Chinese Soviets. The Chinese Soviet governments also strove, with the help of the co-operatives, to organize exchanges of goods between districts and villages into a natural barter trade, attempting by this means to reduce transactions in cash to the minimum and to avoid disturbances of the economy originating from the currency side.

We may also note that the existence of the original private banks and native banks was admitted in the Chinese Soviet Areas, but so strict was the supervision exercised by the authorities that their business was practically brought to a standstill.

The Shanpei Soviet inherited the experience of currency policy in the Chinese Soviets in the period before the move to the North-West, and developed this experience further. We can gain ample insight into this matter by reading Snow's simple account.[9] He

---

9 E. Snow, pp. 221–227.

goes on to seek the reasons for the maintenance of the value of
the purely inconvertible currency of the Soviets, and says that
the standing of the currency appeared to be maintained by the
confidence of the people in the government and by the fact that
it had a certain degree of effective purchasing power in the
market.   He concludes that the people's confidence in the Soviet
currency after five years of war during which the economy had
been maintained and no famines had occurred was not to be
explained in terms of financial administration alone, but must be
understood with reference to its social and political basis.[10]   We
are obliged to say that this testimony is most worthy of our
attention.

CONCLUSION

The above description has provided us with an outline view
of the currency and currency policies of the Chinese Communist
Party in the period before China plunged into war with Japan.
By means of it the general features of the currency and financial
system of the Chinese Communist régime at this period have been
elucidated.   When the war against Japan broke out, this system
of the Shanpei Soviet formed the basis for the war-time institutions
of the Chinese Communist régime in these spheres, while with
the development of the war against Japan the area subject to this
régime was expanded, and the new currency and financial system
developed on the basis of the currencies issued in the Border
Areas.   This matter will be examined in the next chapter.

We may also observe that after the establishment of the
People's Republic of China, the government of new China called
in the notes, bonds, and food-notes issued by the Chinese Communist armies in the period of the Chinese Soviets.   We shall
mention this point later when we discuss the unification of the
Chinese currencies by means of the People's Currency.

---

[10]   E. Snow, pp. 223 and 227.

CHAPTER II

THE ECONOMIES OF THE BORDER AREAS
AND THE BORDER CURRENCIES

INTRODUCTION

THE OUTBREAK of war between China and Japan after the Lukou-ch'iao Incident on the 7th of July, 1937, ushered in a second period of co-operation between the Chinese Communist Party and the Chinese Nationalist Party, the Kuomintang. This co-operation was formally established on the 22nd of September in that year (the day of the signing of the agreement). On the next day, the 23rd of September, the Central Committee of the Chinese Communist Party published a " Declaration of Sincere Solidarity and Unity in Resistance to the Enemy" in which it declared its intention (1) to fight for the realization of Three Principles of the People, (2) to put a stop to all violent acts and bolshevization policies aiming at the overthrow of the Kuomintang government, and to abandon the policy of expropriating landlords' lands, (3) to liquidate the Soviet government, and (4) to reorganize the Red Army. Before this, on the 25th of August, 1937, the Chinese Communists had declared that they (1) had abolished the Soviet government and reconstituted it as Special Area Government, and (2) had reorganized the Red Army as the National Revolutionary Eighth Route Army. Again, Chu Te and P'eng Te-huai had been appointed Commander-in-chief and Second-in-command of the National Revolutionary Eighth Route Army respectively by the National Government of China on the 22nd of August of that year.

It was in October, 1935, that the Central Red Army, led by

Mao Tse-tung, arrived in the area centred on Yenan in north Shensi Province after its "long march of 25,000 *li*" from the Chinese Soviet Republic Area in Kiangsi Province, centred on Juichin. Chu Te, leading the remainder of the Communist armies, arrived in the same Area in November, 1936. Before this, the Shanpei Soviet government had been established here by Liu Chih-tan and Kao Kang, but with the arrival of the Central Red Army northern Shensi became a revolutionary base, and the location of the Central Committee of the Chinese Communist Party. The government of the Shanpei Soviet was then dissolved, and became the North-West Office of the Chinese Soviets. With the renewal of co-operation between the Communists and the Kuomintang in September, 1937, this Office was renamed "The Government of the Shan-Kan-Ning Special Area." However, after this time the Chinese Communist Party generally avoided the use of the term "Special Area," and used the appellation of "Border Area." Consequently, the Shan-Kan-Ning Special Area was also called the Shan-Kan-Ning Border Area.

By etymology, the term "Border Area" (邊區) means an area situated on the frontiers of China, but in these contexts it is used to refer to the areas which were designated as Communist spheres of influence on the basis of co-operation between the Communists and the Kuomintang in the period of the war against Japan, which became revolutionary bases, and which eventually had administrative organs established in them. Communist spheres of influence pure and simple were called Guerrilla Areas (遊擊區).

The first of the Border Areas established in this way was the Shan-Kan-Ning Border Area, but later, as an accompaniment to the expansion of the power of the Eighth Route Army, several of these Border Areas were set up in the area of the Provinces of north China and frontier areas of them. In the region south of the Yellow River, too, a number of Border Areas were established after May, 1938, as operational bases for the New Fourth Army. About the end of 1941 (about the time of the outbreak of the Pacific War) the power of the Chinese Communists comprised 800,000 party members, 440,000 members of the regular forces (305,000 in the Eighth Route Army and 135,000 in the New Fourth Army), and three Border Area governments. In August, 1945 (at the time of the armistice in the Pacific War), there were 1,210,000 party members, 900,000 members of the regular forces, 2,500,000 militia, and 18 governments of Border Areas of various sizes.[11]

During the period of the war against Japan the Chinese Communist armies used the Border Areas as bases in carrying on guerrilla war against the Japanese Army and the forces of the pro-Japanese régime of China. Inspite of the agreement for co-operation between the Kuomintang and the Communists, relations between them became strained after two years, and Chiang Kai-shek's armies too began to surround and blockade the Border Areas. The most manifestation of this state of relations took place in January, 1941, when the Wannan Incident occurred.[12] The Chinese Communist armies, attacked in this way from two sides by two enemies, adopted the policy of looking for the places where attacks or resistance on the enemy side were weakest, there to establish bases and set up Border Areas from which they might carry on their favourite guerrilla warfare and thus gradually expand these areas. Consequently, each base or Border Area was essentially independent of other bases and Border Areas, both geographically and economically.

The financial administration of the Chinese Communist armies in the Border Areas also maintained a position independent of the financial administration of the Centre. It was the general rule in each Border Area for a bank engaged in ordinary business to be established as an issuing bank and for this bank to carry on a currency war against currencies belonging to the Japanese or Kuomintang sides, as well as issuing bank-notes and meeting the needs of the economy and financial administration of the Border Area. Currency of a similar kind was also issued by the state trading companies and co-operative stores. Such finance

---

11 Shigezō Yoshikawa, *A Guide to Chinese Communism* (Tokyo, 1950), p. 20. In *An Outline Account of the State of the Liberated Areas During the War Against Japan* (Peking, 1953), edited by the People's Publishing Company, it is stated that by the spring of 1944 the strength of the Chinese Communist armies had reached 470,000 troops, more than 2,000,000 militia, and 15 Border Areas (pp. 3-4).

12 In this incident the headquarters of the New Fourth Army in southern Anhui Province sustained an annihilating assault in a surprise attack by the army of Ku Chu-t'ung, a general on the side of the army of Chiang Kai-shek. On this occasion the commander of the New Fourth Army, Yeh T'ing, was taken prisoner. However, the New Fourth Army was at length rebuilt by Ch'en Yi.

currency, economic currency and strategic currency issued as paper-money by the Chinese Communists was generally known as " Border Currency " (邊幣) or " Border Notes " (邊鈔), or, occasionally, as " Resistance Currency " (抗幣).

However, with the armistice in the Pacific War the power of the Japanese Army in China collapsed, and later the civil war with the Kuomintang broke out. Consequently the Border Areas which had hitherto been isolated from one another were linked up, and as the power of the Chinese Communist armies expanded and gained strength these areas were incorporated in a number of areas of greater size, the Liberated Areas (解放區). As an accompaniment to this there began the process of integrating the Border Currencies, culminating in the establishment of the People's Currency as the sole form of currency in use in mainland China.

In the following sections we propose first to make a detailed examination of the Border Currency and the economy in the Shan-Kan-Ning Border Area, and then to present a general view of the development of the Border Currencies in other areas.

I. The Border Currency and the Economy in the Shan-Kan-Ning Border Area

1. The Border Currency of the Shan-Kan-Ning Border Area

In regard to the currency of the Chinese Communists after the outbreak of war with Japan, we may first draw attention to the issue of the small-denomination notes called " Kuang Hua Notes " (光華票) by the Kuang Hua Commercial House, a government trading agency in the Shan-Kan-Ning Border Area, a measure which coped with the scarcity of subsidiary paper currency. Later, the Shan-Kan-Ning Border Area Bank (陝甘寧邊區銀行) was established at Yenan in this Area, and it started issuing the Shan-Kan-Ning Border Currency (陝甘寧邊幣) on the 18th of February, 1941. As we shall show later, however, Border Currency had been issued before this date in some of the other Border Areas.

It is not clear when the Kuang Hua Notes were issued. However, if we assume that this currency was issued as a measure designed to make up the deficiency of subsidiary paper currency, we will probably not be much mistaken if we assign the date of issue to the second half of 1938. This is probably the case because it was at this time that a financial panic based on a scarcity of subsidiary currency was beginning to spread over the whole of China. As causes for the occurrence of a financial panic at this time we may mention first, the fact that the intrinsic value of the copper cash (銅錢), copper cents (銅元) and nickel coins which made up by far the greater part of the subsidiary currency of China rose above the nominal value of the coins as an accompaniment to currency instability and the development of inflationary tendencies which accompanied the outbreak of war, so that these coins disappeared from the market at a greatly increased rate; second, the fact that forms of trade which had hitherto been conducted on a credit basis as the general rule in Chinese society changed to cash trading as an accompaniment to the development of the Incident; and third, the widespread speculative manipulation of subsidiary currency by money-changers and other dishonest traders.[13] According to the account given by Harrison Forman, the British journalist, of his conversations with Nan Han-ch'en, the Head of the Financial Administration Office in the Shan-Kan-Ning Border Area, and others during his six months' stay in the Shan-Kan-Ning Border Area in the autumn of 1944, the Kuang Hua Notes were issued in denominations ranging from one *fen* to seven *chiao* five *fen*, and the total amount issued did not exceed 1,000 *yüan* in Kuomintang Legal Tender Notes (法幣) or 25 American dollars.[14]

Forman clearly states that the date of issue of the Shan-Kan-Ning Border Currency was the 18th of February, 1941. There is some discrepancy between this statement and the date given by Nagao Watanabe—the 30th of January, 1941—but we are prepared, in the meantime, to follow Forman's account of the matter.[15] Forman's account of the currency of this Border Area suggests that the cause of the bad relations between the Kuomintang and

[13] See Tadao Miyashita, "Chiang Kai-shek's War-time System of Currency Issue," *Kokumin Keizai Zasshi*, Vol. LXXVI, No. 4 (1944), p. 64 ff.

[14] Harrison Forman, *Report from Red China* (London, 1946), p. 81.

[15] See Nagao Watanabe, *On the Currency of New China* (Tokyo, 1948), p. 98.

the Chinese Communists was connected with the issue of new currency by the Communist side. He relates that it was the contention of the Kuomintang (and in particular, of Ho Ying-ch'in, the Chief of the Military Council in the Kuomintang government) that the outlawing of the Eighth Route Army and the cessation of payment of salary to the Eighth Route Army by the Kuomintang government were due to the fact that the governments of the Border Areas had begun to issue illegal currency, and asks Nan Han-ch'en and others about the views of the Communist side on this point. The reply made to this by Nan Han-ch'en and others was as follows. The issue of Border Currency by the Communist side took place after the Kuomintang government had put into effect a military and economic blockade of the Border Areas, and that, in precise terms, this took place on the 18th of February, 1941. It was agreed that the Kuang Hua Notes had been issued before this, but these were of the nature of subsidiary currency, and the issuing authority, the Kuang Hua Commercial House, was no more than a semi-official trading company, and for this reason the issue of these notes could not be regarded as the issue of bank-notes by the Border Area government in its public capacity. Furthermore, the amount issued was only 1,000 *yüan* in Kuomintang Legal Tender Notes or 25 American dollars. Our personal view is that, leaving aside the question of whether or not the bad relations between the Kuomintang and the Communists were due to the issue of currency by the Communists, the attempt to place the date of issue of their own currency by the Communists after the beginning of the bad relations between the Communists and the Kuomintang (1939) must be considered an attempt to evade the question by narrowing the matter down to a discussion of the Shan-Kan-Ning Border Area alone. We are of this opinion because Border Currency had been issued in another Border Area, the Hsin-Ch'a-Chi Border Area, since March, 1938.

At present we do not possess detailed information about the actual state of the Shan-Kan-Ning Border Currency. The following passages can be read in Mao Tse-tung's report on government trading carried on by 359 Regiment which is included in *Economic Problems and Government Financial Problems* (a report to a meeting of senior cadres in the Shan-Kan-Ning Border Area in

December, 1942). "It is a precondition for the development of business that the currency system should be stabilized and financial conditions made firm. In the last three years there have been frequent fluctuations in the value of the currency of the Border Area and financial conditions have been thrown into confusion, with the result that the buying and selling of goods has been affected and many inconveniences experienced. This has also allowed speculative merchants to make great profits out of the manipulation of the currency, and has affected the economy of the Border Area."[16] We may see from this that the maintenance of the value of the Border Currency was no easy matter. The fact is that in the work by Mao Tse-tung from which we have quoted above there is frequent mention of measures for the stabilization of the Border Currency.

On the basis of personal experience in the autumn of 1944, Forman points out that 1 *yüan* of the Yenan Border Currency was worth one-eighth of 1 *yüan* of the Chungking Legal Tender Notes.[17] The measures for increasing the circulation of Border Currency which were adopted in the other Border Areas generally began with the setting up of a parity relation between the Border Currency and the Chungking Legal Tender Notes, and of the admission of the use of both forms of currency within the Border Area. If parity between the two currencies were broken (usually as a result of a bad balance of payments with outside areas) the circulation of the Chungking Legal Tender Notes in the Border Area was forbidden, and efforts were made to make the Border Currency the only currency in use. It is not clear what form of the measures was employed for increasing the circulation of the Border Currency in the Shan-Kan-Ning Border Area, but if we assume that they commenced with policies similar to those adopted in the other Border Areas, this will imply that during a period of more than three years beginning in February, 1941, the value of the Border Currency declined to one-eighth of the value of the Chungking Legal Tender Notes. Further, the Chungking Legal Tender Notes themselves were also declining in value.

Some light will be thrown on the problem of maintaining

---

[16] Mao Tse-tung, *Economic Problems and Government Financial Problems*, Third Edition (Hong Kong, 1949), p. 150.

[17] H. Forman, p. 76.

the value of the Shan-Kan-Ning Border Currency by a description of the financial administration and the economy of the Area. Therefore the requirements of our attaining an understanding of this matter will lead us from the currency problems of this Area to an examination of the economy which supported the currency system.

2. *The Economy of the Shan-Kan-Ning Border Area*

There are two reasons for examining the economy of the Shan-Kan-Ning Border Area. The first, which we have already mentioned, is the fact that it will make clear the financial and economic basis on which the Border Currency system in this Area rested, and the second is the fact that an elucidation of the economy of the Area will serve as a means whereby we may visualize the general condition of the economies of the other Border Areas and their systems for the maintenance of the value of the Border Currencies. In comparison with other Border Areas, the Shan-Kan-Ning Border Area had a longer history, and from the political point of view it was an area in which the authority of the Chinese Communists was comparatively well established, while its economy, too, was increasing most in strength and stability. We must bear these facts well in mind when we try to visualize the economies of the other Border Areas, but the differences in the basic economic conditions among the Border Areas may be regarded as being only differences of degree.

On the subject of the economy of the Shan-Kan-Ning Border Area, the work of Mao Tse-tung to which we have referred above is particularly useful. Let us now examine the general aspect of the economy of this Area, using this work as the principal source and supplementing it with materials printed in the Japanese edition of *The Selected Works of Mao Tse-tung* and with Forman's *Report from Red China*. We must add that in respect to the work of Mao Tse-tung to which we have referred above all notes will be omitted, except when there is necessity to do otherwise.

The Shan-Kan-Ning Border Area was made up from 23 *Hsien*, and included the Provinces of Shensi, Kansu and Ninghsia, together with some adjacent territory. According to Mao Tse-tung, the population of the Border Area in 1943 was 1,400,000. According to Forman, this Border Area was originally recognized by Chiang Kai-shek as covering an area of approximately 130,000 square kilometres, but when, after two years of co-operation, relations between the Kuomintang and the Communists deteriorated and the armies of Chiang Kai-shek began to blockade the Border Areas and went on to strengthen this blockade, this Border Area declined in size until in the autumn of 1944 it covered approximately 90,000 square kilometres and had a civil population of 1,500,000, to which were added 80,000 government officials and military personnel.[18] According to Mao Tse-tung, more than 90% of the population of 1,400,000 were peasants, and less than 10% were landlords and merchants. Further, pastoralism (principally sheep-rearing) was the most important side-occupation among the peasantry. Again, according to Mao Tsetung, the population of Yenan, the centre of this Border Area and its largest city, was 35,000 in 1937, and was about 70,000 in 1943. These facts indicate that the size of the economy of this Border Area was narrow and its principal elements were agriculture and pastoralism.

As is well known, it was in the resolutions passed at a conference held by the Politburo of the Central Committee of the Chinese Communist Party on the 25th of December, 1935, that the Communist Party switched its Party line to " the building of New Democracy " and adopted the various policies associated with " New Democracy."[19] This took place immediately after the Central Red Army's arrival in the Shanpei Area after the " long march of 25,000 li." Consequently, from the time of the Shanpei Soviet to the period of the Shan-Kan-Ning Border Area, the ideal of the revolution of New Democracy in politics, economies and culture was gradually brought to realization in this northern area. Mao Tse-tung's " The Chinese Revolution and the Chinese Communist Party " (December, 1939) and his " On New Democracy " (January, 1940), are concerned with plans for the future, but we must give full attention to the fact that the theory of the revolution of New Democracy set out from the social reality which we have described. However, a point which is truly worthy of our attention is the fact that the agreement on co-operation between the Kuomintang and the Communists which was concluded in September, 1937,

---

18 H. Forman, p. 56.
19 See T. Miyashita, *Mao Tse-tung's New Democracy* (Kōbe, 1951), pp. 23, 33, and 38.

made inevitable a change in one important element in the revolutionary line of New Democracy. This was the shelving of the overthrow of the feudal class of landlords and the implementation of land reform by this means, and the substitution of these policies for reduced rents and reduced rates of interest (policies for the peasantry aiming at the lowering of rents and the lowering of rates of interest). However that may be, according to Mao Tse-tung, in 1943 more than half of the Chinese peasants in the Shan-Kan-Ning Border Area had been given land. Further, the Border Area government gave firm assurances in regard to the results achieved in distributing land to the peasants by means of land reform.

According to Mao Tse-tung, " The guiding principles in our work in the fields of economy and financial administration are those of developing the economy and assuring our supplies." What he was seeking to convey by these words was, in sum, that it was a mistake to attach exclusive importance to state finance and ignore the importance of the economy. The suitability or otherwise of the government's policy in financial administration does of course exert an influence on the economy, but it is financial administration, on the contrary, which is determined by the economy, and it is impossible to make decisions in questions of financial administration without the necessary economic foundations.

According to Mao Tse-tung, the economy of the Border Area was divided into two great sectors, the private sector and the public sector. The private sector of the economy comprised all agriculture, industry and commerce carried on by private persons, and the public sector of the economy comprised all agriculture, industry and commerce carried on by the government and the Army, as well as by organs and schools. In relations between the public and private sectors, it was necessary to follow the slogans " Equal Consideration for the Public and the Private " and " Equal Consideration for the Army and the People." These slogans had an importance which ranked with the guiding principles in the fields of economy and financial administration to which we referred above. Only when both the public and private sectors of the economy were caused to develop would it be possible to be assured of supplies in the realm of financial administration. In the Border Areas at this period, private capitalism, which was already one of the elements in the economy of the New Democracy, was permitted and encouraged.

The private sector of the economy included agriculture, pastoralism, handicrafts, co-operative enterprises, salt enterprise and commerce.

Looking first at agriculture, Mao Tse-tung states that the estimated food production including rice, wheat, sesame, etc., in the Border Area in 1942 was 1,500,000 piculs, the picul (*tan*) in the Border Area being equivalent to 300 catties (*chin*). The target increase of food production for 1943 was 80,000 piculs. It was expected that if labour were properly employed it would be possible to increase food production in the Border Area up to 2,000,000 piculs. According to information which Forman received from Lin Tsu-han (Lin Po-ch'ü), the Chairman of the government o the Shan-Kan-Ning Border Area, the annual food-consumption of the Border Area was estimated at 1,620,000 piculs, and the total production in 1943 was 1,840,000 piculs, leaving a surplus of 220,000 piculs.[20]

Mao Tse-tung sets out the guiding principles in agricultural policy in 1943 under the following eight heads.

(1)   The reduction of rents and rates of interest.

Of the population of 1,400,000 in the Border Area, half had been given land, but half had not yet distributed land. The latter were found in such districts as the Suimi Defence Area, Lungtung, Fuhsien and Sanpien. In these districts the policies of reducing rents and rates of interest must be put into effect in order to encourage peasants' positive desire for agricultural production.

(2)   The reclamation of uncultivated land.

For this purpose the peasants must be organized, immigrants brought in, and the Army also caused to participate. It may be said in this connection that the area of land newly brought under cultivation between 1939 and 1942 amounted to 2,373,263 *mu*, and as an accompaniment to this reclamation the area devoted to cotton cultivation rose from 3,767 *mu* in 1939 to 94,405 *mu* in 1942. The numbers of cattle, asses, sheep and other domestic animals also increased. Further, the increase in food production which resulted from this increase in the cultivated area amounted to one-sixth of total

---

20   H. Forman, p. 83.

food production.

(3)　The extension of the area of cotton planting.

The total demand for raw cotton in the Border Area was 3,000,000 catties. In 1943 it would be necessary to complete the reclamation of 56,000 *mu* of land to be used for cotton cultivation, making a total of 150,000 *mu* when combined with the existing 94,000 *mu*, and to produce 2,500,000 catties of raw cotton. More than 200 machines would be required for ginning these 2,500,000 catties of raw cotton, but at that time there were only 100 dilapidated cotton-ginning machines in the Border Area, and only 50 of them were fit to be in continuous use. The problems of cotton-ginning are thus included in the policy for the extension of the area of cotton planting. Further, when 2,000,000 catties of raw cotton could be obtained, 4,000,000 catties of cottonseed could be obtained, and from 100 catties of cottonseed 12 catties of oil could be extracted. At that time, however, the peasants did not know how to extract the oil. This problem must also be solved.

(4)　Refraining from mistaking the seasons of agriculture.

Conferences should be held and personnel mobilized only during the slack seasons, and it should be permitted to stop all conferences or mobilizations of personnel not connected with agriculture during the busy seasons in agriculture in order to direct all human and animal power to agricultural production.

(5)　A proper employment of labour power.

This included the encouragement of immigration, mutual aid by exchanging labour, the mobilization of women, the mobilization of the *lumpen proletariat*, giving labour-priority to the assistance of the families of soldiers in the Anti-Japanese Army, giving holidays to the staff of organs, school teachers, students and school-children and causing them to co-operate in production, and the assistance of the Army in production. Encouragement was to be given to elementary forms of mutual-aid organization such as the seasonal labour exchange arrangements called *cha kung* (扎工) or *pien kung* (變工).[21] Forman states that 24% of the Border Area's agricultural labourers of

---

[21]　In connection with this point, Mao Tse-tung's famous speech entitled "Organize !", made on the 29th of November, 1943, is worthy of note. See *MTTS*, Vol. 6.

338,760 were spontaneously taking part in arrangements for the exchange of labour and that it was expected that this number would be almost doubled in 1944.[22]

(6)   An increase in loans to agriculture.

In 1942 the Border Area Bank made loans to agriculture amounting to 3,110,000 *yüan*. Of this sum, 1,580,000 *yüan* were loaned in respect to cultivation and implements, and 1,530,000 *yüan* in respect to cotton planting and buying cotton crops before the harvest. In the light of the results achieved by loans to agriculture in 1942, 17,000,000 *yüan* were newly loaned, making a total of 20,110,000 *yüan* when combined with the 3,110,000 *yüan* loaned in 1943 and now repaid. Of this sum, 14,000,000 *yüan* were to be loaned in respect to implements and ploughing-oxen, and 3,000,000 *yüan* were to be loaned in respect to cotton planting.

(7)   Raising the level of agricultural technology.

Under this head attention is drawn to 1) the building and repair of effective water-supply facilities, 2) the extension of the use of improved varieties of seed, 3) the reclamation of uncultivated land in autumn and the digging-over of the soil, 4) causing the peasants to weed their crops twice after extending the organization of labour exchange associations, 5) the holding of exhibitions, 6) the advocation of the productive movement associated with the name of Wu Man-yu, the Chinese Stakhanov,[23] 7) elementary instruction in agriculture in primary and secondary schools, and 8) the chemical treatment of the water run out from bushes.

(8)   The application of the system of progressive taxation to

---

22   H. Forman, p. 85. When Forman speaks of " agricultural labourers " he probably refers to the peasants.

23   Wu Man-yu was one of the refugees from famine who came into Yenan before the arrival of the Central Red Army in the Shanpei Soviet. In order to maintain the livelihood of his family he sold his three-year-old daughter in exchange for six pounds of food-grains, and his wife died of hunger while he was imprisoned by his landlord for failure to pay his rent. Shortly after this the Chinese Communist army arrived and a land reform was carried out, as a result of which he was allotted a hill. Starting from this land, he succeeded as an industrious and skilful peasant and as a user of labour exchange arrangements, so that he became a rich peasant. The Border Area government gave him the laudatory title of " Number One Hero of Labour," and propagandized the slogan " Take the lead from Wu Man-yu ! " (H. Forman, pp. 63–66.)

agriculture.

Taxes levied on agriculture in the past had been of the nature of " Public Food for the Salvation of the State," but although they had been levied in accordance with the progressive principle, the total amount levied in each year was uncertain, and the amounts levied from each household differed from year to year. In 1941 the levying of taxes by tax-allocations appeared. In 1942 the deliberation system was adopted, and although taxation became comparatively fair, some injustices still remained. The main defect was that the rate of tax was not definitely fixed, and this was inimical to the positive desire in production on the part of the peasants. To deal with this situation, the Party would make the following recommendations to the government. In 1943 the land held by the people should be surveyed and registered and a simple system of progressive taxation laid down. The rate of tax should be calculated with reference to defined quantitative and qualitative attributes of the land, so that the peasants would be able to calculate how much tax they would be required to pay by reference to the quantity and quality of their holdings. After carrying out this preliminary work in 1943, the new progressive taxation system might be able to be put into operation in 1944. The new system would be tried out experimentally in 1943 in the *Hsien* where the preliminary work had been carried out comparatively early.

The pastoral industries were one of the three main kinds of side-occupation carried on by the peasantry side by side with the sale of salt and the textile industry. In 1942 the peasants of the Border Area had an income of more than 1,000,000 catties of sheep's wool and cashmere, and when exports of sheep were added, peasants' income reached more than 20,000,000 *yüan*. In order to care for domestic animals and to increase their numbers, it would be necessary to devote efforts to (1) the prevention of epidemics, (2) the extension of cultivated pastures, (3) the prohibition of the slaughter of mother-animals and the prohibition of the export of the same, and (4) improvement of breeds of stock.

The greater part of the handicrafts carried on in the Border Area took the form of domestic industry pursued as a side-occupation, but some part of them existed as independent handicrafts.   The principal handicrafts were spinning native cotton yarn and weaving native cotton cloth by women.   The textile industry had recently accomplished a gradual recovery, but the output was not enough to make the Border Area self-sufficient, and large quantities of machine-made cotton yarn and cotton cloth were being imported with the help of sales of surplus agricultural produce, hides and animal hair.

In regard to the cotton textile industry, the annual demand for cotton cloth by the peasants, the Army and the officials of the government amounted to 250,000 rolls (*p'i*), one roll measuring 2 *chih* 4 *t'sun* by 10 *chang*.   Of this, the Army and government officials required 50,000 rolls, and the peasants 200,000 rolls.   The amount which could be supplied from within the Border Area was 100,000 rolls, leaving a deficit of 150,000 rolls.   Some parts of the 100,000 rolls of cloth produced in the Border Area were expected to come from seven publicly-operated mills producing approximately 11,000 rolls, from seven privately-operated textile manufacturing co-operatives producing approximately 18,000 rolls, and from private weaving of native cloth by women, amounting to 30,000 rolls.   In order to attain self-sufficiency in cotton yarn and cotton cloth it was proposed (1) that private textile production should be readjusted and developed, (2) that imports of machine-made cotton yarn should be reduced by improving the production of native yarn, (3) that the production of woollen cloth in the publicly-operated mills should be improved and that woollen fabrics should be used to replace cotton uniforms worn by the Army, and (4) that government officials should all be made to wear native cloth and that the people should also be encouraged to use native cloth, so that the importation of cotton cloth from outside the Border Area might be reduced.

In regard to cottonseed oil production, 3,000,000 catties of cottonseed were harvested in 1942 and about 360,000 catties of oil extracted.   It was thought that, with the increased area of cotton cultivation, it should be possible to obtain between 5,000,000 and 6,000,000 catties of cottonseed in 1943 and so to increase the production of oil.

In regard to the sericultural industry, many of the peasants in Suite, Ch'ingchien, Anting, Yench'uan, Kulin and other *Hsien* practised sericulture, and this was a side-occupation of considerable importance. A further development of the sericultural industry was considered necessary.

In 1943 the government intended to invest 2,600,000 *yüan* in the textile industry, cottonseed oil production and the sericultural industry (1,000,000 *yüan* for cotton spinning, 1,000,000 *yüan* for cotton cloth, 300,000 *yüan* for cottonseed oil extraction, and 300,000 *yüan* for sericulture) and to take steps to develop these industries in a positive manner.

Let us next look at the co-operatives. There had been co-operatives in this Border Area since the period of co-operation between the Kuomintang and the Communists. In the five years of trial since the outbreak of the war against Japan the co-operatives in the Border Area gradually developed with government encouragement.

In regard to the consumers' co-operatives, these increased in number from 130 to 155 in the four years between 1937 and 1941, while their members increased from 57,847 to 140,218, their funds from 55,525 *yüan* to 693,071 *yüan*, their consumption from 260,189 *yüan* to more than 6,008,000 *yüan*, their profits from 4,800 *yüan* to more than 1,020,000 *yüan*, and their reserve funds from more than 3,500 *yüan* to more than 173,000 *yüan*. According to the statistics covering 19 cities and *Hsien*, up to the end of October, 1942, the number of members of co-operatives had increased from 97,297 in 1941 to 115,899, while their subscribed funds had increased spectacularly from more than 712,900 *yüan* to more than 6,000,000 *yüan*, and their profits, too, had risen from more than 858,000 *yüan* to more than 3,398,000 *yüan*. The largest amount of funds subscribed by individual members rose as high as 10,000 *yüan*, and the smallest were of the order of 4 or 5 *yüan*.

In regard to the producers' co-operatives, 10 producers' co-operatives were set up with the encouragement of the government and the assistance of the North-Western Office of the Chinese Industrial Co-operatives after 1939. Then some of the consumers' co-operatives which had comparatively large holdings of funds undertook the functions of producers' co-operatives in addition to their normal activities. By October, 1942, the 10 producers' co-operatives had increased in number to 50 and the number of workers engaged in production among them had increased from 199 to 563, while their subscribed funds had increased from 11,130 *yüan* to 2,491,600 *yüan* and the value of their production per month from 60,000 *yüan* to more than 2,300,000 *yüan*. Among the 50 producers' co-operatives there were 27 textile co-operatives employing 497 persons and having subscribed funds of 1,700,000 *yüan*, 5 dyeing co-operatives employing 13 persons and having subscribed funds of 128,000 *yüan*, 5 producers' co-operatives running cottonseed oil plants employing 19 persons and having subscribed funds of 245,000 *yüan*, 9 flour mill co-operatives employing 24 persons and having subscribed funds of 262,000 *yüan*, 4 carpet-making co-operatives employing 42 persons and having subscribed funds of 152,000 *yüan*, and 1 china and porcelain producing co-operative employing 7 persons and having subscribed funds of 3,000 *yüan*.

We may see from the above how rapidly the co-operatives developed in the Shan-Kan-Ning Border Area, but their operations were on a small scale and their development uneven. The co-operatives passed through three stages of development. The first stage was before 1939, when co-operatives were set up in all parts of this area with the help of government funds, and the funds which were to be contributed by the masses were allotted to them. At this period the co-operatives partook of the nature of publicly-run bodies, and in many cases the co-operative was a publicly-operated trading house run by the *Hsien* authorities or by the Border Area government. The second stage dates from 1939, and during it the amount of funds allotted to the masses under the established form were increased, under the slogan of " the popularization of the co-operatives." The third stage dates from January, 1942, when, on the basis of the experience of the Yenan Southern Area Co-operative, the system of allotting quotas of funds to the masses was done away with, and the co-operatives were brought into close relations with the masses. The Southern Area Co-operative exhibited a straight course of development from the first, and was considered a model for the development of a co-operative.

In regard to salt enterprises, the production of salt was one of the greatest sources of wealth in the Border Area, and was of radical importance in achieving a balance between imports and exports, in maintaining the stability of currency and credit, and in adjusting prices. The greater part of the people exchanged salt for goods produced outside the Border Area, and a considerable proportion of the Army and the Party workers maintained or supplemented their livelihood by means of salt. Salt was also an important source of government revenue. Consequently, salt had an extremely important effect on the Border Area. The quantity of salt exported from the Border Area also rose from year to year. In 1938 the amount exported was only 70,000 horse-loads (1 horse-load weighing 150 catties, and 1 catty being equivalent to 24 taels), but in 1939 this was suddenly increased to 190,000 loads, while in 1940 it rose to 230,000 loads, and in 1941 again rose steeply to 299,068 loads. It was expected to reach 230,000 or 240,000 loads in 1942.

The planned production of salt in 1943 was 400,000 loads, and aimed at having a surplus available for export of between 300,000 and 360,000 loads. (In this connection, Forman states that the production of salt in 1943 reached to 600,000 loads.[24]) Of the expected export of between 300,000 and 360,000 loads, 40,000 loads were to be exported under unified management through the channels used by the publicly-operated salt producing company, 50,000 loads were to be taken by transporters from outside the Border Area, and between 210,000 and 260,000 loads were to be exported by organizing human and animal transport in the Border Area. The publicly-operated salt producing company was charged with the duty of expanding exports of salt, enlarging the sales-outlets for salt, and adjusting the price of salt, but at this period it had not yet succeeded in bringing salt exports under unified management. On the basis of 40,000 loads assured for its own export, it carried on a partially unified export trade in salt by buying up as much as it could of the salt produced by small private producers. The salt-tax was set at 100,000 loads in 1943. In places near the site of government the salt tax might be collected in kind, while in distant places it was permissible to pay it in money.

In connexion with the question of the export of salt, the following remarks of Mao Tse-tung on the question of balancing imports and exports in the Border Area are of particular interest from the viewpoint of the maintenance of the value of the Border Currency. " If we can carry out our plans for cotton growing and textile producing in 1943 we should be able to reduce our

---

[24] H. Forman, p. 84.

imports of raw cotton, cotton yarn and cotton cloth. If we can export between 300,000 and 360,000 loads of salt in 1943, we should make an income of between 450,000,000 *yüan* and 540,000,000 *yüan*, assuming the average price of 1 catty of salt to be 10 *yüan*, and 1 load to weigh 150 catties. If, in this way, there is a decrease on the one side and an increase on the other, the question of balancing imports and exports will be completely solved."[25]

According to Mao Tse-tung, all the agriculture, pastoral industry, handicrafts, co-operative enterprises and salt enterprises which we have described above were economic activities carried on by the people. The Party and the government gave them guidance and assistance within the sphere in which this was possible and necessary, took steps to ensure the development of these industries, and undertook to satisfy the demands of the people. At the same time, people handed over part of their production to the government in the form of taxes, thus assuring the government of the satisfaction of part of its requirements (for example, by means of levies of public food, public salt, and other taxes), and also handed over another part of their production to the government in the form of sales of produce, thus assuring the government of the satisfaction of another part of its requirements (for example, by selling raw cotton, cotton yarn, cotton cloth, wool, etc., to the government). The basic characteristic of these activities was that they were carried on by the people. However, in the single case of salt enterprises, a part of that industry (one-seventh of the whole) was under public management, since it involved the export of 40,000 loads of salt organized by the publicly-operated salt producing companies and the 5,000 loads of table salt required for the public use.

We may consider it strange for Mao Tse-tung to have divided the elements in the economy of the Shan-Kan-Ning Border Area into the two great categories of the public and private sectors and to have included the co-operatives in the private sector. However, at this period the agricultural producers' co-operatives had as yet not appeared in any numbers, and we must also give due attention to the special character of the circumstances surrounding this matter, to the fact that the majority of these co-operatives operated under a form of " joint state-private operation,"

[25] Mao Tse-tung, *Economic Problems and . . .* , p. 99.

in which public (government) capital had been invested. In " On New Democracy " the co-operative sector of the economy is ranked alongside the state-operated sector and the private capitalist sector, but here the co-operative sector refers to the producers' co-operatives built on the foundations provided by land reform in the rural areas.[26]

The public sector of the economy included the following three parts. (1) Salt enterprises, industry, and commerce carried on under government management, (2) agricultural, industrial and commercal enterprises carried on by the Army, and (3) agricultural, industrial and commercial enterprises carried on by the organs of the Party and the government. According to the settlement of accounts for 1942 and the budget for 1943, these parts of the economy supplied more than the amount supplied by the people to the government in the form of taxes (including levies of public food). The enterprises of the public sector of the economy were thus one of the two principal bases for assuring the supply for the government finance.

It was in 1938 that attention was given to publicly-operated enterprises. At that time the Army began productive activities as a result of a scarcity of funds. Next the government started to operate a number of small factories. In 1939, the supply of funds for military purposes from the Kuomintang government was cut off, and the Border Areas came under blockade. Hereupon it became necessary to meet the demands of the war against Japan by means of self-sufficient production. Thus, in 1939 Party organs and schools also began productive activities. In the past, publicly-operated enterprises had passed through three stages. The first stage extended over the three years 1938, 1939 and 1940, and during this period Army units, Party organs, and schools accorded importance to agriculture, while the government brought about the development of industry. The second stage extended over the two years 1941 and 1942, and during this period commerce came to be regarded as being of importance. These developments took place in response to the pressing need to meet economic demands. During this period some of the Army units, Party organs and schools adhered firmly to the policy of according first importance to agriculture, but all the others practised commerce, and

26 *MTTS*, Vol. 4, pp. 240–241.

agriculture was not accorded as much importance as during the
first stage.   The government, Army units, Party organs and schools
all brought about the development of manufacturing industries
and handicrafts.   The third stage began from December, 1942.
During this stage, it became firmly established for agriculture to
be accorded first place, for industry, handicrafts, transport and
pastoral industries to be accorded second place, and for commerce
to be accorded third place.

After describing the development of the enterprises in the
public sector of the economy, Mao Tse-tung gives the following
interesting characterization of these enterprises.   " . . . We built
up a model for a new type of state economy.   The reason why
it was a new type of state economy was that it was neither a
state economy of the old Bismarck type, nor a state economy of
the latest USSR type, but was a state economy of the New
Democracy type or the Three Principles of the People type."[27]
In this context Mao Tse-tung did not go so far as to say that
the public sector of the economy was a socialist economy.   His
discussion of the question differs on this point from his treatment
of it in " On New Democracy."

In April, 1942, the following seven industries were being
carried on under public management.
  (1)   18 textile mills. Funds 26,900,000 *yüan*. 1,427 employees.
  (2)   8 clothing and shoe factories.   Funds 1,000,000 *yüan*. 405
        employees.
  (3)   12 paper mills. Funds 4,100,000 *yüan*. 437 employees.
  (4)   3 printing works. Funds 5,200,000 *yüan*. 379 employees.
  (5)   12 chemical plants (pharmaceuticals, soap, leather, china
        and porcelain, petroleum oil, etc.).   Funds 17,030,000 *yüan*.
        674 employees.
  (6)   9 tool-making factories.   Funds   3,662,792   *yüan*.   237
        employees.
  (7)   12 coal-mines. Funds 1,777,070 *yüan*. 432 employees.
  Total : 74 factories and mines.   Funds 59,669,862 *yüan*. 3,991
  employees.

These factories and mines were small, and the greater part
of them were still in the stage of " manufacture."   Only part of
them were operating mechanized production.   " However," Mao

---

[27] Mao Tse-tung, *Economic Problems and . . . ,* p. 104.

Tse-tung says, "After five years of effort we have laid the first foundations and have produced results in assuring our supplies and adjusting prices."[28]

Among these industries textile mills occupied the most important place. In 1942 they produced more than 22,000 rolls of cotton cloth, but the demand was for 40,000 to 50,000 rolls, and in order to attain self-sufficiency it would be necessary to make even greater efforts in the future. At that time the annual production of the paper industry amounted to more than 5,000 *lien* of Ma Lan paper, and this could be increased to 7,000 *lien* in 1943. In the chemical industries, self-sufficiency had already been attained in the production of soap, and soap was being exported from the Border Area.

Among the industries in the public sector of the economy, government-run factories held the principal place. Thus, government-run textile factories produced 56% of the yearly production of 22,000 rolls of cotton cloth in the textile factories in the public sector of the economy, while government-run paper mills produced 70% of the total production of paper in the public sector of the economy and government-run soap factories produced 70% of all the soap produced in the Border Area.

In the plan for 1943, a call is made for increases in funds, the establishment of a unified direction of the whole of self-sufficient industry, the establishment of a system of economic accounting and the improvement of organization and supervision in factories, and in addition to this the plan calls for the attainment in 1944 of complete self-sufficiency in the supply of cotton cloth for public use, as well as in printing and stationery paper. A call is also made for the attainment of self-sufficiency in petroleum oil by means of an increase in production, and, further, for the attainment of the export of the production of petroleum oil.

We have already shown how important salt was for the maintenance of the external balance of payments in the Shan-Kan-Ning Border Area by our quotations from the writings of Mao Tse-tung. However, Forman stresses that petroleum oil was as important as salt in its rôle of one of the principal means of obtaining foreign exchange. He notes that the Chinese Communist

---

[28] Mao Tse-tung, *Economic Problems and...*, p. 110.

authorities made the most strenuous efforts to develop the Yen-ch'ang oilfield, discovered by a Japanese oil engineer in 1906 but abandoned by him and, at a later date, by the Socony Vacuum Oil Company of the United States.[29]

In the work for the attainment of economic self-sufficiency carried out by the various units of the Army stationed in the Shan-Kan-Ning Border Area, the results produced by 359 Brigade (stationed at Suite) are particularly striking. In the productive enterprises carried on by this unit, the policy was adopted of giving first place to agriculture, second place to industry and transport, and third place to commerce. In the three years between 1940 and 1942 the unit was able to attain 82% self-sufficiency in all its expenses, apart from the food supplies which it received from the government. Among the enterprises carried on, we may note that in the sphere of commerce, the Brigade's activities begin with the establishment of the 359 Brigade Military and Civil Co-operative at Yangwu in 1937, a merchant of the locality, Li Man-jen, being appointed manager. In 1940 this Co-operative moved to Suite, changing its name to the Ta Kuang Commercial House, and became a profit-making enterprise. Some of the factories run by the Brigade also had the words "Ta Kuang" prefixed to their designations. An example is the Ta Kuang Textile Factory. The Ta Kuang Commercial House maintained friendly relations with merchants outside the Border Area, and carried on trade with the enemy in a positive manner. Further, in addition to undertaking the conversion and withdrawal of the Kuang Hua Notes, the Ta Kuang Commercial House endeavoured to stabilize commodity prices by selling its own salt at 4 taels for 2 catties when the market price was 4 taels for 1 catty.

Thus, according to Mao Tse-tung, in 1942 the public sector of the economy came to occupy three-fifths of the supply for government finance. Forman states that in 1944 the public sector of the economy was producing 64% of the food and clothing required by the Army, government personnel and Party workers.[30]

The first of all the payments which the people had to make

---

29   H. Forman, pp. 81–83.
30   H. Forman, p. 85.

to the government was the payment of levies of public food called *Kung Liang* (公糧). These levies of public food stood at 10,000 piculs in 1937 and 1938, 50,000 piculs in 1939, 90,000 piculs in 1940, 200,000 piculs in 1941, and 160,000 piculs in 1942. After 1943 these levies were set at 180,000 piculs, and it was made clear that for several years thereafter the policy was to maintain them at this level. In addition to public food, there were also public levies of public fodder (*Kung Ts'ao*: 公草) (26,000,000 catties in 1941 and 16,000,000 catties in 1942) and of public salt (*Kung Yen*: 公鹽) (100,000 loads in 1943). Other taxes were also levied in addition to these. It is not clear from the writings of Mao Tse-tung what kinds of taxes were comprised, but in the same work he mentions a "sheep tax" and a duty on imports and exports. We may also note that in 1941 government bonds were issued to the value of 50,000 *yüan*.

According to N. Watanabe, the total revenue in the Shan-Kan-Ning Border Area in 1943 was 9,000,000,000 *yüan*, and of this sum 64% (or 5,760,000,000 *yüan*) represented the value of production carried on in the public sector of the economy and by public organs, 10% (or 900,000,000 *yüan*) represented the revenue from the unified progressive tax, 8% (or 720,000,000 *yüan*) represented the income from government trade and commerce, and the remaining 18% (or 1,620,000,000 *yüan*) was made up by the issue of government bonds and by borrowing from the Border Area Bank, that is to say, by increased issues of Resistance Currency. Among these latter sources of revenue, the government bonds were allotted on a compulsory basis among the rich peasants, so that it may be said that some part of the 18% was made up by the issue of paper currency.[31]

As a result of our examination of the Shan-Kan-Ning Border Area we may draw attention to the following points as being of particular importance as factors which may be supposed to have contributed to maintain the value of the Border Currency in this Area.

(1) This Border Area was of comparatively small size and had a comparatively small population. It was a backward economic area principally devoted to agriculture and pastoralism.

(2) There were no large urban centres of consumption in the

---

31 N. Watanabe, pp. 99–100.

Area. It was a producing area and as far as food supplies were concerned it had enough and to spare.

(3) The Chinese Communist régime made great efforts to develop the private sector of the economy under the principles of " Equal Consideration for the Public and the Private " and " Equal Consideration for the Army and the People."

(4) The government, the Army and the organs of the Party all carried on public enterprises of their own, and by this means sought to increase the self-sufficiency of the economy.

(5) In relation to outside areas, the necessity of importing manufactured goods such as cotton cloth was the principal cause of an adverse balance of payments, but exports of salt and petroleum oil contributed greatly to compensating this adverse balance.

(6) The Border Currency had no direct connections with foreign currencies or foreign exchange such as the American Dollar or the Pound Sterling.

We may also note that in the Shan-Kan-Ning Border Area " Shan-Kan-Ning Border Area Trading Company Circulatory Notes " (陝甘寧邊區貿易公司流通券) were later issued in addition to the Shan-Kan-Ning Border Currency.[32]

II. The Appearance of Border Currencies and Liberated Area Currencies

The first Border Currency to be issued was that of the Chin-Ch'a-Chi Border Area. This was issued on the 20th of March, 1938.[33] At this time Kuomintang Legal Tender Notes (法幣) and Hopei Currency (河北幣) were circulating in the western parts of Hopei, and the Kuomintang Legal Tender Notes were the most

---

[32] Tseng Ling & Han Lei, " The Circulation of Currency in the Liberated Areas, 1948–1949," *CCYC*, No. 3, 1955, p. 113.

[33] The sources referred to in writing this section are presented below. When we quote these sources, footnotes have been omitted from the text of this section.

S. Yoshikawa, pp. 177–180; N. Watanabe, Chap. 5; Ch'en Yang-ch'ing et al., *Some Theoretical Problems Connected with the People's Currency* (Peking, 1954), pp. 57–62; P'eng Ti-hsien & Ho Kao-chu, *Principles of the Theory of Currency and Credit* (Peking, 1955), Chap. 15, Sect. 1, and Tseng Ling & Han Lei, op. cit.

important of them. In the eastern parts of Shansi, currency issued by the Shansi Provincial government (such as the Shansi Provincial Bank Notes: 山西省銀行票, and the Railway Bank Notes: 鐵路銀號票) and Kuomintang Legal Tender Notes were in circulation. All these currencies were exchangeable at par.

In this situation, the Administrative Commission for the Chin-Ch'a-Chi Border Area (established on 10th of January, 1938) set up the Chin-Ch'a-Chi Border Area Bank (晋察冀邊區銀行), and instructed the Bank to issue the Chin-Ch'a-Chi Border Currency (晋察冀邊幣). When this currency was first put into circulation it was determined that 1 *yüan* of Chin-Ch'a-Chi Border Currency had to have the same value as 1 *yüan* of Kuomintang Legal Tender Notes in the market. On the 1st of October, 1941, the Kuomintang Legal Tender Notes were called in at this value, and the circulation of Kuomintang Legal Tender Notes, Hopei Currency and Shansi Currency was prohibited in the Chin-Ch'a-Chi Border Area. In this way the Border Area established its own currency system. Previous to this, the Provisional Government of the Republic of China, a pro-Japanese régime which had been established at Peking, had set up the Federal Reserve Bank of China (中國聯合準備銀行), and on its instructions this Bank issued the Federal Reserve Bank Notes (聯銀券) on the 10th of March, 1941. The Administrative Commission for the Chin-Ch'a-Chi Border Area no doubt had its own reasons for beginning the issue of Border Currency in its Area, but it is certain that it was also a measure adopted by the Chinese Communists for the protection of their own economy at the time when the attack on the Kuomintang Legal Tender Notes by the issue of the Federal Reserve Bank Notes was begun. The head office of the Chin-Ch'a-Chi Border Area Bank was at first established in Wut'ai *Hsien*, Shansi Province, but after the end of the Pacific War it moved to Changchiak'ou. According to N. Watanabe, in 1944 this bank issued paper currency to the value of 200,000,000 *yüan*.

The next Border Currency to be issued was the Chinan Currency (冀南幣). This was first issued in October, 1939, in the T'aihang Area by the Chinan Bank (冀南銀行). When first put into circulation, 1 *yüan* of the Chinan Currency was determined to have the same value as 1 *yüan* of the Kuomintang Legal Tender Notes, and later, after the spring of 1941, the Kuomintang

Legal Tender Notes were called in at this value, and their circulation prohibited.   Later the Chinan Area, the T'aihang Area, the Yüpei Area and the Luhsi Area were combined to form the Chin-Chi-Lu-Yü Border Area.   The government of the Chin-Chi-Lu-Yü Border Area was formally constituted in July, 1941.   Hereupon the Chinan Currency extended its circulation to the Chinan and Yüpei Areas, and at the same time it replaced the Shangtang Notes (上黨票) which had been in circulation in the Shangtang Area until that time.   However, the Luhsi Area, which was cut off by the war, continued to issue its own Luhsi Currency (魯西幣). The head office of the Chinan Bank was established at Nankung *Hsien*, Hopei Province, and according to Watanabe, in the summer of 1944 the Chinan Currency issued amounted to 200,000,000 *yüan*, and showed a comparatively marked depreciation in value.

The next currency to be issued was the North-West Peasants' Currency (西北農民幣) in the Chin-Sui Area.   The issue of this currency took place in May, 1940.

TABLE II-1   Border Currencies and Liberated Area Currencies

Period	Issuing-Bank	Area of Circulation	Name of Currency	Date of Issue
	Shan-Kan-Ning Border Area Bank	Shan-Kan-Ning Border Area	Shan-Kan-Ning Border Currency	18 Feb., 1941
	North-West Peasants' Bank	Chin-Sui Border Area	North-West Peasants' Currency	May, 1940
	Chinan Bank	Chin-Chi-Lu-Yü Border Area	Chinan Currency	Oct., 1939
I	Chin-Ch'a-Chi Border Area Bank	Chin Ch'a-Chi Border Area	Chin-Ch'a-Chi Border Currency	20 March, 1938
	Ch'ang Ch'eng Bank	Chi-Je-Liao Border Area	Ch'ang Ch'eng Currency	
	Peihai Bank	Shantung Area	Peihai Currency	1 Apr., 1942
	Huachung Bank	Huachung Area	Huachung Currency	
		Tungchiang Anti-Japanese Base, Kwangtung Province	Yumin Currency, Hsinlu Currency	
	North-East Bank	North-East Liberated Area	North-East Currency	The Summer of 1946
	Chungchou Peasants' Bank	Chungyüan Liberated Area	Chungchou Currency	1948
II	Kuantung Bank	Lüshun-Talien Area	Kuantung Currency	Oct., 1948
	Southern People's Bank	Ch'aomei Liberated Area	Southern Currency	Sept., 1949
	Inner Mongolian People's Bank	Inner Mongolia	Inner Mongolian Currency	

After these currencies came the issue of the Shan-Kan-Ning Border Currency (陝甘寧邊幣) which we have already described.

Later, when the Chinese Communist armies had established bases in different parts of northern and central China, they issued currencies of their own in these areas. We present above a table listing the Chinese Communist currencies, dividing into two categories, namely those in circulation at the end of the Pacific War (Period I) and those put into circulation after the end of the Pacific War (Period II).

We may add the following in connexion with the table.

(1) In the Shan-Kan-Ning Border Area, Shan-Kan-Ning Border Area Trading Company Circulatory Notes were also issued.

(2) In the Chin-Chi-Lu-Yü Border Area, Shangtang Notes were in circulation in the Shangtang Area, and Luhsi Currency in the Luhsi Area.

(3) Apart from the Ch'angch'eng Bank's issue of the Ch'angch'eng Currency (長城幣), the sources also mention the circulation in the Chi-Je-Liao Border Area of Chin-Ch'a-Chi Border Currency overprinted " Chi-Je-Liao " and known as " Chi-Je-Liao Border Currency " (冀熱遼邊幣), as well as a form of currency known as " Jehol Bank Notes " (熱河銀行票).

(4) In the New Fourth Army base in central China, subsidiary currency was issued by the Yü-O Construction Bank (豫鄂建設銀行) in the Yü-O Border Area in June, 1941. Later, between the spring and summer of 1942, various sorts of Chinese Communist currency were issued. This period coincides with the time when the National Government of the Republic of China, the pro-Japanese régime in central and south China which had its capital at Nanking, had started to replace the Kuomintang Legal Tender Notes with the Reserve Bank Notes (儲備券) throughout its territory, after the attack on the Kuomintang Legal Tender Notes by issuing notes from the Central Reserve Bank of China (中央儲備銀行). The New Fourth Army issued their own currencies as a defence against this move. Note-issuing banks which were established in the Chinese Communist areas at this time include the Yenfu Bank (鹽阜銀行), the Huaihai Bank (淮海銀行) and the Chianghuai Bank (江淮銀行) in the Supei Area, the Suchung Bank (蘇中銀行) in the Suchung Area, the Huinung Bank (惠農銀號) in the Sunan Area, the

Huaipei Local Bank （淮北地方銀號） in the Huaipei-Su-Wan Border Area, the Huainan Bank （淮南銀行） in the Huainan-Su-Wan Border Area, and the Tachiang Bank （大江銀行） in the Wanchung Area. The present writer carried out an on-the-spot survey of the state of the currency in this area about this time. As a general rule, these Chinese Communist currencies started from parity exchange with the Kuomintang Legal Tender Notes and extended their areas of circulation, and at length the Kuomintang Legal Tender Notes were called in and their circulation forbidden. Thus, in June, 1943, the Chianghuai Bank was calling in Kuomintang Legal Tender Notes and exchanging them at par with Border Currency, the Huainan Bank, and Huinung Bank and the Huaipei Local Bank were calling in the Kuomintang Legal Tender Notes at an exchange rate of 1 *yüan* of Border Currency for 2 *yüan* of Kuomintang Legal Tender Notes, and the Yenfu Bank was calling in the Kuomintang Legal Tender Notes at an exchange rate of 1 *yüan* of Border Currency for 5 *yüan* of Kuomintang Legal Tender Notes. Thereafter, as an accompaniment to the decline in the value of the Kuomintang Legal Tender Notes, Chinese Communist authorities gradually raised the exchange-value of their currencies. Taking an example from this period, we may observe that the Huaipei Local Bank Notes were issued in denominations of ten *yüan*, five *yüan*, one *yüan*, five *chiao*, two *chiao* and one *chiao*. The writer has in his possession a five *yüan* note and a one *yüan* note of the Huaipei Local Bank. The quality of the paper is inferior to that of the low denomination (one *yüan* and below) notes issued by the Kuomintang government about this time, the printing is poor, and it appears that it may have been done by lithography. On the face of these notes there appeared the figure of a carpenter (on the five *yüan* note), a miner and a peasant (on the one *yüan* note), each engaged in his work, together with the inscription, " Printed in the Thirty-First Year of the Chinese Republic " （中華民國卅一年印）. On the back of these notes there appeared the letters XUAIBEI DIFONG IENXAO (on the five *yüan* note) or YWONSUBION DIFONG IENXAO (on the one *yüan* note). The five *yüan* note measures 11.5 cm. by 6.0 cm., while the one *yüan* note measures 13.0 cm. by 6.7 cm. Both notes are of smaller size than the normal paper currency, and this may be supposed to have been due to a desire to economize in paper. It is also interesting that the five *yüan* note is of smaller size than the one *yüan* note. However, the value of paper currency is unaffected by its material value. Such paper currencies gradually increased their value relative to the Kuomintang Legal Tender Notes as time went on. Be that as it may, at the end of the Pacific War these isolated Chinese Communist areas were linked up, and as an accompaniment to this the Huachung Currency (華中幣) appeared in the rôle of a unified currency for the areas occupied by the Huachung New Fourth Army. The Huachung Bank (華中銀行) is said to have been the successor of the Yenfu Bank.

From the above we may see that during the period of the Border Areas and the period of the Liberated Areas there were at the least about 20 kinds of Chinese Communist currency in circulation.

All these currencies were issued independently of one another in the various Border Areas. This form of currency issue was adopted because of the geographic and economic separation of the Border Areas among themselves, but it was accompanied by the advantage that any effects produced in a particular Border Area did not spread to other areas. This was particularly so since there was no small number of occasions on which the Chinese Communist armies were obliged to retreat (for military operations were carried on under very difficult conditions, not only, as need hardly be said, in the anti-Japanese war but also in the war against the armies of Chiang Kai-shek after the end of the Pacific War), and we must note that the multiplicity of currencies made it impossible for the enemy to gain possession of goods in the Chinese Communist areas with the help of currency obtained as the result of the occupation of one of these areas, or to attempt to attack the currencies in use on the Communist side. In this way the Border Currencies, besides fulfilling the demands of financial administration and economies in the various Border Areas, also served as important instruments for carrying on economic warfare and currency warfare against the enemy.

In March, 1946, the Chinese Communist armies were already stepping up their military offensive in Manchuria. This took place simultaneously with the withdrawal of the armies of the Soviet Union from Manchuria. It is also from this period that the Chinese Communist armies attacked the cities of north China— Ts'ingtao, Chinan, Tat'ung, T'aiyüan, K'aifeng, Hsüchou, etc.— and undertook the conquest of the area north of the Yangtze. As an accompaniment to these developments the area under the control of the Chinese Communist armies was expanded. About the end of the Pacific War the conquest of areas formerly occupied by the Japanese Army or by the armies of Chiang Kai-shek was described as the " liberation " of these areas, and these occupied areas began to be styled " Liberated Areas." At length the older Border Areas were merged with the Liberated Areas in a process of unification, and the areas under the control of the Chinese Communist armies came to be designated as the North-East Liberated Area, the North China Liberated Area, the Shantung Liberated Area, the North-West Liberated Area, the Chungyüan Liberated Area, the P'ingchin Liberated Area, etc.[34] Before this could be accomplished the Chinese Communist armies had to suffer such setbacks as the temporary occupation by the armies of Chiang Kai-shek of Changchiak'ou (in October, 1946) and of the Communist capital, Yenan (in March, 1947), but throughout this period the power of the Chinese Communist armies and the area of territory under their control went on steadily expanding. In the course of the development of this situation there were issued the currencies of the period after the end of the Pacific War, the North-East Currency (東北幣), the Chungchou Currency (中州幣), etc., listed in the table above. These currencies were not described as Border Currencies, but they possessed the same functions and character as the Border Currencies, at least when they were first issued.

---

[34] In Mao Tse-tung's " On United Government," written in May, 1945, the areas in which the Chinese Communist armies were active in the war against Japan are referred to in general as " Liberated Areas." See *MTTH*, Vol. 6, p. 207. Later the " Great Administrative Region " system was put into force, and the area under Communist control was divided up into the North-East Great Administrative Region, the North China Great Administrative Region, the East China Great Administrative Region, the Central and Southern Great Administrative Region, the North-West Great Administrative Region, and the South-West Great Administrative Region.

CONCLUSION

The above considerations have enabled us to make some examination of the general outline of the economies and currencies of the Chinese Communist Border Areas. Let us conclude with a brief discussion of people's confidence in these currencies and the maintenance of their values.

The areas under the control of the Chinese Communist armies in the period of the Border Areas were direct producing areas occupied wholly by rural populations, and each of these areas was small in size. In this they differed greatly from the areas occupied by the Japanese Army, for the latter were very large, and included cities of various sizes containing a large unproductive population. Again, they were not to be compared with the vast area of territory under the control of the armies of Chiang Kai-shek. This was the first factor contributing to the maintenance of the value of the Border Currencies. Unlike the Legal Tender Notes of the Chiang Kai-shek régime, the Chinese Communist currencies had no direct connexion with the American Dollar or other foreign currencies. As a matter of course the Chinese Communists regarded the Legal Tender Notes of the Chiang Kai-shek régime and the currencies associated with the Japanese Army as foreign currencies, and they were obliged to take steps to maintain the value of the Communist currencies in relation to these currencies, but they had no need to worry over a depreciation in value relative to the currencies of foreign countries. This was the second factor contributing to the maintenance of the value of the Chinese Communist currencies. The third factor was the system of dispersed, local currency issues on an independent basis. Lastly, we must add to these the extension of the planned economy, centring on increasing the self-sufficiency of the public sector and the accompanying measures for the maintenance of the value of these currencies within and outside the Communist areas in a manner which we have seen in the course of our examination of the economy of the Shan-Kan-Ning Border Area. These various circumstances combined to give the Chinese Communist currencies a greater degree of stability than was enjoyed by the Kuomintang Legal Tender Notes and the currencies associated with the Japanese Army.

CHAPTER III

THE ESTABLISHMENT AND STABILIZATION OF THE PEOPLE'S CURRENCY SYSTEM

INTRODUCTION

THE PEOPLE'S CURRENCY, which is the present unitary currency of the People's Republic of China, came into being about one year before the People's Republic of China was established. The People's Currency was created in the midst of the civil war against the Kuomintang. Consequently, the People's Currency fulfilled the primary function of being a military currency or operational currency, and at the same time performed the rôle of an economic currency, simultaneously accomplishing the unification of the currency system. When at length the People's Republic of China was established the People's Currency was set on firmer foundations and it played a most important part in relation to economic recovery and the building up of the national economy. In this chapter we propose to examine the process through which the People's Currency came into being and brought about the unification of the currency system in China, as well as the structure of the People's Currency system and the manner in which it achieved stabilization.

I. The Process of Unifying the Currency System under the People's Currency

It was on the 1st of December, 1948, that a great step towards the unification of the Chinese currency under the People's Currency was taken with the establishment of the People's Bank of China at Shihchiachuang. Previous to this, the following complex of preparatory work for unification of the currency had been undertaken in the Liberated Areas.

(1) In the North-West Liberated Area (comprising the Shan-Kan-Ning Border Area and the Chin-Sui Border Area) the issue of the Shan-Kan-Ning Border Currency was stopped in January, 1948, and the North-West Peasants' Currency was made the unitary currency of the North-West Liberated Area.

(2) On the basis of a joint declaration by the governments of the Chin-Ch'a-Chi and Chin-Chi-Lu-Yü Border Areas on the 15th of April, 1948, the Chin-Ch'a-Chi Border Currency and the Chinan Currency were made interchangeable at an exchange ratio of 10 : 1.

(3) On the 5th of October, 1948, the Peihai Currency (北海幣) of the Shantung Liberated Area was made interchangeable with the two currencies circulating in the North China Liberated Area as described above. The Peihai Currency and the Chinan Currency were to be exchangeable at par, and the Peihai Currency and the Chin-Ch'a-Chi Border Currency were to be exchangeable at an exchange ratio of 1 : 10.

(4) On the 20th of October, 1948, the interchangeability of the North-West Peasants' Currency of the North-West Liberated Area and the currencies of the North China was declared. The exchange ratios were 1 : 20 between the Chinan Currency and the North-West Peasants' Currency, and 1 : 2 between the Chin-Ch'a-Chi Border Currency and the North-West Peasants' Currency.

(5) On the 15th of November, 1948, the Peihai Currency and the Huachung Currency were declared interchangeable at par.

The following statement made by the Head of the People's Bank of China, Nan Han-chen, on the 10th of January, 1949, shows how well the currencies of the Liberated Areas retained their stability at the time of the fierce currency war between the Kuomintang currency and the Chinese Communist currencies in 1948. " Last year (1948) the rate of price inflation in the areas under the rule of the Kuomintang was more than 1,000 times (50 times before the currency reform, and 25–30 times after the currency reform). The rate of price inflation in the Liberated

Areas south of the Great Wall was only 1–3 times. The currencies of the Liberated Areas were always more stable than those of the Kuomintang. When Japan surrendered, 1 *yüan* of the currency of the Shantung Liberated Area was worth 5 *yüan* of the Kuomintang Legal Tender Notes, and 1 *yüan* of the currency of the Chinan Liberated Area was worth 2 *yüan* of the Kuomintang Legal Tender Notes. In August, 1948, about the time when the Kuomintang government implemented its currency reform, 1 *yüan* in the currencies of these two Liberated Areas became worth 800–2,000 *yüan* of the Kuomintang Legal Tender Notes, and at present is worth more than 10,000 *yüan* of Kuomintang Legal Tender Notes. To make a comparison with the Gold Yüan Notes (金圓券), about September, 1948, 1 *yüan* in Gold Yüan Notes was worth 3,000 *yüan* of the currencies of the Shantung Liberated Area or Chinan Liberated Area, but at present it stands at less than 300 *yüan*. In some localities it is worth about 100 *yüan* of these currencies."[35]

We may add that the Kuomintang régime's currency reform was carried out on the 19th of August, 1948, and that the Kuomintang régime then called in the Legal Tender Notes in exchange for Gold Yüan Notes at the rate of 1 *yüan* in Gold Yüan Notes for 3,000,000 *yüan* in Legal Tender Notes.[36]

One aspect of the currency war which the Chinese Communists were waging against the Kuomintang régime at this time may be

---

[35] *Hua Shang Pao* (6 Dec., 1948).

[36] Among the currencies of the Chiang Kai-shek régime in use at this period there were, in addition to the Legal Tender Notes, the Bank-notes in Customs Gold Unit (關金券), the North-East Circulatory Notes (東北流通券), and the Bank of Taiwan Notes (臺幣). The Bank-notes in Customs Gold Unit came into use as a general currency in April, 1942, and their official value was set at 1 *yüan* in Bank-notes in Customs Gold Unit for 20 *yüan* in Legal Tender Notes. The North-East Circulatory Notes were issued after the end of the war with Japan when the Chiang Kai-shek régime took over Manchuria, and the Bank of Taiwan Notes were issued when they took over Taiwan. Under this currency reform the Bank-notes in Customs Gold Unit and the North-East Circulatory Notes were called in together with the Legal Tender Notes (the period of exchange ending on the 20th of November), but the continued circulation of the Bank of Taiwan Notes was allowed. North-East Circulatory Notes were called in at the rate of 300,000 *yüan* for 1 *yüan* in Gold Yüan Notes, and the official exchange rate for Bank of Taiwan Notes was 1 *yüan* in Gold Yüan Notes for 1,835 *yüan* in Bank of Taiwan Notes.

Nominally at least, the mint par value of the Gold Yüan Notes was fixed at 0.2217 grammes of pure gold, or one-fourth of the mint par value of the American Dollar.

seen from the following A. P. News report from Shanghai, dated the 18th of October, 1948.

" Taking advantage of their victories at Chinan, Chinchou and elsewhere, the Chinese Communists are opening an offensive against the Kuomintang government on the economic front. Whenever the Chinese Communist armies capture a town they confiscate all the Gold Yüan Notes on the market. These are then sent to the great cities, to Shanghai, Tientsin, Tsingtao or Peip'ing. Communist organs in these cities use these notes in buying up rice, cotton cloth, woollen goods, drugs, radios and other articles of daily use. They will pay 3–4 times the normal market prices in buying up these goods. As a result, the prices in the great cities have risen all the more, and material resources in short supply have become even more scarce."

Previous to this, on the 15th of June, 1948, the Chin-Ch'a-Chi and Chin-Chi-Lu-Yü Border Areas were combined to form the North China Liberated Area, and on the 19th of August—the day on which the Kuomintang régime implemented its currency reform—the North China People's Government was established at Changchiak'ou (Hopei Province) as a result of deliberation by the North China Provisional People's Congress. This government was formed by a combination of the Chin-Ch'a-Chi and Chin-Chi-Lu-Yü Border Areas, while the military forces in these two Border Areas were reorganized into two Field Combined Armies of the North China People's Liberation Army and the two committees of the Chinese Communist Party in these Border Areas combined to form a North China Central Bureau. The appearance of the North China People's Government at Changchiak'ou represents the beginning of a new epoch in the history of the Chinese Communist Revolution. At this time the Chin-Ch'a-Chi Border Area Bank (the head office of which had already moved to Changchiak'ou) and the Chinan Bank were combined to form the North China Bank (華北銀行).

In the autumn of the same year there was an intensification of military operations by the Chinese Communist armies, and they went on to conquer not only the cities of the North China and North-West regions, but also Manchuria. We may list the cities occupied by the Chinese Communist armies in chronological order as follows: Chinan (24th September), Chefoo and Chinchou

(15th October), Ch'angch'un (19th October), Chengchou (22nd October), Paot'ou (23rd October), K'aifeng (24th October), Shanhaikuan and Ch'inhuangtao (27th November), and Hsüchou (4th December). Thus, by the end of 1948 the occupation of Peip'ing and Tientsin was regarded as being only a question of time.

While this situation was in course of development, the People's Government of the North China Liberated Area issued the following order on the 22nd of November. "With the agreement of the governments of Shantung Province, the Shan-Kan-Ning Border Area and the Chin-Sui Border Area, the currency circulating in the North China, East China and North-West Areas is to be unified, and the North China Bank, the Peihai Bank, and the North-West Peasants' Bank are to combine to form the People's Bank of China. The head office of this bank is to be located at the head office of the former North China Bank, and, from the 1st of December, 1948, the bank will issue People's Bank of China Notes (abbreviated designation " People's Currency ") which will be put into circulation as the unitary standard currency in the North China, East China and North-West Areas."

Thus, on the 1st of December, 1948, the People's Bank of China began business at the address of the former North China Bank at Shihchiachuang. Work began on the calling in and exchange of the old currencies for People's Currency. The legal rates of exchange against 1 *yüan* of People's Currency were 100 *yüan* for Chinan Currency (including Luhsi Currency) and Peihai Currency, 1,000 *yüan* for Chin-Ch'a-Chi Border Currency, and 2,000 *yüan* for North-West Peasants' Currency. It was at first intended to issue the People's Currency in six denominations—one *yüan*, five *yüan*, ten *yüan*, twenty *yüan*, fifty *yüan* and one hundred *yüan*, but for the meantime only three denominations were issued : ten *yüan*, twenty *yüan* and fifty *yüan*—and the existing local small-denomination currencies were used as substitutes for small-denomination currency of the People's Currency.[37]

We have no detailed information as to the system governing

---

[37] Later, as a consequence of the inflation of the People's Currency in 1949, People's Currency was issued in the denominations of five hundred *yüan* and one thousand *yüan* on the 15th of August of that year. Previous to this, two hundred *yüan* notes were in circulation in Shanghai. The highest denomination in People's Currency, issued in the later period of inflation, was that of fifty thousand *yüan* (issued in 1954).

the issue of the People's Currency, but on this point the Head of the People's Bank of China, Nan Han-chen, declared on the occasion of the opening of the Bank that it was not based on precious metals or foreign exchange, but was backed by the things which the people required—grains, cotton cloth, raw cotton, and other such means of livelihood and fruits of production.[38]

1949 was the year in which the Chinese Communist armies achieved basic dominance over the continent. In January of that year they liberated Peking (after the liberation Chinese Communist authorities changed the name from Peip'ing to Peking) and Tientsin, in April Nanking, in May Shanghai, in October Canton, and in November Chungking. On the 9th of December the Chiang Kai-shek régime moved from Ch'engtu to Taiwan. During this period, on the 1st of October, the People's Republic of China was established at Peking. Up to that time the head office of the People's Bank of China moved to Peking. For the present we shall postpone our examination of the calling in or adjustment of the Kuomintang currencies and foreign currencies which took place at this period, and shall examine the Chinese Communists' activities which brought about the unification of their currencies.

Tientsin was occupied by the Chinese Communist forces on the 15th of January, 1949. The city of Tientsin was the first great city to be liberated by the Chinese People's Liberation Army. At that time the city of Tientsin was a part of the North China Liberated Area, but since the Fourth Field Army had come into this area from Manchuria to carry out military operations, Chinan Currency, Chin-Ch'a-Chi Border Currency, North-East Currency and Ch'angch'eng Currency were circulating alongside the People's Currency. On the 18th of January, the Tientsin branch of the People's Bank of China began to call in and exchange these currencies in conformity with the instructions from the North China People's Government. The exchange rates, which are said to have been based on market values, were as follows.

For exchange against 1 *yüan* of People's Currency

	(*yüan*)
Chinan Currency	100
Chin-Ch'a-Chi Border Currency	1,000

---

[38] *Hua Shang Pao* (6 Dec., 1948).

North-West Peasants' Currency   2,000
Peihai Currency   100
Shan-Kan-Ning Border Area
    Trading Company Circulatory Notes 2,000
North-East Currency   200
Ch'angch'eng Currency   200
Jehol Bank Notes   1,000
Chi-Je-Liao Border Currency   5,000
Huachung Currency   100
Chungchou Peasants' Currency   3

Among these currencies, temporary permission was given for the circulation of the North-East Currency and the Ch'angch'eng Currency in Peking and Tientsin, but on the 15th of April, 1949, the North China People's Government prohibited the circulation of these currencies in Peking and Tientsin, and took steps to ensure that they should be gradually returned to the North-East.

In March of the same year the Chungchou Peasants' Bank (中州農民銀行) became the Chungyüan Area branch of the People's Bank of China, the issue of the Chungchou Currency was stopped, and People's Currency came into circulation in this area. The official exchange rate against 1 *yüan* in People's Currency was 3 *yüan* of Chungchou Currency. The calling in of the Chungchou Currency at this exchange rate began on the 13th of November, 1949, and the circulation of the Chungchou Currency was prohibited after the 1st of January, 1950.

In the North-East Liberated Area the North-East Currency became the unitary currency of the area both in name and in fact about the end of 1948. In addition to North-East Currency and other currency issued by the Chinese Communists (such as the Ch'angch'eng Currency and the Chi-Je-Liao Border Currency), Central Bank of Manchuria Notes (滿洲中央銀行券), USSR Army Notes, and Kuomintang currency issued in the North-East were also in circulation in this area. It is thought that the head office of the North-East Bank (東北銀行) was at first located at Harbin, and moved to Shenyang about the end of 1948. Special conditions prevailed in the Lü-Ta Administrative Area (the Lüshun-Talien Area), and here the circulation of the Kuantung Currency (關東幣) was permitted, a currency peculiar to this area. Since the end of the Pacific War the Lü-Ta Area had been under the command of the armed forces of the USSR, while the civil administration had been carried on by a Chinese Communist organ called the Lü-Ta Administrative Office, and the Kuantung Currency had been issued from the Kuantung Bank (關東銀行) on instructions from the Chinese Communist authorities. Nevertheless, in June, 1950, it was decided to call in the Kuantung Currency in this area in exchange for North-East Currency. The exchange rate was 1 *yüan* of Kuantung Currency for 270 *yüan* of North-East Currency.

In South China, the Yümin Currency (裕民幣) and Hsinlu Currency (新陸幣) were in circulation in the Tungchiang Anti-Japanese Base Area and the Ch'aomei Liberated Area in Kwangtung Province, having been issued in these areas, but when the Southern Currency (南方幣) was issued from the Southern People's Bank (南方人民銀行) in September, 1949 the issue of both these currencies was stopped, and for the time being they all circulated at par. Later, on the 3rd of November, the People's Bank of China, Canton, fixed the exchange ratio between the People's Currency and these three currencies at 1 : 250, and on the 18th of November the Kwangtung Military Control Commission published an order prohibiting the circulation of Southern Currency in the city of Canton, and permitting its circulation only in the inner parts of Kwangtung Province. On the 15th of June, 1950, the Southern Currency was called in throughout the Yüeh-Kan-Hsiang Border Area and the Min-Yüeh-Kan Border Area. The exchange rate was 250 *yüan* of Southern Currency against 1 *yüan* of the People's Currency circulating in these areas.

The final measures taken by the Communists for the unification of the currencies which had been in circulation since the time of the outbreak of war with Japan were centred on the " Order for the Calling in and Exchange of Currency Circulating in the North-East and Inner Mongolia " issued by the Administrative Council of the Government of the People's Republic of China on the 31st of March, 1951. This Order made the following provisions.

(1) Within a certain period beginning on the 1st of April, 1951, the People's Bank of China was to undertake the calling in and exchange of the local currencies issued by the North-East Bank and the People's Bank of Inner Mongolia, the Bank

being made responsible for carrying this out. The rate of exchange was to be the current official rate. Nine *yüan* five *chiao* of these local currencies were to be exchanged against 1 *yüan* of People's Currency.

(2) With effect from the 1st of April, 1951, all of the commodity prices, accounts, contracts, etc., in the North-East Area and Inner Mongolia must employ the People's Currency as the official standard of currency. In all credits and debts before the 1st of April, 1951, the sums to be repaid would be calculated in People's Currency on the basis of the rate of exchange stipulated in this order.

(3) With effect from the 1st of April, 1951, the North-East Bank and the People's Bank of Inner Mongolia were to be reorganized to become subordinate agencies of the People's Bank of China.

The head office of the People's Bank of China fixed the period for the calling in and exchange of the North-East Currency under the provisions of the above order at two months from the 1st of April, 1950. For the first of these two months the North-East Currency was to be allowed to circulate on the market, but after the 1st of May its circulation on the market was to be stopped. The period for the calling in and exchange of the local currency issued by the People's Bank of Inner Mongolia was to be three months after the 1st of April, and the currency was to go out of use on the 1st of June.

An editorial in the *Jenmin Jihpao* on the 31st of March, 1951, gave the following reasons why the currency of the North-East had not been unified under the People's Currency until that time. "This was because the liberation of the whole of the North-East Area was accomplished at a comparatively early date and prices there achieved stability before those of any other area, but nevertheless the liberation of the area south of the Great Wall was not finished, and so it was still necessary to devote efforts to the stabilization of prices in the North-East Area. In order that the North-East Area should not be affected by the military operations and the instability of the prices which affected the area south of the Great Wall, and in order to restore production as far as possible, to advance the work of construction in the North-East Area, and so to facilitate this area's contributing to the support of the whole country in an improved financial and economic condition, it was decided that this North-East Area should retain for the time being the independent currency system which was in force there." Why, then, had the currency system of the North-East now been unified? On this point the editorial said, " The reason is that now that prices have been stabilized throughout the whole country, that industry and agriculture have been rapidly restored and have shown some development, and now that the purchasing power in the hands of the people has been universally increased, there is an urgent necessity for a normal interchange of goods throughout the whole country, and it would be an obstacle to such an interchange of goods if the North-East Area were to retain its independent currency system."

It is clear from the above that a bank called " The People's Bank of Inner Mongolia" (內蒙古人民銀行) had been established, and that it had issued a form of currency differing from the People's Currency, but it is not known when these events took place. The issue of paper currency by the People's Bank of Inner Mongolia appears to be analogous to the issue of the Southern Currency by the Southern People's Bank, and this issue of currency may have taken place some time after the People's Bank of China began business at Shihchiachuang in 1948 and may have been undertaken in the absence of any direct connexion with that institution. We may note in passing that the People's Government of the Inner Mongolian Autonomous Region was established in May, 1947.

We must also make mention of the fact that the paper currency, bonds, and food-notes issued by the Red Army in the Red Areas in Kiangsi, Fukien, and other Provinces during the period of the Chinese Soviets were called in after the establishment of the People's Republic of China. For example, in December, 1952, the People's Government of Fukien Province disbursed 1,700,000,000 *yüan* in People's Currency in exchange for such paper currency, bonds and food-notes.[39] This measure was carried out on the basis of a decision of the Financial and Economic Committee of the Administrative Council of the Central

---

[39] *H-TKP* (18 Dec., 1952). See also Ministry of Finance & the People's Bank of China, "Notice Regarding Bonds Issued in Former Soviet Areas and in Liberated Areas which Are to be Called in by the People's Bank of China," in *Collected Legal Enactments of the People's Republic of China* (Peking, 1958), Series VIII, pp. 120–123.

People's Government, and it would appear that the People's Government of Kiangsi Province carried out similar measures. According to the decision mentioned above, 12 *yüan* of paper currency during the period of the Chinese Soviets was to be considered equal to 1 silver *yüan*. The values in silver *yüan* were then converted into People's Currency, and the paper currency was exchanged for People's Currency at this value.

The above account enables us to understand how more than a score of Communist currencies were at last unified under the People's Currency as an accompaniment to the growth of the strength of the Communist régime and the expansion of the territory under its control. However, there was another important aspect of the unification of the currency system under the People's Currency. This aspect consists of the policies of the Communist régime in regard to the currencies associated with the Chiang Kai-shek régime, the currencies of foreign countries, and gold and silver. Let us now give a brief account of these matters.

Table III-1 shows the measures taken by the Communists in regard to the currency of the Chiang Kai-shek régime in 1949 in the principal cities liberated by the Communist armies.

TABLE III-1
Communist Measures in Regard to the Currency
of the Chiang Kai-shek Régime (1949)

City	Date of Liberation	Period of Conversion for Gold Yüan Notes	Rates of Exchange (Gold Yüan Notes per *yüan* of People's Currency)	Remarks
Tientsin	15 Jan.	17 Jan.–4 Feb.	At first 6 *yüan*, later 8 *yüan*	Special favourable rates for workers and students applied.
Peking	24 Jan.	2 Feb.–22 Feb.	10 *yüan*	
Nanking	24 Apr.	28 Apr.–5 May	2,500 *yüan*	
Shanghai	25 May	30 May–5 June	100,000 *yüan*	
Canton	15 Oct.			No exchange made.

In this manner the Communists first called in the Gold Yüan Notes during a defined period, and then prohibited their circulation. However, the rates of exchange were fixed at levels which were unfavourable to the Gold Yüan Notes in the light of prevailing market prices. Besides serving to drive the Gold Yüan

Notes out of the Liberated Areas, this measure was also in the nature of a positive attack on the Gold Yüan Notes. The Gold Yüan Notes which had been called in were also used in obtaining material resources and in attacking the Gold Yüan Notes. It is said that the amount of Gold Yüan Notes called in in Shanghai was 36,000,000,000,000 *yüan* and that this was equivalent to 53% of their total issues at that time.[40] Again, on the 2nd of July of the same year the Chiang Kai-shek régime issued "Silver Yüan Notes" (銀元券) in Canton.[41] Hereupon the Communist régime declared that the Chiang Kai-shek régime's Silver Yüan Notes would be worthless in the Liberated Areas in the future, and that the Communist government would give no money inexchange for them.

In regard to foreign currencies the Communists forbade their circulation on the market and either caused them to be converted to People's Currency at official rates, or caused them to be deposited with the People's Bank of China or the Bank of China as "foreign currency deposits." Foreign exchange was subject to control. The people were allowed to be in possession of gold and silver, but their export was forbidden, while permission was

---

[40] Tseng Ling & Han Lei, "The Circulation of Currency in the Liberated Areas, 1948-1949," *CCYC*, No. 3, 1955, p. 118.

[41] According to the "Instructions for the Issue of Silver Yüan and Silver Yüan Notes." The Silver Yüan Notes were put into circulation on the 4th of July, 1949. According to the above-mentioned Instructions, the Gold Yüan Notes were to be called in and exchanged against Silver Yüan Notes between the 18th of July and the 31st of August, and the Gold Yüan Notes would become invalid after the 1st of September. According to a cabinet decision of the Kwangtung government dated the 22nd of June, the rate of exchange was to be 500,000,000 *yüan* in Gold Yüan Notes for 1 silver *yüan*. At that time 300,000,000,000,000 *yüan* of Gold Yüan Notes had been issued, and it was anticipated that the whole could be called in against 600,000 silver *yüan*. We will do well to reflect that when the Gold Yüan Notes were issued by the Chiang Kai-shek régime in August, 1948, 2 *yüan* in Gold Yüan Notes were declared equal to 10 silver *yüan*. Thereafter, on the 10th of October, the Kuomintang government began its move from Canton to Chungking. The Chinese Communist armies liberated Canton on the 15th of October and Chungking on the 30th of November, after which the Kuomintang government moved to Ch'engtu. It was on the 8th of December that the Kuomintang government transferred its capital to Taiwan. Previous to this, on the 15th of June, the New Bank of Taiwan Notes had been issued in Taiwan, and the Old Bank of Taiwan Notes were called in at an exchange rate of 40,000 *yüan* for 1 *yüan* in New Bank of Taiwan Notes. One American Dollar was declared equivalent to 5 *yüan* in New Bank of Taiwan Notes.

required for their importation and for their movement within the country. The People's Bank of China has been accustomed to buy gold and silver from the people at official rates of exchange.

The present writer has given a detailed account of the policies of the government of New China in regard to foreign exchange and gold and silver in his "Foreign Exchange Control System," Chapter 8 of *China's Foreign Trade Machinery* (Asian Economic Studies Series No. 17, 1961). Accordingly only a short account has been given here.

On the 1st of November, 1951, the Administrative Council of the Central People's Government instructed the People's Bank of China to issue People's Currency inscribed in the Uigur language and to replace the Silver Yüan Notes issued by the Sinkiang Provincial Bank with this currency. The rate of exchange was 1 *yüan* in Silver Yüan Notes for 350 *yüan* in People's Currency.

It was more or less in this fashion that the People's Currency became the unitary currency of the whole of China, apart from the silver *yüan* and Tibetan Notes (藏票) circulating in the Tibetan region and the Bank of Taiwan Notes (臺幣) circulating in Taiwan, the seat of the Chiang Kai-shek régime.

However, in the period since the appearance of the People's Currency, prices in this currency have risen. This rise was greatest during 1949, and at the end of that year the prices in People's Currency rose to 75 times the price level at the beginning of 1949.[42] A stop was put to this acute inflation by the "Unified Policy for State Financial and Economic Work" which was put into effect by the New China régime in March, 1950.

The currency reform of New China carried out on the 1st of March, 1955, which was based on the foundation of the stability of the value of the People's Currency established over the previous five years and which sought to sweep away the vestiges of the acute inflation and at the same time to unify and adjust the huge volume of People's Currency, was a devaluation in the form of the change of the denominations of the notes. The Old Currency

---

[42] P'eng Ti-hsien & Ho Kao-chu, *Principles of the Theory of Currency and Credit* (Peking, 1955), p. 339. In Campbell & Gordon C. Tullock, "Hyperinflation in China, 1939–49," *Journal of Political Economy*, Vol. LXII, No. 3 (June, 1954), it is stated that prices rose by 70 times in that year (p. 239). Refer also to statistical tables given in the following section.

was called in at an exchange rate of 1 *yüan* of New Currency for 10,000 *yüan* of the Old Currency, while not only the currency but all prices, contracts, and other expressions of economic value in terms of currency were changed to the New Currency standard at the same rate of exchange.

The New Currency instituted by this currency reform was issued in eleven denominations. Five denominations of standard currency were issued—one *yüan*, two *yüan*, three *yüan*, five *yüan* and ten *yüan*—and six denominations of subsidiary currency—one *fen*, two *fen*, five *fen*, one *chiao*, two *chiao*, and five *chiao*. The exchange of currency began on the 1st of March, notice being given that the exchange of Old Currency bearing the denominations of ten thousand *yüan* and fifty thousand *yüan* would be stopped on the 1st of May, and that the date for the cessation of the exchange of Old Currency bearing the denominations of five thousand *yüan* and below would be announced later. The ten *yüan* denomination of the New Currency was not to be issued for the meantime. The paper of the New Currency was better than that of the Old Currency, and there was uniformity in the designs, colours and sizes of the paper currency in each of the denominations. The notes were also inscribed in the Chinese, Tibetan, Mongol and Uigur languages, these inscriptions facilitating their circulation throughout the country and symbolizing the equality and unity of the various nationalities. The rate of 1 *yüan* of New Currency against 10,000 *yüan* of the Old Currency was derived from the fact that the prices of gold, silver, and foreign exchange in China were, on the whole, about 8,000 to 10,000 times higher than they had been before the outbreak of war with Japan and that the ten thousand *yüan* note of the Old Currency had attained the position of the principal denomination of circulating currency, and it was not arrived at by considering the rise of a price index.[43] Again, at the time of the currency reform the new official foreign exchange rate was stated to be 685.90 *yüan* of People's Currency for £100 sterling bought, and 692.70 *yüan* for £100 sterling sold.

In this way the new People's Currency system came into being, a system of which the people of New China could be proud

---

[43] See Editorial, "Protect the Newly Issued People's Currency!" *Jenmin Jihpao* (21 Feb., 1955).

as an "independent, unitary and stable currency system."[44]

We may add that since the 1st of December, 1957, the People's Bank of China has been issuing three denominations of coined subsidiary currency, one *fen*, two *fen* and five *fen* (described in the original sources as "metal fen currency" (金屬分幣), and sometimes referred to by the abbreviated designation "hard fen currency" (硬分幣), and these have been put into circulation at values equal to the old subsidiary paper currency of the same denominations. Further, the ten *yüan* currency, the issue of which was postponed at the time of the currency reform, was actually issued at the same time as the issue of these coins.[45]

II. The Value of the People's Currency and Its Stabilization

It was in March, 1950, that prices in New China moved towards stabilization. Among the important factors contributing to the checking of the rising trend of prices and to the establishment of the stabilization of the People's Currency we may mention, first, the virtual conclusion of military operations on the continent with the subjugation of Yünnan Province in March, 1950, and second, the implementation of the "Unified Policy for State Financial and Economic Work" by the government of New China during the same month. The Unified Policy for State Financial and Economic Work was popularly known as the *San P'ing* (三平) policy, "Three Balances" policy, since the policy aimed at (1) balancing the finances of the government, (2) balancing supply and demand in regard to important material resources, and (3) balancing the cash accounts of government organs. The word *P'ing* in the expression *San P'ing* is used in the sense of "balancing." The later policies for maintaining the value of the People's Currency, and, consequently, for assuring price stability,

---

[44] Detailed knowledge is lacking in regard to the currency systems of Tibet, Ch'inghai, etc. It appears that silver *yüan* were circulating in these areas in 1951.

[45] According to the announcements made by the People's Bank of China, dark blue one *yüan* notes were issued from the 25th of March 1961, and thus put into circulation along with the red one *yüan* notes already in use. Again, brown five *yüan* notes and dark red one *chiao* notes were issued from the 20th of April, 1962.

may be said to have been pressed forward with this *San P'ing* policy as their starting-point and nucleus.

The first element in the *San P'ing* policy was the balancing of the finances of the state. Steps were to be taken to increase government revenue and to reduce expenditure. In 1950 the finances approached a balance, and in 1951 and the succeeding years they achieved a complete balance, leaving a surplus which increased from year to year. Up to 1956 this surplus, besides being employed as loan funds by the People's Bank of China and for other special purposes, was also allotted to the balancing of the government finance, so that there were no outstanding balances left. Thus, in the few years preceding 1955 no new issues of currency designed to cover financial deficits were made in New China. We must also add that socialist planning now entered the fields of revenue-collection and the distribution of expenditure in the financial administration of the government of New China.[46]

The second element in the *San P'ing* policy was the balancing of the cash accounts of state organs. This policy was at first styled " cash control," and later " currency control." " State organs " included state enterprises, organs, military units, co-opera-tives and other bodies, and joint state-private enterprises were made subject to the provisions of " currency control " in the same manner as " state organs." As an accompaniment to the socializa-tion of China, the economic transactions centring on these state organs have come to assume a greater and greater importance in the national economy, and as a general rule the greater part of these transactions are settled through the accounts which the state organs have with the People's Bank of China, the use of cash by state organs being reduced to the minimum. The currency ac-counts of the state organs are, in themselves, a reflection of the implementation of socialist economic planning, and in particular their cash accounts are subject to direct control by the People's Bank of China. With these policies as the nucleus, in regard to currency, finance and the international balance of payments,

---

[46] On the state finances of New China, see T. Miyashita, " A Review of Income and Expenditure in the State Finances of the Chinese Communists, and a Con-sideration of Their Future Prospects," *Aziya Kenkyū*, Vol. III, No. 2 (1957), and T. Miyashita, " Financial Administration," in Aziya Seikei Gakkai, *A Handbook of Chinese Politics and Economics* (Tokyo, 1962), Part IV, Chap. 4.

policies were adopted for enlarging and strengthening the powers of the People's Bank of China for reorganizing the financial organization centred on the Bank, for the strengthening of the Bank's powers for the financial control and for the putting into use of units for conversion of currency to real values (see below), for the control of foreign trade and foreign exchange, for the encouragement of remittances from overseas Chinese and the investment of overseas Chinese capital, and for the control of gold, silver, etc.

The third element in the *San P^xing* policy was the attainment of a balance of supply and demand in regard to important material resources. This policy started out with the establishment and operating of state commercial companies which dealt with certain types of material resources, their exclusive duty being that of buying up and selling or distributing certain important material resources. The number of state commercial companies increased as the range of material resources grasped by the government increased, and in 1955 the number of state commercial companies directly attached to the Centre was 37.[47] The supply and marketing co-operatives worked together in collecting the principal agricultural products and in distributing and selling material resources in the rural areas as the assistants of state commerce. The industrial products grasped by state commerce at first were the products of state industry, but as time went on state commerce acquired favoured positions in the procurement of raw materials, and by making use of these positions it gave out orders and entrusted processing work to capitalist industry, and undertook planned purchases of the goods produced as well as planned marketing of such products. On the other hand, state commerce also acquired favoured positions for dealing in the commodities handled by capitalist commerce, and by making use of these positions it began to make private commercial enterprises retail distributors and commission agents of its commodities. The above policies, as well as the birth and development of joint state-private enterprises in the capitalist commerce and industry, were nothing other than a manifestation of a development of these enterprises in the direction of state capitalism, while from the point of view of state commerce they constituted an enlarge-

---

[47] On the development of the mechanisms for state commerce, see T. Miyashita, *China's Foreign Trade Machinery* (Tokyo, 1961), Chap. 4.

ment of the extension of state commerce, curbing the insatiable pursuit of money profit on the part of capitalist commerce and industry, suppressing their speculative activity in the market, and at the same time serving to bring about a planned adjustment of supply and demand in regard to material resources and to assure the stability of prices. In November, 1953, the state instituted planned systems for the purchase and distribution of foodstuffs, and at the same time introduced systems for planned purchase and distribution of edible oil products and of the raw materials for edible oils. In September, 1954, a planned system for the purchase of raw cotton and for the distribution of cotton cloth was put into effect. Again, in order to block speculative activities by private commerce in the towns and in the countryside, the local People's Governments co-operated with the relevant organs in maintaining a close supervision of the markets in their several areas of jurisdiction.

We have now briefly reviewed the development of the price policies of New China, centring our attention on the *San P'ing* policy. To this we may add some words about the nature of the People's Currency system. The People's Currency system is a managed currency system, but it is the currency system of a state governed by the principles of New Democracy or People's Democracy, and is a system of currency which operates under the conditions of an economy run in accordance with the principles of New Democracy and oriented to socialist construction. Consequently, the acceptability and value of the People's Currency is upheld by the political and economic power in the hands of the state. Economic power is of particular importance in this connexion, and in this sense the rehabilitation and development of the productive forces in the period since the foundation of the new state have been the basic element maintaining the value of the People's Currency, and, consequently, maintaining the stability of prices. When the People's Bank of China opened, the then Head of the Bank, Nan Han-chen, declared, " The issuing system of the People's Currency is not based on precious metals and foreign currencies, but is backed by the things which the people of the Liberated Areas require—grains, cotton cloth, and other such means of livelihood and fruits of production," and it would appear that his words refer to this situation. Further, in an article published in the first issue of *Hung Ch'i* (Red Flag) for the year 1960, Li Hsien-nien, the Minister of Finance, made the following notable remarks about the policy of issuing the People's Currency. " The volume of currency issued in the market should be designed to increase from year to year along with the development of production and the enlargement of the sphere of commerce. Under conditions in which currency issues are not made for the purpose of covering government financial deficits or for giving credit unsupported by material resources, it is entirely necessary that suitable increases in the volume of currency issued should be made for the purposes of buying up commodities, and such increased currency issues, being suitable to the demands of the market, are a legitimate and normal form of currency issue. Provided only that the state has control over commodities, it will be possible for the state to sell these commodities in exchange for currency, and also to preserve the stability of prices in the market. If the state fails to make currency issues of this kind it will be disadvantageous for a rapid development of the national economy."[48] There is a comparatively large number of Chinese writers who hold that it is necessary for commodities to be granted an existence parallel to that of currency issues and circulation.[49]

On the other hand, however, we must note that as currency theory has developed in New China, and as studies of Marxist currency theory have advanced, the question of the relation between the People's Currency (or the People's Currency system) and precious metals has become the object of discussion.[50]

From statements made to representatives of the New China News Agency by responsible persons from the People's Bank of China on the 20th of February, 1955, we may learn the follow-

---

[48] Li Hsien-nien, " Some Problems in the Practical Aspects of Financial Administration and Credit Provision," *HC*, No. 1, 1960, p. 10.

[49] For example, Huang Ta, " The Principles Governing Bank Loans and Their Relation to Currency Circulation," *CCYC*, No. 9, 1962, and Lin Chi-k'en, " On the Operation of the Laws Governing Currency Circulation under a Socialist System," *CCYC*, No. 2, 1963.

[50] For an example of those who attach importance to the significance of gold for the essential quality and the value of the People's Currency, and for the People's Currency system, see the works made by Ch'en Yang-ch'ing et al., *Some Theoretical Problems Connected with People's Currency* (Peking, 1954). For a writer who ignores these questions, see the paper by Shih Wu, "An Essay Regarding the Basis of the People's Currency in Marxist Currency Theory,'" *CCYC*, No. 2, 1957.

ing regarding the state of China's international balance of payments at this time. Taking the total of international receipts and payments in the year 1950 as 100, this total stood at 221.5 in 1954, and since 1950 there had always been a favourable balance. Between 1950 and 1952, payments stood at 90% of receipts, and in 1953 and 1954 at 98.6%. In 1954, gold reserves had increased more than 10 times over 1950, and the proportion occupied by international trade in China's international balance of payments was 70.8% in 1950, and 83.9% in 1954. We may note in this connexion that in the report made to the National People's Congress by the Minister of Foreign Trade, Yeh Chi-chuang, in July, 1955, it is stated that the total of New China's foreign trade in 1954 was 8,486,730,000 *yüan* (in American Dollars, $ 3,620,000,000), so that the scale of New China's international balance of payments in 1954 was 10,111,500,000 *yüan* (or, in American Dollars, $ 4,310,000,000).

We have already pointed out that the acceptability and value of the People's Currency was basically assured by economic power grasped by the government of New China, and in this connexion one of the important factors determining the suitability or otherwise of the operation of socialist economic planning is the suitability or otherwise of price-policies. By 1956 the basic processes of the socialist transformation of capitalist commerce and industry as well as that of agriculture and handicrafts in New China had been completed, and in this way favourable conditions were provided for the operation of socialist economic planning in that country. However, each economic unit was linked to other economic units by exchanges of commodities, and, consequently, by prices, except in the case of the procurement and distribution of commodities within the state economies (or between state enterprises). Such exchanges of commodities and such prices had by now come to differ in their nature to some degree from exchanges of commodities and prices as these exist under a capitalist economy, but at this period, as in the past, the effects of prices on the national economy of New China could not be disregarded. For this reason prices were fixed for the procurement and distribution of commodities within the state economies, too, and the level of these prices, as well as that of the official and specified prices for important commodities fixed by the state had an important significance for the operation of Chinese socialist economic planning.[51]

We present below some collected statistics showing the trends of the value of People's Currency.

Tables III-2 and III-3 may serve to show how prices in People's Currency rose in Shanghai and Tientsin after liberation and how they were stabilized after the *San P'ing* policy came into effect in March, 1950.

Table III-4, which we present below, may serve a similar purpose. In the Table the term *chech'u p'aichia* (折儲牌價) means the official monetary price per unit calculated in terms of commodities, which is used for the purpose of saving. *Chech'u* (折儲) is an abbreviation of *cheshih ch'uhsü* (折實儲蓄). *Cheshih* (折實) means "calculated in terms of commodities." During the period in which the prices in People's Currency were not yet stabilized the Communist authorities adopted a system for the calculation of stabilized values which was based on commodities. For example, a fixed quantity of staple food grains was laid down as the unit to be used in connexion with wages and salaries. This unit was called a *kungtz'u-fen* (工資分) or "wage-unit." Wages and salaries expressed in this unit were paid in currency after multiplying the prevailing market price of the unit of staple food grains by the appropriate number of units. There was also a system for the payment of wages and salaries in which half of the wage or salary was paid in currency and half in kind. Commodity-units were also employed in connexion with bank deposits and loans, and in connexion with bonds issued by the government. In all these cases the units were called "*fen*" (分). In the case of the *chech'u p'aichia* price officially fixed every day by the People's Bank of China in Tientsin, the unit was calculated from the wholesale prices for one catty of T'ungchou flour of the brand called "*litzu*" (利字), one foot of calico of the quality called

[51] Since Stalin discussed the laws of value in socialist society in his *Economic Problems of Socialism in the USSR* (Moscow, 1952), discussion has been carried on in China on the subject of the operation of these laws in the Chinese economy under New Democracy. For example, see Chu Chien-nung, "The Operation of the Laws of Value in Our Country during the Transition Period," *CCYC*, No. 5, 1955; Sun Chih-fang, "Let Planning and Statistics Be Set on the Foundation of the Laws of Value," *CCYC*, No. 6, 1956, and Hsieh Mu-ch'iao, *Economic Planning and the Laws of Value* (Peking, 1957).

TABLE III-2

Wholesale Price Index for Shanghai, after Liberation (July, 1949–1957)

(June, 1949=100)

Month / Year	Yearly Index	January	February	March	April	May	June	July	August	September	October	November	December
1949	529.05	—	—	—	—	—	—	204.61	231.11	270.29	383.58	892.41	1,192.28
1950	2,179.47	1,434.80	2,097.90	2,242.93	1,871.29	1,806.83	2,015.20	2,206.46	2,293.78	2,384.27	2,522.74	2,655.61	2,621.94
1951	2,875.03	2,667.56	2,647.44	2,651.97	2,764.05	2,810.37	2,884.05	2,948.34	2,997.74	3,038.39	3,038.68	3,078.54	3,073.15
1952	2,903.77	3,033.20	2,975.12	2,904.43	2,863.25	2,867.86	2,880.16	2,882.61	2,893.99	2,896.75	2,891.53	2,886.00	2,870.32
1953	2,859.70	2,888.12	2,884.38	2,878.36	2,845.06	2,833.87	2,833.29	2,840.47	2,850.23	2,859.70	2,856.83	2,872.33	2,874.34
1954	2,871.18	2,867.16	2,861.42	2,859.99	2,862.28	2,867.16	2,870.32	2,872.90	2,876.06	2,875.20	2,876.63	2,875.49	2,888.69
1955	2,881.23	2,898.16	2,898.16	2,882.38	2,880.37	2,879.51	2,881.51	2,881.51	2,880.37	2,874.05	2,872.04	2,873.48	2,873.76
1956	2,873.48	2,873.76	2,873.76	3,873.48	2,872.33	2,872.04	2,872.04	2,871.47	2,871.47	2,873.48	2,875.77	2,876.63	2,876.63
1957	2,886.39	—	—	—	—	—	—	—	—	—	—	—	—

Source: Institute of Economic Research, Academia Sinica, Shanghai, and the Institute of Economic Research, Shanghai Academy of Social Science, *Collection of Materials Relating to Prices in Shanghai Before and After Liberation* (Shanghai, 1958), pp. 448–453.

TABLE III-3

Wholesale Price Index for Tientsin, after Liberation

(July, 1936–June, 1937=100)

Month / Year	Yearly Index	January	February	March	April	May	June	July	August	September	October	November	December
1949	3,589.354*	First half 105.558 Second half 173.778	281.176	372.522	468.450	913.095	982.425	1,588.533	3,108.041	3,228.740	3,938.953	10,501.885	14,099.571
1950	23,815.600	16,266.58	24,182.21	28,828.95	24,334.69	21,624.84	21,806.89	23,056.61	23,942.65	23,310.32	25,170.39	26,164.05	26,448.97
1951	29,269.430	27,009.09	27,137.03	27,325.79	27,742.01	28,187.81	28,278.84	28,656.18	29,345.36	30,161.51	30,503.76	30,861.52	31,024.42
1952	30,841.270	30,944.66	30,839.73	30,739.42	—	—	—	—	—	—	—	—	—

Note: * Index calculated from data covering February to December.

Source: Institute of Economic Research, Nank'ai University, *Nank'ai Index Materials, 1913–1952* (Peking, 1958), pp. 20 and 44–47.

"*wufu*" (五福), and one catty of maize-flour starch, as published in the *Tientsin Jihpao*, a newspaper published in Tientsin. When dealing with deposit withdrawals, this Bank at first applied values of commodity-units derived from the commodity prices five days prior to the date of the transaction, but after the 3rd of April, 1950, it applied values of commodity-units derived from the prices prevailing on the day of the transaction. The unit for the *chech'u p'aichia* price fixed by the People's Bank of China, Shanghai, was calculated from the previous day's wholesale prices of 1 *sheng* (升) of polished non-glutinous rice of medium quality (emended to 1.56 Shanghai local catties of the same commodity with effect from the 1st of October, 1950), 1 foot of twelve-pound *Lungt'ou* (龍頭) cotton cloth, 1 tael of Pench'ang peanut oil, and 1 catty of ordinary oval briquettes (emended to 12 taels of coal waste with effect from the 2nd of November, 1950). From these instances we may understand how the People's Bank of China used different bases for the calculation of the *chech'u p'aichia* prices in different parts of China. Further, the *chech'u p'aichia* prices were fixed daily, but it is worthy of note that it is the figure for the monthly average of these prices which appears in Table III-4. Again, in the case of the commodity-unit employed in connexion with the issue of government bonds, when, March, 1949, the Administrative Commission for the North-East issued " Commodity-Unit Incentive Bonds for the Production and Construction " the unit employed (described as a "*fen*") was calculated from the total Mukden market prices of 5 local catties of kaoliang, 1 foot of calico with the brand *wufu*, 5 local catties of granular salt, and 34 local catties of coal. The unit or "*fen*" (share) employed in connexion with the issue of the People's Victory Commodity-Unit Bonds by the Central People's Government of the People's Republic of China in January, 1950, was based on the total of average wholesale prices of 6 catties of polished rice (of millet in Tientsin), of 1.5 catties of wheat flour, of 4 feet of calico and of 16 catties of coal in the 6 cities of Shanghai, Tientsin, Wuhan, Hsian, Canton and Chungking. The market price of this unit was uniformly published at 10-day intervals by the People's Bank of China. With the stabilization of the value of the People's Currency these commodity-units lost their function, and on the whole they were abolished by the end of 1955.

TABLE III-4

Chech'u P'aichia Prices Fixed by the People's Bank of China
in Seven Great Cities (Monthly Averages)

(unit: *yüan*)

Year	Month	Shanghai	Tientsin	Wuhan	Canton	Peking	Chungking	Hsian
1949	March	—	90.40	—	—	—	—	—
	April	—	106.61	—	—	100.66	—	—
	May	—	221.89	—	—	227.79	—	—
	June	341	247.67	518	—	252.69	—	—
	July	733	409.08	766	—	390.03	—	480
	August	823	781.63	729	—	753.24	—	765
	September	793	749.28	709	—	764.62	—	811
	October	821	827.39	897	—	847.08	—	985
	November	1,993	2,277.75	1,973	—	2,043.66	—	2,399
	December	2,861	3,003.44	3,102	4,074	3,130.08	—	3,570
	Average	1,195	871.51	1,242	4,074	945.54	—	1,502
1950	January	3,973	3,487.35	2,552	4,132	3,616.21	2,254	4,880
	February	5,799	5,216.06	4,047	7,374	5,117.60	4,709	7,674
	March	6,229	6,099.13	5,021	9,887	6,408.58	6,976	8,329
	April	5,680	5,587.35	4,019	7,205	5,626.57	5,584	6,479
	May	5,386	5,161.21	3,700	6,511	5,135.00	5,171	5,305
	June	5,238	5,017.22	3,525	6,195	5,017.00	5,291	4,841
	July	5,181	4,801.48	3,571	6,415	4,863.00	5,155	4,779
	August	5,200	4,737.61	3,505	5,931	4,723.00	5,192	4,800
	September	5,036	4,731.30	3,227	5,673	4,715.00	4,748	5,042
	October	4,967	4,894.50	3,326	5,456	4,893,00	4,832	5,331
	November	5,003	5,091.00	3,532	5,379	5,131.00	4,930	5,644
	December	4,982	5,142.01	3,649	5,393	5,149.00	4,858	5,872
	Average	5,223	4,997.19	3,639	6,296	5,033.00	4,975	5,748
1951	January	5,027	5,491	3,703	5,157	5,392	4,961	6,149
	February	5,036	5,495	3,695	5,178	5,404	5,002	6,175
	March	4,994	5,492	3,764	5,180	5,380	5,189	6,175
	April	5,215	5,723	3,768	5,377	5,512	5,492	6,408
	May	5,291	5,755	3,781	5,565	5,511	5,718	6,425
	June	5,331	5,718	3,810	5,570	5,511	5,823	6,425
	July	5,403	5,713	3,840	5,587	5,505	5,926	6,434
	August	5,458	5,869	3,758	5,634	5,671	5,795	6,584
	September	5,455	5,986	3,723	5,545	5,841	5,498	6,646
	October	5,452	6,063	3,741	5,530	5,861	5,510	6,688
	November	5,452	6,110	3,753	5,574	5,873	5,813	6,701
	December	5,452	6,123	3,791	5,507	5,880	5,794	6,763
	Average	5,297	5,795	3,761	5,450	5,612	5,543	6,464
1952	January	5,452	6,122	3,705	5,495	5,841	5,792	6,763
	February	5,499	6,117	3,697	5,542	5,845	5,926	6,794
	March	5,527	6,152	3,744	5,574	5,871	5,993	6,813
	April	5,521	6,155	3,738	5,590	5,814	6,018	6,738
	May	5,520	6,017	3,726	5,602	5,704	6,101	6,568
	June	5,520	5,934	3,717	5,585	5,657	6,094	6,524
	July	5,520	5,928	3,686	5,565	5,682	6,045	6,524
	August	5,499	5,974	3,615	5,533	5,733	5,890	6,524
	September	5,424	6,054	3,566	5,525	5,812	5,812	6,637
	October	5,392	6,081	3,538	5,471	5,830	5,809	6,668
	November	5,380	6,152	3,549	5,386	5,891	5,810	6,782
	December	5,371	6,152	3,594	5,347	5,899	5,845	6,782
	Average	5,469	6,070	3,656	5,518	5,798	5,928	6,676
1953	January	5,412	6,226	3,629	5,437	5,974	5,927	6,931
	February	5,416	6,234	3,638	5,465	5,982	5,939	6,941
	March	5,416	6,234	3,624	5,461	5,982	5,939	6,941
	April	5,477	6,307	3,694	5,519	6,004	6,098	6,932
	May	5,487	6,310	3,649	5,589	6,005	6,096	6,932
	June	5,488	6,310	3,639	5,601	6,042	6,092	6,932
	July	5,488	No further	3,651	5,512	6,055	6,100	6,932
	August	5,488	figures	No further	5,451	6,055	6,071	6,819
	September	5,488	issued	figures	5,427	6,055	6,008	6,811
	October	5,473		issued	5,420	6,021	5,977	6,789
	November	5,467			5,410	5,962	6,011	6,782
	December	5,466			5,496	5,913	6,057	6,785
	Average	5,464			5,482	6,004	6,026	6,877
1954	January	5,466			5,648	5,905	6,069	6,785
	February	5,466			5,733	No further	6,069	6,785
	March	5,466			5,767	figures	6,069	6,785
	April	5,466			5,796	issued	6,069	6,785
	May	5,482			5,796		6,069	6,785
	June	5,492			No further		6,069	6,785
					figures			
					issued			

Source: *Jenmin Shouts'e*, 1952 Edition, pp. 298-299, 1953 Edition, p. 299, and 1954 Edition, pp. 471-472.

Foreign exchange dealings in the People's Currency are sub-ject to control, but the form in which this control was exercised differed to some degree from region to region when the People's Republic of China was first established. At first there were frequent changes in the official foreign exchange rates for the People's Currency, and these also differed from region to region. In was on the 8th of July, 1950, that the official foreign exchange

TABLE III-5

All-China Price Indices (1)

(Average for previous year=100)

Index Year	All-China Wholesale Price Index	All-China Retail Price Index	All-China Agricultural Products Purchase-Price Index	All-China Index of Retail Prices of Industrial Products in Rural Districts
1952	100.1	99.9	101.7	99.5
1953	98.7	103.2	110.1	98.5
1954	100.4	102.2	103.4	101.7
1955	100.6	100.8	99.5	101.2
1956	99.5	100.0	103.0	99.0
1957	100.9	102.2	105.0	101.1
1958	100.0	99.7	102.2	99.4

Source: State Statistical Bureau, *Ten Great Years* (Peking, 1959), pp. 152–154.

TABLE III-6

All-China Price Indices (2)

(Average for 1952=100)

Index Year	All-China Wholesale Price Index	All-China Retail Price Index	All-China Agricultural Products Purchase-Price Index	All-China Index of Retail Prices of Industrial Products in Rural Districts
1953	98.7	103.2	110.1	98.5
1954	99.1	105.5	113.8	100.2
1955	99.7	106.3	113.2	101.4
1956	99.2	106.3	116.6	100.4
1957	100.1	108.6	122.4	101.6
1958	100.1	108.3	125.1	101.0

Note: The reason why the retail price index appears to be a little too high is that the prices of supplementary foods were too low in the past, and the figures were adjusted from year to year. The rise in the purchase-prices for agri-cultural products is due to the fact that these prices were systematically revised for a few years, since it had been found that the relative values between agricultural products and industrial products were irrational.

Source: Same as TABLE III-5.

TABLE III–7

All-China Price Indices (3)

(Average for March, 1950=100)

Index Year	All-China Wholesale Price Index	Retail Price Index for Eight Great Cities
1951	92.4	94.6
1952	92.6	93.7
1953	91.3	98.3
1954	91.8	100.2
1955	92.4	101.1
1956	91.9	101.1
1957	92.7	102.2
1958	92.7	101.4

Source: Same as Table III–5.

rates in different regions, official foreign exchange rates for overseas Chinese buying the People's Victory Commodity-Unit Bonds and unified all-China official foreign exchange rates for foreign trade were abolished, and that unified all-China official foreign exchange rates came to be published. At first the unified all-China official foreign exchange rate was changed two or three times in each month, but as time went on the changes became less frequent. The following Table shows the changes which took place in the official foreign exchange rates for the People's Currency in the early years after the establishment of the People's Republic of China. It should be noted that the People's Currency at this period is the Old People's Currency.

On the 1st of March, 1955, the Chinese government began the calling in of the Old People's Currency, exchanging it for New People's Currency at the rate of 10,000 *yüan* of Old People's Currency for 1 *yüan* of New People's Currency. The official foreign exchange rates published by the People's Bank of China on the same day were 685.90 *yüan* of People's Currency for £ 100 Sterling bought, and 692.70 *yüan* for £ 100 Sterling sold, and 42.70 *yüan* for HK $ 100 bought and 43.10 *yüan* for HK $ 100 sold. These rates were arrived at merely by converting the values of the Old People's Currency into those of the New People's Currency by the official exchange rate. Among these foreign exchange rates, at least those in relation to Sterling and the Hong Kong Dollar, have been maintained up to recent times.

We may add that the most recent official purchase-prices for gold and silver published by the People's Bank of China are 3.04 *yüan* for 1 gramme of gold, and 0.40 *yüan* for 1 gramme of silver.

TABLE III-8

Changes in the Official Foreign Exchange Rates for the
People's Currency

(unit : *yüan* of Old People's Currency)

Date of Change in Exchange Rate	Against One American Dollar	Against One Pound Sterling	Against One Hong Kong Dollar
1 Jan., 1950	21,000	48,000	3,000
6 Jan., 1950	23,000	64,400	3,498
24 Jan., 1950	25,000	70,000	3,816
1 Feb., 1950	27,500	77,000	4,167
8 Feb., 1950	29,000	81,200	4,538
23 Feb., 1950	31,000	82,150	4,733
24 Feb., 1950	34,500	89,500	5,267
2 March, 1950	39,000	97,500	5,990
11 March, 1950	42,000	98,708	6,460
2 Apr., 1950	41,000	98,400	6,400
10 Apr., 1950	40,000	96,000	6,244
19 Apr., 1950	39,000	97,194	6,310
24 Apr., 1950	37,500	93,000	6,000
26 May, 1950	37,500	98,900	6,120
3 July, 1950	35,500	94,280	5,870
8 July, 1950	35,000	93,200	5,800
26 July, 1950	35,000	91,440	5,690
7 Aug., 1950	32,200	81,220	4,950
5 Sept., 1950	31,000	78,210	4,750
28 Sept., 1950	31,000	78,210	4,750
25 Dec., 1950	27,360	73,570	4,500
4 Jan., 1951	24,900	68,370	4,200
20 Jan., 1951	22,890	63,350	3,880
22 May, 1951	22,270	62,350	3,880
6 Dec., 1952	—	68,590	4,270

Note: After the 28th of September, 1950, buying and selling rates were fixed in place of the former single rate for buying and selling. The figures given in the Table are those for the buying rate.

Sources: Article by Chao Yi, "Movements of the Official Foreign Exchange Rates," *H-TKP* (26 Jan., 1951); Cheng Chu-yüan, *The Financial Institutions of the Chinese Communist* (Hong Kong, 1954), pp. 115–118, and the news in the Hong Kong *Ta Kung Pao* (7 Dec., 1952).

CONCLUSION

The above considerations have enabled us to get a general view of the manner in which the People's Currency system was established and later developed, as well as of the manner in which this currency system was established on a firm basis and the value of the People's Currency stabilized. However, doubt and confusion arose in regard to the acceptability and value of the People's Currency system during the latter part of the First Five-Year Plan, and in the following chapter we shall enter upon an examination of this question.

CHAPTER IV

THE QUESTION OF PRICES REVEALED

INTRODUCTION

IN 1956 the relations of supply and demand in regard to material resources in New China had become strained, the decline in the quality and the decrease in the number of kinds had become all the more marked in the products of light industry, the prices of one type of material resources after another had begun to rise, and the question of prices became pressing. Faced with this situation, the government authorities and the organs of opinion associated with them emphasized repeatedly that the stability of the general price levels had not been disrupted, but the very fact of their doing so revealed that doubt, confusion and lack of confidence had appeared among the masses in regard to the future of price levels, and even in regard to the acceptability and value of the People's Currency itself. We must consider this to be a truly extraordinary situation, compared with the brilliant results achieved on the production side of the economy, chiefly in the development of heavy industry, and with the rapid leap forward towards the socialization of the socio-economic structure. Truly, we are obliged to say that as New China approached the fourth year of the First Five-Year Plan great contradictions were revealed in the realm of maintaining a balance between production and consumption and between supply and demand.

In this chapter it is intended to analyse this question of prices in the latter part of the First Five-Year Plan, and to attempt some examination of the basic line underlying the price policies adopted by the New China authorities.

I. The Intensification of the Unbalance between Supply and
Demand in Regard to Material Resources

It had been the practice to stress and laud the stability of
prices in New China and the stability of the value of the People's
Currency, attention being drawn to price indices and to the trends
of foreign exchange rates in order to establish this point. However, after the second half of 1956 the unbalance between supply
and demand in regard to material resources widened and became
more intense, and the future of the value of the People's Currency
was called in question.

Before this, an unbalance between supply and demand had
already raised problems in connection with a number of kinds of
material resources. In 1953 and 1954 a rationing system had to be
introduced for foodstuffs, edible oils and cotton cloth because a
severe unbalance had developed in the demand for these articles.
At the Second Session of the First National People's Congress in
July, 1955, Yeh Chi-chuang, Minister of Foreign Trade, was at
pains to rebut the suggestion that the unbalance in the demand
for foodstuffs, edible oils, pork, hen's eggs, tea, silk cloth, fruit,
etc., was due to exports of these commodities. (On this point see
below.) At the Third Session of the First National People's Congress
in June, 1956, Li Fu-ch'un, Chia T'o-fu, Yao Yi-lin, Sha Ch'ien-li,
Ch'en Yün and others spoke at length alternately on (1) the
necessity for increasing production in light industry, (2) the decline
in the quality of the products of light industry and the decline
in the number of kinds of goods produced, (3) the shortages of
meat, vegetables, and other supplementary foods and the question of rising prices in the cities, and (4) the poor results achieved
by state commerce. Reading through these speeches, we may
perceive that New China's economic construction, centred as it
was on heavy industry, was at length giving rise to contradictions in those parts of the economy which were directly connected
with the life of the masses.

However, the unbalance between supply and demand in
regard to material resources in the period beginning from the

second half of 1956 was of a vastly different order, for a larger number of types of goods were in short supply and the degree of unbalance was intensified. According to a statement made at the Third Plenary Session of the Second National Committee of the People's Political Consultative Conference of China held in March, 1957, by Ch'en Yün (who had been appointed Minister of Commerce in November, 1956), the material resources in short supply could be classified in three categories. The first comprised meat and supplementary foods. There had been shortages of these commodities in many areas for several years past, but shortages had appeared in an even larger number of areas in 1956. The second category comprised a number of articles of daily use, such as bicycles, paper and cotton cloth. In the second half of 1956 the supply of woollen cloth, leather bags, wool thread, radios, etc., had been unable to meet the demand. The third category comprised production materials, including pig-iron, rolled steel, timber and cement. As a result, the supply of metal materials was strained, and in the North the supply-and-demand relations in regard to stoves and fuel were strained. Augmenting the list of goods in short supply given in Ch'en Yün's speech with the items mentioned in the Chinese newspapers, we may add vegetables, salt, oils, sugar, powdered milk and milk products, alcohol, canned goods, egg products, etc. to the first category, camphor and pharmaceutical products, pots and pans, domestic utensils, cultural and recreational articles, articles used in physical culture, surgical appliances, etc. to the second category, and electricity, bamboo, and the smaller agricultural implements to the third category. The shortage of material resources in the third category was holding up economic construction and house construction, and was checking the supply of material resources in the second category.

In the new industrial cities such as Kunming, Yunnan Province, Sian, Shensi Province, Lanchow, Kansu Province, etc. supply-and-demand relations were also strained in the catering trade and the service industries (hotels, hairdressers, bath-houses, photographers, dry cleaners, etc.), as well as in regard to furniture, clock and watch repairs, etc. There was a great deal of overcrowding, not only on urban transport facilities, but also on local railways and long-distance buses, and transport facilities were holding up economic development.

Each state enterprise carried on its own accounting on the basis of prices fixed by the state, and fixed procurement prices were applied in dealings between these enterprises. A coupon system was in force for food, cotton cloth and edible oils. The buying-up and distribution of other kinds of material resources was also centred on state commerce and was subject to official or fixed prices. Under such institutions and policies the unbalance between supply and demand in regard to material resources was not immediately made manifest by a rise in prices, but took the form of " repressed inflation."

According to a news commentary article on the question of prices published in the Peking *Ta Kung Pao* on the 1st of May, 1957, the index figures for retail prices in the eight great cities (taking 1952 as 100) were 103.7 in 1953, 104.1 in 1954, 105.5 in 1955, and 105.8 in 1956, while in comparison with the previous year prices in 1954 stood at 100.4, in 1955 at 101.3, and in 1956 at 100.3. In 1957 the same retail price index showed the following figures in comparison with the prices in the previous month :— January 101.2, February 100.0, and March 100.9. In comparison with the prices of the same month in the previous year the figures were :—January 101.6, February 100.9, and March 101.7. On the basis of these figures the article maintained that in spite of the enlargement of the unbalance between supply and demand in regard to commodities, price levels in general had remained stable. The government authorities of New China were at one with this newspaper on this point. According to statements made by Hsin Yüan-hsi, the Chief of the Fifth Staff Office of the People's Commission of Shanghai, published in the same newspaper on the 30th of May, 1957, the Shanghai prices of 168 articles necessary for livelihood rose by 9.12% in the four years between 1953 and 1956, taking 1952 as the base. Hsin Yüan-hsi states that within this period prices rose by 5.28% during 1953 and by about 1% in each of the following three years. He also stresses the basic stability of prices in Shanghai.

However, such price indices were based on prices which were mainly official or fixed prices, and the question lies in whether it was possible or not to buy the commodities at these prices, in how many of the articles it was possible to buy, and in the degree to which the quality of the articles could be assured. Up to the first half of 1956 there were queues only for pork and other forms of meat, but after the second half of that year there was an enlargement of the number of kinds of goods for which queueing became necessary. (This was of course so in the case of queues for urban and local transport facilities.) Even in these cases there was no end to the extreme scarcity of goods and services available for purchase.   In circumstances such as these the people contended for priority in buying up articles while they were still available, thus causing a greater worsening of supply-and-demand relations. The decrease in the amount of manufactured articles and the decline in their quality[52] remained the objects of discussion, and there were not a few instances of old vegetables being sold at the prices charged for fresh vegetables.   Leaving aside the question of the original cause of the decline in the quality of these articles, the main question at issue was the objective situation of goods shortage which made it possible for such goods to sell in the market.   Dealings in mixed lots of good-quality goods and bad-quality goods were also called in question, and there appeared the malpractice of not allowing customers to bring back goods for exchange, even if these should have proved to be of bad quality.   In a situation

[52]   At the Third Session of the First National People's Congress in June, 1956, Chia T'o-fu, Head of the Fourth Staff Office of the State Council, spoke of the deterioration of the quality of the products of light industry in 1955, and in the course of doing so made the following interesting remarks.   The wine was so muddly and weak-tasting that the people said, "It is not sour enough to be vinegar, nor sharp-tasting enough to be wine."   Some pills were "stubbornly insoluble."   Many cigarettes were loosely rolled, and too thin, and their acrid taste hurt the nose and throat. Certain lines of cotton cloth showed increasing rates of sub-standard goods, and the people called cotton cloth of this kind "Huma-pu" (probably meaning 'cloth of rough texture'—Miyashita).   Some of the dyed cloth was very liable to shrinking and the patterns were not clearly printed, while the designs were said to be in preternaturally bad taste.   Certain poor-quality vacuum-flasks were called "cold bottles" or "time bombs" by the people.   Some of the fountain pens were bent in the middle, or had bad writing points, or leaked, and the people called them "snivel."   Some of the soap "had a good smell on the surface, but not inside."   This was in 1955, but in spite of calls for the improvement of quality after this time, it proved impossible to call a halt to the decline in the quality of the products of light industry.   An editorial in *Jenmin Jihpao* (28 Apr., 1957), set forth the necessity of getting rid of the phenomenon of a decline in quality, and on the following day the Peking *Ta Kung Pao* reported that there had been a decline in the quality of such goods as rubber boots, gym shoes, paper, enamel ware, vacuum-flasks, educational supplies, and china in Shanghai, Tientsin, Shenyang, Chungking, T'aiyüan, and in the Hunan and Kiangsu areas.

such as this, in which demand was comparatively strained, those who had possession of goods were able to attain a position of economic dominance in which they might obtain the goods they desired by means of barter dealings. It appears that barter dealings were carried on fairly widely and in a most gross manner inside the state enterprises, not only in the case of consumer goods but also in that of production goods. It is said that in some of the departments of production carried on under state management special offices were set up for the purposes of going around from place to place to buy up the material resources in short supply which were required by many departments of production, in order that they might be assured of a dominating position in securing necessary goods and raw materials. It also happened that departments of state commerce were required to provide state managed departments of production with raw materials in return for the acquisition of the products of these departments of production, or were pressed to supply these departments of production with consumer goods which they needed. In general the disposition of the factors of production and the distribution of their products in the departments carried on under state management should have been carried out in accordance with the prescriptions of state planning, so that if there were a shortage of certain factors of production in one branch of industry and a surplus of these factors in another it would be allowable for them to equalize their surpluses and scarcities since this would be the means of assuring the most efficient use of these factors, but the widespread practice of barter dealings such as those which we have noted above was attacked as having a serious effect on state planning.[53]

The question is whether black-market prices came into being or not, and, if they did, to what degree. We may suppose that when the situation had worsened to the degree we have described it would be impossible to prevent black-market prices coming into being, even with the help of the political power at the disposal of the government of New China, but we are vouchsafed only fragmentary information regarding this point. According to state-

[53] On the subject of the widespread resort to barter transactions, see the piece by Lan Tsung-mien in the *Jenmin Jihpao* (30 Dec., 1956), the article by Yang Li in the same paper (2 Apr., 1957), the account in the Peking *Ta Kung Pao* (21 March, 1957), and the piece by Ch'ien Ch'ing-yen in the same paper (22 Apr., 1957).

ments made by Yao Yi-lin, Vice-Minister of Commerce, at a
session of the National People's Congress, in June, 1956, if the
retail prices for all the great cities in China in 1952 are taken
as 100, in 1955 the price of pork stood at 127, edible oils at
120, and hens' eggs at 133. Again, taking the retail price of
vegetables in 1951 as 100, in 1953 these prices stood at 148, and in
1955 at 126. Although Yao Yi-lin makes no explicit statement
about the matter, it is probable that he was speaking of black-
market prices. If this was in fact the case, then we may say
that there were black-market prices for these goods in 1955. In
this connexion we must give full consideration to the fact that,
as we shall show below, in the period beginning from the second
half of 1956 a free market for the native products and handicraft
products was allowed and, in this sense, some degree of freedom
was permitted in the formation of the prices of these goods, but
we may give our attention to the following two pieces of news
regarding the state of prices in the period beginning from the
second half of 1956. The first of these is a following passage
from an editorial in the Peking Ta Kung Pao published on the
9th of February, 1957, and entitled " On the Strained Balance."
" In some areas there have been scrambles to buy up scrap-iron
and bamboo, and black markets have come into being." The
second is an article published in the same newspaper on the 27th
of May, 1957. According to this article there had been considerable confusion in the state food market since February in Hopei,
Anhui, Shantung, Kiangsu and elsewhere, and the merchants
dealing in food had been breaking official prices at will. The
market prices in Kiangsu, Shantung, Anhui and elsewhere were
in general about twice the official prices, in Hopei Province they
were in general about three times the official prices, and in certain
markets they were four to five times the official prices. The peasants sold their rations at high prices, and at the same time called
upon the state to increase the rations. There were some peasants
who had abandoned agricultural production and were engaging
in speculation in the food market. Of these two pieces of evidence, the second article is of particular importance.[54]

---

[54] In Shanghai, speculative dealings in machinery and other capital goods were
being carried on by brokers. *Jenmin Jihpao* (17 Dec., 1956). The scrap-metal merchants of Peking were using the most unscrupulous means of buying up metal goods.
Jenmin Jihpao (11 March, 1957).

It also appears that there were abuses of the coupon system. According to an article in the Peking *Ta Kung Pao* of the 6th of December, 1956, edible oils had been sold without coupons in Wuhan, Hangchou, and in Hsinyi *Hsien,* Kwangtung Province. They had also been sold for coupons which were out-of-date or not yet valid in these places. Some of the garment-making co-operatives, commission sales shops and cotton cloth shops under joint state-private management in the city of Chinan had been using the same cotton-cloth coupons which had been collected time and time again (the same coupon being used seven times or twelve times), in order to buy up cotton cloth. Again, in the issue of the Peking *Ta Kung Pao* dated the 22nd of May, 1957, a reporter named Kao Shou-lan wrote that at one of the food distribution centres in the T'iench'iao area in Peking people did not like to go to the food distribution centres at the end of the month, because when they did so they had a fair number of coupons taken from them. We may add that this reporter's account of the sufferings of the consumers contains passages which remind the reader of the scarcity of material resources in Japan towards the end of the last war and immediately after it.

There were also certain units of state industry which sent in false returns and received excessive allocations of coal under state rationing, and which bought up coal for ordinary consumption in the market, thus causing an intensification of the strain on the market.[55]

II. A New Development in Price Policy

The men who first took up officially the question of prices in New China at the beginning of the period of the enlargement of the unbalance in the supply and demand in regard to material resources were Li Hsien-nien, Vice-Premier of the State Council and Minister of Finance, and Ch'en Yün, Vice-Premier of the State Council. Li and Ch'en, each from their own particular points of view, raised questions concerning past price policies at

[55] *Jenmin Jihpao* (4 Apr., 1957).

the Eighth National Congress of the Chinese Communist Party in September, 1956, and consequently the proposals which they put forward were distinct from one another, but they were completely in agreement on the point that in the new situation created by the basic completion of socialist transformation the price policies hitherto employed were now unnecessary and unsuitable in certain spheres, and, in particular, were an impediment to the development of production, and that for this reason an elastic price policy should be adopted under the understanding that it should not endanger the stability of prices. Let us examine the views of Li and Ch'en.

1. The Adjustment of Unsuitable Prices
   —Li Hsien-nien's Proposals

Li Hsien-nien considered that the price policies of the Chinese Communist Party had been correct, and that the results of the implementation of these policies had been basically successful. His reasons were as follows.

(1) Market prices had been basically stabilized.

(2) The purchase prices for the principal agricultural products, that is, foodstuffs, cotton, tobacco, sugar-cane, etc., (these commodities made up 70% of the agricultural products handled by commerce) and the relations between these purchase prices had been basically suitable.[56]

(3) The price differences between the products of industry and agriculture had been narrowed. According to material drawn on by Li, these price differences had narrowed by 17.25% between 1950 and 1955.[57]

(4) The price policies had served socialist transformation of capitalist commerce and industry. This refers to the fact that

---

[56] The suitability of purchase prices for agricultural products is determined with reference to the standard of pre-war food prices, reviewed in the light of new conditions. According to statements made by Yang Shen and Hsiao Kuo-chin of the Price Bureau, Hupei Province, the purchase prices for the principal agricultural products in the village markets of Hupei Province in 1956 were 37.65% above those of 1950. P-TKP (11 May, 1957)

[57] In an example of five village markets in Hupei Province given in the same source, in 1956 the price differences between agricultural and industrial products are said to have narrowed by 9.65% in comparison with those of 1955, and by 22.61% in comparison with those of 1950.

capitalist industry had been caused to acquire profit up to suitable levels by means of the sub-contracting of processing operations, the placing of orders, planned purchases and planned marketing, while the narrowing of price differences between the various areas had rendered it impossible for the wholesale sector of capitalist commerce to carry on business over long distances, and the narrowing of the price differences between wholesale and retail dealings had made it impossible for the large-scale retailers to make excessive profits.

(5) Seasonal variations had been eliminated from the prices of the principal agricultural products. By this means speculative buying and hoarding were prevented.

Nevertheless, Li believed that price policies had not been entirely devoid of mistakes and shortcomings. In particular, exclusive attention had been paid to the price-stabilization aspect of price policy, and no provision had been made for rational adjustments (when and where required) in response to changes in the general situation, while some unsuitable measures had been taken in the fixing of prices in commerce and also in the control of institutions by the authorities responsible for prices and commerce. As a result the following six problems had arisen in regard to prices.

(1) Price levels as a whole had remained stable, but a problem had been created by a deficiency in the supply of certain supplementary foods (vegetables, meat, edible oils, bean curd, etc.) and a rise in their prices.

(2) The purchase prices for the principal agricultural products were suitable, but those for a certain range of agricultural products (tung oil, camellia oil, rape-seed, pigs, peanuts, sesame, tea, etc.) were too low.

(3) In the case of a certain number of commodities, it sometimes happened that there was too great a gap between the purchase prices and the local selling prices for agricultural products in a particular locality. For example, the raw materials for oil-pressing might bè bought at low prices while the selling prices of edible oils were high, or there might be a great gap between the purchase price for pigs and the selling price of pork.

(4) The prices for agricultural products in certain mountain areas and distant border regions were too low.

(5) No " good quality, good price " policy (a policy of attaching
     high prices to good-quality articles) had been put into effect,
     nor had any policy for the encouragement of new products
     been adopted, and for this reason the number of kinds of
     industrial products had decreased, and their quality had
     declined.   In the case of agricultural products, too, unsuitable
     measures had been taken in determining standards of quality
     and price differences between classes of produce, and in par-
     ticular the peasants were dissatisfied with the alleged practice
     of " depressed classes and depressed prices " (purchasing pro-
     duce cheaply by lowering the class of the produce below its
     actual class).

(6) Some price differences between regions were unsuitable.[58]

On the subject of the reasons why such unsuitable prices for
agricultural and industrial products had not hitherto been discovered and adjusted when and where required, Li said, " This is due
to the fact that since in general there was no price competition
from elsewhere in our country the problem did not easily become
manifest." However, now that socialist commerce had become
the only form of commerce in China, price policy had come to
assume an especially important position in state commerce, and
the question of whether the prices fixed were suitable or not had
a direct effect on production at large, as well as on the people's
consumption and the state's accumulation of capital. Consequently
Li went on to propose the following seven measures, " on the
basis of the general principle that, under the basic policy of assuring the stability of prices, they would be profitable for the development of production and the circulation of commodities, due
consideration being given to state capital accumulation and the
people's consumption."

(1) The purchase prices for live pigs, rape-seed, tung oil and
     camellia oil should be raised by a wide margin, while suitable
     increases should be made in the purchase prices of sesame, tea,

---

[58] Li Hsien-nien states that the prices of industrial products in the Provinces of
the North-West were determined with reference to the Shanghai prices, additions
being made to cover costs of various kinds, but since industry had now developed in
the North-West also, and certain kinds of cotton cloth produced in Sian could fully
satisfy demand in the Provinces of the North-West, such an arrangement had now
become irrational.

and, in certain areas, in the purchase prices of peanuts and cocoons.

(2) The differences between the purchase prices and selling prices of the articles purchased and sold in any locality should be narrowed.

(3) When making purchases of goods in mountain areas or distant border regions where communications were very inconvenient, subsidies should be given in respect to transportation when the goods had to be transported over some distance.

(4) The prices of the smaller coarse grains should be raised to suitable levels. In areas where food prices were too low, these should be raised.

(5) In order to reform the mistaken policy of " depressed classes and depressed prices," unsuitable quality standards and price differences between classes of produce should be revised.

(6) In respect to the industrial products, great pains should be taken to apply the principle of determining prices with reference to quality, and a " good quality, good price " policy should be put into effect with great thoroughness. Factories producing articles of good quality should be encouraged in terms of prices, while factories producing poor quality articles should be penalized in terms of prices. Effective incentives should be adopted in respect to new products, and some compensation should be made for increased costs incurred by factories trying out new products, while suitable encouragements should also be given to the devisers of new products and to all the factory staff and workers.

(7) The differences from region to region in the prices for industrial products should be suitably adjusted and rationalized.

Li Hsien-nien went on to speak of the following notable lines of policy in the realm of government price policy.

The first such line of policy was the necessity of raising the prices of agricultural products and of the products of agricultural side-occupations which hitherto had been set at low levels, but since the manufactured articles which were dependent on these products as raw materials were indispensable for the livelihood of the people the selling prices of these manufactured articles must not be raised. However, in order to put this policy into effect, not only must state commerce practise economy in its expenditures,

but the state must reduce the rates of taxation on these manufactured articles and must lighten the duties of making payments
to the state out of profits by state commerce which handles such
manufactured articles, and, in the last analysis, the state must be
prepared to accept some reduction in its revenue income. Li
Hsien-nien estimated this reduction in revenue at between
1,000,000,000 and 2,000,000,000 *yüan*. It was acknowledged that
if this policy were put into effect it would eventuate in an increase in revenue income as a result of an increase in the production of agricultural products, but this would take some considerable
time. Of necessity, the reduction in the revenue income would
be accompanied by a corresponding reduction in expenditure, and
thus could not but affect the relations between the various items
of state expenditure. On the other hand, since a rise in the
purchase prices of agricultural products would increase the incomes
and purchasing-power of the peasants, it would be necessary to
make available to the peasants an increased supply of materials
for production and consumption, and consequently it would also
be necessary to make suitable changes in the proportion of industrial investment devoted to heavy industry and in expenditures
in other fields. These views of Li Hsien-nien may be regarded
as hinting that the low price policies hitherto employed in relation
to the purchase prices of agricultural products and the products
of agricultural side-occupations had provided a fixed sum of state
revenue which had contributed to the implementation of the policy
of priority for heavy industry in state expenditures, and that the
new policies put forward by Li were in the nature of a call for
a re-examination of the policy of priority for heavy industry in
government expenditures, since their implementation would bring
about a certain degree of reduction in the revenue resources of
the state.

The second line of policy was that in principle it was impossible to adopt a policy of lowering the prices of industrial products
or a policy of selling a large volume of such products at a low
profit margin, except in the case of industrial products with a
high volume of production (such products were few in China),
and that steps should be taken to assure the basic stability of
the prices of industrial products. In this connexion we must
note that Li Hsien-nien states that when the prices of commodities

are to be fixed it is necessary to take the importance of the commodities and the question of state accumulation of capital into
consideration, and that basic stability in the prices of industrial
products means fixing the prices of industrial products with reference to the principle of maintaining an overall balance between
the purchasing-power of the people and the supply of commodities.
Taking a synoptic view of the views of Li Hsien-nien, we may
regard them as hinting that, apart from certain industrial products
closely related to the livelihood of the masses, the prices of other
industrial products in New China would go on rising in the future,
in consideration of the tendency for the people's purchasing-power
to increase and of the tendency for the necessity for state accumulation of capital to increase.

The proposals put forward by Li Hsien-nien were later put
into effect one after the other. Rises in purchase prices took
place in the cases of rape-seed (September, 1956), sesame, tung
oil, camellia oil, creosote, wax tree oil, and soybeans produced in
the three Provinces of the North-East and the Inner Mongolian
Autonomous Region (January, 1957), and live pigs (March, 1957).
On the other hand, selling prices were also raised, as in the cases
of table salt (January, 1957), pork (March, 1957), woollen textiles
and high-class tobaccos (March, 1957), edible and other oils, and
oil materials (April, 1957). Among the articles whose selling
prices were raised, woollen textiles and high-class tobaccos were
industrial products which were also treated as luxury articles, and
their prices were raised by a fairly high margin. To take the
example of woollen textiles, pure wool articles had their prices
raised by around 25%, while the prices of mixed wool articles
were raised by around 15%. In contrast, the rise in the prices of
table salt and other goods was kept at a lower level, in consideration of the fact that these material resources were necessary
for the livelihood of the masses. We have already noted that Li
Hsien-nien maintained that the prices of such goods should not
be raised, and it is probable that they were raised to some degree
because of the condition of the state finances. The retail prices
for pork were raised by a smaller margin than the purchase
prices of live pigs, and the selling prices for oils and oil materials
were lower than their purchase prices. The differences between
these two sets of prices meant an eventual increase in the burden

laid upon the state finances.[59]

The prices listed above were those fixed by the central government. In addition to these, it appears that the selling prices of goods held by local state commercial departments were also raised.[60]

2. Official Recognition of a Free Market under State Control —Ch'en Yün's Proposals

Ch'en Yün, a Vice-Premier of the State Council, maintained that the system of controlled purchase and selling of material

---

[59] The following is a collection of the fragmentary information regarding price rises and related prices reported in the Chinese press.

Live pigs had risen by a national average of 14% (some papers reported a rise of 14.26%). Pork had risen by 7% (according to certain papers by 8.42%). The differences in these prices had been made up by the state by a reduction in the slaughtering tax (a reduction of 8%) and a reduction in commercial profits. To do this the state had been obliged to disburse 180,000,000 yüan. In this connexion we may add that in Peking the price of pork had risen from 7 chiao to 8 chiao 2 fen per catty, while in Canton superior quality pork had risen from 8 chiao 7 fen per catty to 9 chiao 4 fen, and side meat of the pig had risen from 8 chiao 3 fen to 9 chiao.

In the past the price of salt had been set at a lower level than the prices of other articles. The rise in the price of salt at this time was due to a rise in the rate of tax imposed on salt, a measure adopted with a view to balancing the state finances. However, the adjusted price of salt was still lower than the pre-war price. The adjustment of the price of salt also involved inter-regional adjustments of salt prices. The range covered by these adjustments in respect to the wholesale prices of 1 catty of table salt was, at the maximum 1.7 fen, at the minimum 0.1 fen, and on the general average 1.45 fen.   The retail price of table salt in Peking rose from 1 chiao 4 fen per bag of fine salt to 1 chiao 7 fen.

Prices for sesame rose by a national average of 25.0%. The rise in the purchase prices for oils, oil materials and other agricultural products increased state expenditure by 345,410,000 yüan, while the rise in their selling prices yielded an income of 236,100,000 yüan, the difference between these figures being charged to the state. In the case of edible oils the state alleviated the rise in prices at the expense of some financial loss, and also lowered the rate of tax on rape-seed oil. The burden imposed on the state finances by these two items amounted to around 30,000,000 yüan. In the majority of areas the rise in the price of edible oils was between 6 fen and 1 chiao per catty, in a certain number of areas between 1 fen and 4 fen, and in certain special areas around 1 chiao 3 fen.

[60] In Shanghai, in addition to the rises in the prices of table salt, pork, woollen textiles, high-class tobaccos, etc., ordered by the Centre, rises occurred in the prices of about 20 items under the control of the local state commercial department including salted meats, etc. P-TKP (3 May, 1957).

resources which state commerce and the supply and marketing co-operatives had been operating in the past had been necessary for the purposes of putting limits to the activities of capitalist commerce and industry, but that parts of this system became unnecessary and unsuitable, and, in particular, certain aspects of this system were depressing the development of production, now that socialist transformation had been basically completed. Since this was so, a free price system should be allowed to a certain degree, and steps should be taken to adjust supply and demand through free price movements within certain defined spheres and under state control, so that in this way the healthy development of production might be attained. These views of Ch'en were developed in the following two points.

The first point concerned a reform of the methods of carrying out the sub-contracting of processing operations, the placing of orders, planned purchases and planned marketing which the state commercial departments had been practising in relation to capitalist industry. It appeared that this system caused some factories to have less interest in the quality of the goods they manufactured than when they sold the goods for themselves, as they had been accustomed to do in the past, and was preventing the improvement of the quality of manufactured articles. Again, under this system it was usual in the state wholesale companies for the greater part of commodities to be sent from higher institutions to lower institutions, while the placing of orders to factories was confined to a minority of wholesale companies, and since the shops at the bottom were unable to procure goods directly from the factories in response to the demands of the consumers the types and specifications of commodities ordered from the factories by the state commercial departments had decreased in number, with the result that the types and quantities of commodities put on the market throughout China by the state wholesale companies were not in accord with the state of local demand, so that in some places commodities were piling up unsold, while in others they were sold out. For this reason, the existing system should be emended in the following particulars.

(1) In the case of articles which were closely related to the national economy and the people's livelihood, and which were of simple specification, for example, cotton yarn, cotton cloth,

coal, sugar, etc., planned purchases and planned marketing by the state should be continued in order to assure supply and conduce to the stability of the market.

(2)   In the case of the multifarious types of articles of daily use, a change should be made to "selective buying." Under the selective buying system state commerce would have priority in selective buying from factories. The commodities left over after selective buying had been carried out by state commerce and the commodities which state commerce had not bought could then be sold off by the factories on their own account or they might be entrusted to state commerce as commission agents. The state should undertake the distribution of raw materials required by factories in cases where these were in short supply, but in other cases the factories should be allowed to engage in free selective buying. The higher wholesale companies must not be allowed to force the buying of commodities under the selective buying system on lower institutions, and the shops at the bottom should be allowed to carry on selective buying from any wholesale company in the country, or directly from the factories. The handicraft products were also to be included in the scope of selective buying. Such a system of free selective buying of industrial products was what was signified by official recognition of a free market in the industrial products.

The second point concerned a reform of the methods then in force for the supervision of the market when purchases of agricultural products and of the products of agricultural side-occupations were made. Strict market supervision was exercised in the villages in order to restrain speculative activities on the part of private merchants, and as a result the organs of state commerce and the supply and marketing co-operatives were in the positions of monopolistic buyers, unopposed by any competitors. Due attention was not paid in making purchases of agricultural products and the products of agricultural side-occupations, and in some cases these products were bought up at low prices which tended to bring about a decrease in the production of these goods. Consequently, Ch'en Yün proposed that this system should be emended as follows. (1) Planned purchases of foodstuffs, industrial crops and the important by-products of agriculture by the state,

state commerce and the supply and marketing co-operatives should continue as at present. (2) However, in the case of a certain range of agricultural products, such as local agricultural products produced on a small scale, and the by-products of agriculture, the existing system should be changed, and the state shops, co-operative stores, co-operative groups and supply and marketing co-operatives should collectively be permitted to undertake free buying, free selling and free transportation, and mutual particularism should be prevented. This latter case is what is signified by official recognition of a free market for agricultural products and the products of agricultural side-occupations. If, in these cases, the supply cannot meet the demand in the free market, the sources of supply of these material resources should be distributed according to the degrees of urgency of demand among individual unit organizations, under the direction of the local Party and government authorities. When the opposite situation occurs and supply exceeds demand and prices fall, supply and marketing co-operatives should buy in the usual way at normal prices in order to protect the interests of the peasants.

Ch'en Yün had spoken in some detail about the selective buying system for industrial products when the question of the poor results achieved by state commerce in 1955 was raised at the Third Session of the First National People's Congress in June, 1956. At this Congress the subject was also mentioned in the speech of Yao Yi-lin, Vice-Minister of Commerce.[61]

It is especially worthy of note that the above proposals put forward by Ch'en Yün aim at using a mechanism for the adjustment of supply and demand through the operation of free price movements in a certain defined sphere within a socialist economy. It need hardly be said that this idea is modelled on the Kolkhoz market in the USSR. Ch'en Yün is opposed to " frozen " stability in prices, and maintains that price policy must be such as will favour the development of production. He maintains that high prices should be allowed for high-cost manufactured articles of good quality, and that such prices are the means of giving en-

---

[61] According to Yao Yi-lin, the system of free selective buying for industrial products was first put into effect in the buying side of the Small Stores Wholesale Firm, *Lien Yi*, a joint state-private enterprise in T'aiyüan, and produced notable **results**.

couragement to the production of new products. It is mass production which constitutes the essence of price stability, and what
must be avoided is a rise in prices consequent upon a decline in
production. According to Ch'en, prices might rise for a time when
a free market for some part of the products of light industry and
local agricultural products was permitted, but these prices should
fall when at length production was expanded and supply increased.
Further, the commodities which would come on to the free
market would constitute a little more than one-quarter of the
46,000,000,000 *yüan* of retail commodities covering the whole of
China, while the remaining three-quarters would still remain
under the control of the state. Again, such a free market would
differ from the free market operated in a capitalist society and
would be a socialist free market, and since there would no longer
be any private entrepreneurs in commerce or industry and state
commerce and supply and marketing co-operatives would be able,
under control, to enter the free market (for which reason the free
market was to be called " a free market under state control"), price
changes in the free markets would have no effect on the price levels.

Free markets under state control were opened in all parts of
China from the second half of 1956. In the case of a certain
range of industrial products, too, free selective buying began in
some places, but in January, 1957, it was announced that this
would be temporarily discontinued during 1957 because of lack of
preparation. The goods which came on to the free markets in
the spring of 1957 were chickens, ducks, fish, eggs, vegetables,
dried fruit, bamboo-ware, articles made of wood, ordinary traditional Chinese pharmaceutical products, etc.—the so-called " native
products"—and their monetary value is said to have amounted
to roughly one-quarter of the total amount of the agricultural
products and products of agricultural side-occupations, and to have
been equivalent to 12.5% of the total amount of retail commodities
throughout China.[62] In the free markets of Peking and Shanghai
the handicraft products which arranged the procurement of their
own raw materials and repairs materials for the repair shops were
assigned to the free market.[63] In the free market of Canton the
traditional wholesale merchants (*hangchan*: 行棧) and selling agencies

---

[62] Ch'en Hsing, " The Opening of the Domestic Free Market," *Jinmin Chūgoku*,
No. 49 (May, 1957).

(*taihsiaotien*: 代銷店) were revived, and agency selling of the products of agricultural side-occupations and native products by them began. Their numbers had risen to 41 units by the 10th of April, 1957.[64] As a result of the opening of the free markets there was a general rise in the prices of goods coming on to the markets, production was stimulated, and the quantities of goods coming on to the markets were increased.[65] On the other hand, however, no small number of unhealthy phenomena appeared. There was a great deal of speculative trading, in pursuit of which the peasants neglected their duties at the agricultural co-operatives, and there were some who withdrew from the co-operatives and betook themselves to commerce in the free market, where much profit was to be had. Among handicraftsmen there were some who withdrew from the handicraft producers' co-operatives and set themselves up again as independent handicraftsmen. Again, as a result of the sudden rise in prices in the free market the purchase of material resources under state planned purchases was obstructed. On the 6th of May, 1957, the free market at Peking was abolished. It may be that in such a place as Peking, where there is an absolute scarcity of vegetables because of the restriction of the expansion of the area of the vegetable gardens in the suburbs, the institution of a free market had been found to be attended by more disadvantages than advantages, but at all events the people had once more to put up with the inconvenience of queue-

---

[63] Before joint state-private operation by whole trades was brought into effect throughout private commerce and industry and before the handicrafts were organized in co-operatives, the adjustment of commodity prices could be carried out only with the agreement of the supervisory departments of the administration for industry and commerce. In this way market prices were subject to unified supervision. However, after the peak of socialist transformation had been passed the supervision of the prices of certain goods was left to the relevant Bureau or Company, and in respect to some goods supervision ceased to be exercised. Included in this last category were the industrial products and the handicraft products which were made of the raw materials procured by the producers by themselves. *P-TKP* (11 May, 1957).

[64] *H-TKP* (12 Apr., 1957).

[65] At Tientsin the free market prices for bean curd, oranges and apples were 50–80% above the government prices charged by the state companies. *P-TKP* (3 May, 1957). In Peking the prices of vegetables were 20-30% above the state fixed prices, and in some cases were 2 or 3 times the state fixed prices. *Jenmin Jihpao* (30 Apr., 1957).

ing when making their purchases. In some of the rural free markets, however, the operation of the free market proceeded rationally, since supervision was exercised in a suitable manner.[66]

We may add that the free markets disappeared naturally in the course of the people's commune movement in the villages of China which began in the summer of 1958. However, in the autumn of 1959 the authorities in New China, acting against the background of a new condition of affairs, again urged the development of free markets in the rural areas. Free markets which came into being after this time are still in existence.[67]

III. A Change in State Economic Planning

According to statements published by the governmental authorities of New China, the national income, the total values of agricultural production, the total values of industrial production, and the total values of industrial and agricultural production have increased from year to year, and the standard of living of the Chinese people has risen. If we are to believe the published statements of the governmental authorities, the relations of supply and demand in regard to material resources cannot be said to have been due to a falling-off in production. Examining this question in the cases of particular items of material resources, we find that the decline in the production of live pigs after 1955 must be regarded as a rare exception. In 1956 the production of raw cotton and rape-seed was less than in the previous year, but this is to be regarded as a temporary phenomenon caused by natural damage to crops in that year.

Accordingly, the core of the problem lies in the fact that in spite of this increase in production, production was not able to keep up with demand. The proposals put forward by Li Hsiennien and Ch'en Yün of which we have given an account in the

---

[66] See the instances of the free market in Hupei Province published in the Peking *Ta Kung Pao* (11 May, 1957) and at T'aots'unchen, Ch'ihsia *Hsien*, Shantung Province published in the same paper (23 May, 1957).

[67] The rural free market under the people's communes is examined in T. Miyashita, *The Economic System of New China* (Tokyo, 1964), Chap. 5, Sect. 7.

previous Section are based on the assumption that this was so, and are in the nature of counter-measures put forward with the idea of dealing with factors causing a depression of production or dealing with aspects of distribution which were considered unsuitable. Both Li and Ch'en raise the question of price policy as a factor causing a depression of the development of production. As the unbalance between supply and demand grew, and in spite of the replacement of the Minister of Commerce, voices were raised in an endless succession of criticism of the vastness of the mechanisms operated by the state commercial departments and the unsuitability of certain aspects of the collection and distribution of material resources carried on under their direction. As an episode which reveals such an unsuitable aspect of the management of state commerce, we may cite a case divulged in a leading article in the Peking *Ta Kung Pao* on the 25th of September, 1956. The article states that although vegetables were in short supply, the state-operated China Vegetable Company had dug two great holes outside the Ch'ingan Gate in Peking, into which it was throwing rotten vegetables, and that the peasants were calling these holes "the bloody sweat pits."

As a question concerned with the distribution of material resources, we may consider the export of foodstuffs and other agricultural products. At the Second Session of the First National People's Congress in July, 1955, Yeh Chi-chuang, Minister of Foreign Trade, insisted that the export of these goods would not bring about an unbalance between supply and demand. As the reason why this should be so, Yeh pointed out that the quantities of these various kinds of goods exported amounted to only a small proportion of the quantities produced and consumed. But whatever might be the effects produced in a situation in which the demand of the masses for these goods was more or less satisfied, in a situation in which under-consumption of these goods persisted, a very small amount of exports—even if in the nature of "sacrifice exports" made in order to import production goods considered to be more necessary—would have a great effect on domestic supply-and-demand relations. In the same speech Yeh said that exports of foodstuffs in 1954 and 1955 had maintained the level of 1953 and that it was intended to maintain this level in the following two years, that exports of edible vegetable oils in 1954 had declined by 36% in comparison with those of 1953, and that it was proposed to maintain this level in the future. These words are nothing other than a tacit recognition of the above-mentioned principle. At the National People's Congress in June, 1956, Yao Yi-lin declared that exports of pork in 1956 would decline by 50,000 tons. Further, in a speech made at the Third Plenary Session of the Second National Committee of the People's Political Consultative Conference of China in March, 1957, Ch'en Yün stated that in 1957 exports of pork would be decreased by two-thirds in comparison with 1956, and that it was intended to reduce still further the exports of edible oils. Again, at the conference held by the Heads of the All-China Bureaux for External Trade and All-China Special Representatives in May, 1957, it was laid down as the general line of policy that steps would be taken to facilitate imports of fertilizers, raw cotton and sugar, to reduce the exports of edible oils by 120,000 tons, and to reduce exports of pork by 110,000 tons.

The cases which we have discussed above are concerned with problems of production and distribution, and are merely in the nature of explanations for unbalances between supply and demand in regard to particular items of goods. But as the sphere of un-balance between supply and demand was enlarged and intensified, the fact that total demand had exceeded total supply in the Chinese national economy was at last revealed. In a socialist economy, plans are made for balancing the total supply and total demand for goods over the whole economy, at least during the year in question, so that provided there are no mistakes in the plans total demand should be met by total supply, and even if it should happen that in the year in question the demand for a certain number of individual items is not satisfied this unsatisfied demand will be diverted to other goods. Consequently, the oc-currence of a situation in which total supply is not in balance with total demand must mean that there has been some mistake in the economic planning for that year.

The first frank recognition of this reasoning would seem to have been the long leading article in the Peking *Ta Kung Pao* of the 5th of February, 1957, entitled " On the Strained Balance."[68]

---

[68] This reasoning was also at last recognized in a leading article in the *Jenmin Jihpao* (17 Feb., 1957).

Noting that the government's reserved goods were limited, this article drew attention to the fact that the basic cause of the strain between supply and demand was the excessive increase in the total demand in comparison with the total supply of material resources during 1956, and drew attention to the following three points as causes of the excessive increase in demand.

(1) The scale of capital construction in 1956 had been too large. The enlargement of " capital construction " during that year had indeed been necessary, but of the 14,000,000,000 *yüan* invested, approximately one-tenth, or about 1,500,000,000 *yüan*, had been unsuitably invested.

(2) Too much had been spent on improving the conditions of staff and workers. The increases in wages for staff and workers in 1956 were indeed a necessary measure, but of the increased payments of 3,000,000,000 *yüan* made under this head above the figures for the previous year, approximately 6 or 7 hundred million *yüan* had been unnecessary and unsuitable.

(3) Some of the loans made to agriculture had been unsuitable. It had been necessary to provide vast sums for agricultural loans during the first years in which the completion of the agricultural co-operation was basically attained. Nevertheless, the planned figures for funds to be disbursed as loans were rather too high, and were unsuitable. In 1956 the state had disbursed more than 2,000,000,000 *yüan* in agricultural loans, and with the addition of previous loans as yet unrepaid this amounted to 3,000,000,000 *yüan*.

The article states that the experience of 1956 had provided the following lessons.

(1) In carrying out investment in capital construction it was necessary to give consideration to the state of raw materials, and not only to the balance of revenue and expenditure in the state finances.

(2) In improving the standard of living of the people and raising purchasing-power in society, decisions should be made on the basis of the quantities of consumer goods which could be supplied, and not only on the basis of the balance of financial receipts and payments and the balance of cash receipts and payments.

(3) The scale on which capital construction was planned and the

promotion of economic power should be conformable to the resources in wealth and goods at the disposal of the state, and, if this principle were to be thoroughly applied, it would be necessary to take into consideration not only the balance of the year in question, but also the situation in the next year and the following few years, having due regard to past experience and future consequences.

We may add that it later became apparent that excessive expenditures in the form of loans to peasants had reached the sum of 5 to 6 hundred million *yüan*,[69] which means that in 1956 a total of more than 3,000,000,000 *yüan* of excess purchasing-power was fed into the Chinese national economy.

We may also note that in this year the budgeted state expenditure stood at more than 30,700,000,000 *yüan*, or 31.5% of the national income.

It was in the face of the development of this situation that Ch'en Yün made a speech before the Third Plenary Session of the Second National Committee of the People's Political Consultative Conference of China in March, 1957, in which he explained the necessity of restraining the enlargement of the scale of the state finances and made a strong appeal for the government and people to unite in an effort to increase production and practise economy. From this it would be natural for us to anticipate that in the budget for 1957 restraints would be placed on expenditure for capital construction, agricultural loans and administrative expenses. However, the problem was not merely connected with the economic plans for the year 1957 alone. We may suppose this to have been the case because the problem of the moment would appear to have been the disproportion in the development of the various branches of the national economy. What was now at issue was how to bring about balances between accumulated funds and production goods, between consumption funds and consumption goods, and, in connexion with this, how to determine the ratio between capital accumulation and consumption, and how to determine the ratio between investment in industry and investment in agriculture and other parts of the economy.

What is worthy of note at this point is the fact that it was

---

[69] According to a news commentary article in the Peking *Ta Kung Pao* (1 May, 1957), written by the editorial department of that newspaper.

being recognized that it would be necessary to do something to promote the development of light industry and agriculture, even though the general principle of giving priority to the development of heavy industry were maintained. Looking at state investment in industry, we find that the First Five-Year Plan provided for investment in heavy and light industry in the proportion of 8 to 1, but that this proportion was changed to 7 to 1 in 1956. One of the reasons for this change in policy was the poor results produced by light industry in 1955, but a more important reason was the fact that the functions of capital accumulation by light industrial production had been conceived anew. At the Third Session of the First National People's Congress in June, 1956, Li Fu-ch'un, a Vice-Premier of the State Council and Chairman of the State Planning Commission, explained the necessity of developing light industry, and drew attention to (1) the need to satisfy the demands of the people in regard to their material and cultural lives, and (2) the fact that light industry required a low rate of investment, that it was easily constructed and soon came into effective production, and that the state revenue from the light industry sector, that is, the commercial and industrial profits and tax income accruing from light industry, was the principal source of state capital accumulation. The new situation which arose after 1956 gave an even greater importance to light industrial production. We have already drawn attention to this in connexion with Li Hsien-nien's exposition of the manner in which the implementation of price-adjustment policies was leading to changes in the proportions of the various items of state expenditure. On this point a most notable piece of news is the report that at a meeting of the Supreme State Council at the beginning of March, 1957, Chairman Mao Tse-tung proposed that the ratio between heavy and light industry in state investment should be lowered to 6 to 1.[70]

CONCLUSION

In the previous two sections we have given an outline account of the basic line of policy adopted by the governmental authorities

---

[70] This was revealed in a statement made by Ts'ai Fang-ying, who was present at the meeting. *Jenmin Jihpao* (7 March, 1957).

of New China in relation to the unbalance between supply and demand in the second half of the period of the First Five-Year Plan and the associated problem of prices. We feel that we should say something about the encouragement of pig-rearing, the joint state-private enterprises in commerce and industry and the agricultural producers' co-operatives in the period after the completion of socialist transformation, the adjustment and filling-out of the handicraft producers' co-operatives, the improvement of the quality of commodities by the revival of the old system of branded goods and the encouragement of the production of new products, but for reasons of space we shall leave these subjects untouched.

Viewing the situation as it existed in 1957, the last year of the First Five-Year Plan, these problems were by no means solved, and, at least from the phenomenological point of view, they were getting progressively worse.

The basic policies adopted for the solution of these problems were the adjustment of unsuitable prices and the institution of free markets, but no immediate results were produced by these measures, and for a time they had an unfavourable effect on the problems at issue. The rise in prices on the free market had a striking effect on the daily lives of the mass of the people. From January, 1957, the prices of such consumer goods as table salt, pork, woollen textiles, high-class tobaccos, edible oils, etc., were successively raised. In March it was revealed that the food situation had worsened under the effects of natural damage to crops.[71] In April it was announced that the ration of cotton cloth for the summer period was to be reduced by half,[72] and at the same time a scarcity of sugar came to light in many of the cities. When such situations developed, the people, not being in possession of

---

[71] In a speech by Ch'en Yün at the Session of the National Committee of the People's Political Consultative Conference of China it is said that as a result of damage to crops in 1956 reduction should be made in state purchases of foodstuffs in the food year extending from July, 1956 to June, 1957 in comparison with the previous year, that at the same time the supply of food to the stricken areas should be greatly increased and a saving of half a catty to one catty of foodstuffs per person per month effected throughout the whole country.

[72] This measure passed a General Session of the State Council on the 12th of April, 1957. It was declared to be a measure designed to ensure the satisfaction of the demand for cotton cloth in the winter season of 1957, justified by the failure of the cotton harvest to attain the planned yields as a result of natural damage to the crop and by the easiness of the supply of cotton in the previous two years.

the facts of the case, were filled with doubt as to the future of prices, and it was only natural that they should have been brought to chase after goods from place to place in order to buy them up, actuated by an ideology attaching a low value to currency and a high value to goods.[73] In March a new situation arose, although only temporarily, when there were withdrawals of savings deposits from the People's Bank of China, and the balance of savings fell. By May work had begun on instituting unified supervision of market prices under the People's Commissions in Peking, Tientsin and Shanghai. It is probable that this happened because the price controls exercised by the authorities had lapsed in respect of certain goods in the period after the completion of socialist transformation. Thus, in the fourth and fifth years of the First Five-Year Plan, New China was confronted by problems of no common order. We may reflect that at this time the planned socialist economy of New China, like those of all socialist economies, was passing through its period of trial and error. It was fortunate that as soon as the authorities of New China, in their wisdom and good conscience, discovered any errors, they immediately strove to correct them. The General Line, the Great Leap Forward and the Organization of the People's Communes were developed in 1958, the first year of the Second Five-Year Plan, and a number of problems which had appeared during the First Five-Year Plan proceeded to their solution within the framework of the new Plan. The problem of the unbalance between supply and demand in regard to material resources and the problem of the general rise in prices were no exception. However, we must not overlook the fact that the theoretical and practical experience gained by the Chinese Communist authorities in dealing with the problems in the period of the First Five-Year Plan, and especially in the last years of the Plan, 1956 and 1957, lies in the background of the General Line, the Great Leap Forward and the Organization of the People's Communes.

---

73 See the leading article in the Peking *Ta Kung Pao* (4 May, 1957) and the directive to local banks from the People's Bank of China published in the same issue.

CHAPTER V

A GENERAL DESCRIPTION OF THE SOCIALIST FINANCIAL ORGANIZATION

INTRODUCTION

WITH the establishment of the People's Republic of China, the banks of purely Chiang Kai-shek affiliation, such as the Central Bank of China and the China Farmers Bank, in so far as they existed on the Chinese mainland, fell into the hands of the new state. The banks of the former enemy countries, Japan, Germany, Italy, etc., which had been in the possession of the Chiang Kai-shek régime for a time, also fell into the hands of the new state. The Chinese banks which held some part of the capital affiliated to the Chiang Kai-shek régime (called "bureaucrat capital" in New China) had the capital in question confiscated by the new state, and became joint state-private banks. Further, the new state had a state bank of its own, the People's Bank of China, and it embarked on the establishment of a new socialist system of finance with this bank playing the central role. In this chapter we shall make a general examination of the socialist financial system of New China centred on the People's Bank of China.

I. The State Financial Organs

The state financial organs are socialist financial organs, and owned by the whole people. We can list four types of these institutions in addition to the People's Bank of China.

1. The People's Bank of China

The People's Bank of China started business on the 1st of December, 1948, eleven months before the establishment of the People's Republic of China. The bank was formed around the North China Bank, with which were amalgamated a number of Communist note-issuing banks dispersed as independent units in the former Liberated Areas. It was at this time that People's Currency was first issued in place of the Border Currencies circulating in the various regions of China, and at length the unification of the currency system over the whole of mainland China was accomplished by means of this People's Currency. When the People's Bank of China started business its head office was located in the North China Bank at Shihchiachuang, Hopei Province, but after the Liberation of Peking it was moved to that city.

The People's Bank of China is the state bank of the People's Republic of China. A state bank is defined as meaning a nationalized bank under the direct control of the central government. After the People's Republic of China had been established and until the new Constitution had been laid down the People's Bank of China was one of the central administrative bodies established under the Administrative Council, having a status equal to that of the Ministries (and bodies bearing the titles of *hui*: 會, *yüan*: 院, *shu*: 署 and *hang*: 行), and was subject to the direction of the Financial and Economic Commission of the Administrative Council (Article 18 of the Organizational Law of the Central People's Government of the People's Republic of China). In the state structure set up under the new Constitution the People's Bank of China became a body directly subordinate to the State Council, and was of a character different from the Ministries and Commissions which were the component elements of the State Council, its duties being merely those of attending to its specialized functions. We may interpret this as meaning that, although the People's Bank of China was ranked along with the Ministries, it possessed less than equal status in relation to these Ministries. From the point of view of the allotment of spheres of administrative responsibility within the State Council the People's Bank of China came under the jurisdiction of the Fifth Staff Office, along with the Ministry of Finance and the Ministry of Foreign Trade.[74]

The People's Bank of China is thus one of the administrative bodies of the People's Republic of China, but at the same time it has performed a variety of duties as the nerve-centre of the national currency and financial institutions, and is still charged with the performance of these duties.

Among the functions which have been fulfilled by the People's Bank of China we may list (1) the unification of the Chinese currency system by means of the People's Currency, (2) the direction and supervision of private banks and silver shops,[75] (3) the socialist transformation of private banks, (4) the development and overseeing of co-operative enterprises,[76] and (5) the direction of activities for commercial credit inquiries.[77]

The main functions with which the People's Bank of China is at present charged are as follows.[78]

(1)   It is the sole currency-issuing organ in China.

(2)   It carries out adjustments of the currency, including the cash

---

[74]   See Articles 2, 4, and 6 of the Organization Law of the State Council of the People's Republic of China, and the Communication from the State Council issued on the 10th of November, 1954, concerning Central and Local State Administrative Organs and Related Matters.

[75]   As the Chinese Communist armies expanded the area of the Liberated Areas, the supervision of private financial organs and silver shops was provided for under Provisional Regulations issued in the Regions in North China, East China and South China (Provisional Regulations for the Supervision of the Private Banks and Native Banks, and Provisional Regulations for the Control of Gold and Silver), and the People's Governments in each Region empowered the People's Bank of China to undertake supervision and inspection on their behalf.

[76]   Since the time of the establishment of the People's Republic of China, the People's Bank of China has been occupied with assisting the development of the co-operative works and overseeing the financial plans of the co-operatives and the manner in which loans are employed by the co-operatives, from the side of financial business (See Central Supervisory Bureau of Co-operative Works & the People's Bank of China, "Decisions Concerning State Bank Aid for Co-operatives," in *CTCFH*, II, p.547).

[77]   In accordance with decisions taken at the Federated National Conference of Banking Institutions in August, 1950, United Commercial Inquiry Agencies (徵信所) were established in Shanghai, Wuhan, Canton and in other great cities in all parts of China.   These Agencies correspond to the Japanese *kōshinsho* (興信所), and in the present instance they are organs for investigating the credit of clients in relation to financial business.   The People's Bank of China is the directing organ of these Agencies in all parts of China, and the general manager of the local branch of the People's Bank of China is also the chief director of the local Agency.

[78]   On the subject of the functions of the People's Bank of China see Kao Hsiang, "On the Function of the State Banks in Socialist Construction," *CCYC*, No. 10, 1962, and Tuan Yün, "On a Number of Problems in the Work of China's Socialist Banks," *HC*, No. 1, 1964.

control and currency control.

(3) It is the centre of the settlement in the national economy. All settlements between state enterprises, state organizations, state organs, and bodies are carried on through book transfer on the deposit accounts of the People's Bank of China. This is connected with the cash control.

(4) It is the centre of receipts and payments of cash in China. This is also connected with the cash control.

(5) It is the centre of bank credit in the national economy. The People's Bank of China mobilizes all temporarily unemployed funds in the form of deposits by state organs, bodies and individuals, and, in accordance with the demands of state planning, makes loans to agriculture, industry and commerce, thus facilitating the development of socialist construction. It is to be noted that this state bank, which is the central note-issuing bank, has direct deposit and lending relations with economic units other than financial organs.

(6) It undertakes the overseeing and direction of the making of loans provided by banking institutions.

(7) It represents the State Treasury, and undertakes the issue and redemption of government loans.

(8) It supervises the wage fund. Payment of the wages of staff and workers is the largest item of cash payments normally made by the state. The People's Bank of China is charged by the state with the duty of overseeing and supervising all payments of wages, and payments of monies of the nature of wages (bonuses, allowances, etc.) in state enterprises, state organs, bodies and economic organizations operating under the system of collective ownership.

(9) It undertakes the buying, selling and supervision of gold and silver. The regulations governing gold and silver differ in the North China, East China and South China regions, but in all these regions the People's Bank of China is charged with the buying and selling of gold and silver, and with the supervision of dealings in these metals. The Bank has official prices for buying and selling gold and silver, and sales are restricted to pharmaceutical, industrial and other legitimate uses.

(10) It undertakes foreign exchange control and the effecting of international settlements. Their actual work is carried out

by the Bank of China.

Let us examine later each of these aspects of cash control and currency control stated above.

As we have already pointed out, the People's Bank of China differs from the generality of central banks in other countries in that it is directly involved in ordinary banking business. Further, its business covers an extremely wide range, for besides deposit, loan and exchange business it also undertakes trust, savings, and agency business (for example, acting as agent for the People's Insurance Company of China). It of course undertakes the provision of credit for agriculture, industry and commerce, and in addition also extends its activities to the granting of petty loans direct to the working people.[79] On the subject of petty loans to the working people we may observe that in March, 1953, the People's Bank of China set up a Citizens' Petty Loan Office at Tientsin. This institution was in the nature of a government pawnshop, and was set up with the secondary aim of destroying the power of the established pawnbroking business.[80]

The following is a general representation of the dendritic organization of the People's Bank of China.[81]

(1) Head Office in the capital (Peking).
(2) Regional Banks in major administrative regions (general supervisory functions)
(3) Branch Banks. There are three forms of these, (a) Provincial Branches (located at seats of Provincial administrations), (b) City Branches (located in cities under the direct jurisdiction of the central government), and (c) Branches in Autonomous

---

79 The operation of the People's Bank of China is governed by a variety of regulations. For a general coverage of these, see *CTCFH*, I, pp. 272–276 and 284–311; *CTCFH*, II, pp. 581–587; *CTCFH*, III, pp. 221–240; The Financial and Economic Commission of the Military Administrative Commission in the East China Region, *Collection of Legal Instructions Relating to Financial and Economic Matters in the East China Region* (Shanghai, 1951), Series I, Vol. 1, pp. 485–512.

80 On the Citizens' Petty Loan Office of the People's Bank, Tientsin, see the news report in the Hong Kong *Ta Kung Pao* (19 March, 1953). The Provisional Regulations for the Supervision of Pawnshops in Shanghai, issued by the People's Government, Shanghai, on the 22nd of September, 1950, are worthy of note in connection with the policy of the government of New China in regard to the pawnbroking trade.

81 Liu Liu, "The New Bank System in Process of Growth," *H-TKP* (11 June, 1951).

Regions. The City Branch Banks have no Sub-Branches beneath them, but have direct control of Branch Offices.

(4) Sub-Branch Banks located at the seats of *Hsien* administrations or in comparatively prosperous places within the *Hsien*.

In addition to the above-mentioned, " Central Sub-Branch Banks " were sometimes established between the Provincial Branches and the Sub-Branches. These were of a transitional character, and were established when necessary in areas in which the transportation, political situation, or Party cadre conditions were somewhat different. They acted as representatives of the Provincial Branches, and undertook the direction and overseeing of a number of Sub-Branches.

In addition to the above four grades there was the following subordinate organization beneath the Branches and Sub-Branches.

(1) In the cities—Branch Offices, Savings Offices, Savings Shops, Receiving Offices, and stationary and mobile work-teams.

(2) In the rural villages—Business Offices, Loan Offices, and Rural Finance Small Groups.

By 1951 the business network of the People's Bank of China had extended over the urban and rural areas to a density not inferior to that of the Japanese Third Class Post Office network. The People's Bank of China considered that even this network of Branches, Sub-Branches, etc., was insufficient, and in order to increase its business it delegated agencies to post-offices and co-operatives, especially in the collection of savings. It also engaged the services of special workers, and in the rural areas it used the primary school teachers as important propaganda agents.[82]

Since the Central People's Government abolished the system of major administrative regions in June, 1954, it is probable that the above-mentioned Regional Banks were also abolished at this time. Again, the majority of the " Central Sub-Branch Banks " were established in Special Districts (專區).

Further, as a means of absorbing savings, the People's Bank of China has recently established Branch Offices in the cities, as well as Savings Offices, Agency Offices, Business Stations, Service Stations, Agent Workers and Savings Co-operators under the *Hsien* Sub-Branch Banks.

---

[82] Head Office of the People's Bank of China, " The Principal Forms of Work Performed by the State Banks in the Year 1951," in *CTCFH*, III, p. 200.

In 1957, the last year of the First Five-Year Plan, "the People's Bank of China had 20,000 Branches and Sub-Branches, to which were added 100,000 rural credit co-operatives, and had built up a vast socialist financial network."[83]

About the end of 1952 the People's Bank of China dealt with 90% of the deposits and loans transacted in China, and with the addition of the business conducted by the joint state-private banks this proportion reached 98–99%.[84] In the two and a half years between June, 1950 and December, 1952, the proportion of savings and other deposits held by the People's Bank of China rose from 58.6% to 92.8%, and the proportion held by private banks and native banks fell from 41.4% to 7.2%.[85]

This strengthening and extension of the power of the People's Bank of China was of great service in the implementation of the First Five-Year Plan, which began in 1953.

2. *The People's Construction Bank of China*

This bank is a specialized government bank attached to the Ministry of Finance which began business on the 1st of October, 1954, with head office in Peking and branches and sub-branches in all parts of China. Its duties were (1) to concentrate the funds in the budget to be used by the state in capital construction and the funds provided by state enterprises, state organs, etc., by themselves for use in capital construction and to oversee and disburse these funds in accordance with the plans and budgets, (2) to make short-term loans to the sub-contracting enterprises under state and provincial state operation in accordance with credit plans approved by the state, (3) to carry out the settlement business of funds allotted for capital construction, and (4) to oversee the special use of the Special Funds provided for use in capital construction, and to oversee and inspect the employment of funds, the financial control, the cost-accounting, and the fulfilment of investment plans of construction units and sub-contracting enterprises.

When this bank was established China had already entered the period of planned economic construction, and the funds in-

---

[83] *P-TKP* (6 Oct., 1957).

[84] Hsü Kuang, "The Development and Achievements of Banking in New China in the Past Year," *Chingchi Nienpao*, 1953 Edition, p. 35.

[85] Ts'ao Chü-ju, "Banking in the Last Ten Years," *Jenmin Jihpao* (1 Nov., 1959).

vested by the state in capital construction had increased from year to year. The bank was established because it was found necessary to establish a separate specialized bank which would assure the supply of funds for capital construction at suitable times, oversee the rational use of funds, cause the state departments engaged in capital construction to complete their tasks in capital construction in accordance with the plans laid down by the state, and which would, at the same time, carry out economic accounting, lower the costs of work undertaken, and bring about a saving of construction funds on behalf of the state.[86]

The main duties of the People's Construction Bank of China are those of overseeing disbursements made in respect to capital construction. These duties were transferred to the bank at its inception from the Bank of Communications (concerning which see below). All the regulations and legal instructions which had been distributed by the Bank of Communications in connection with its supervision of disbursement of funds in respect to capital construction were declared to be still in force, and the accounts for the payment of funds, clearing accounts and advance accounts, etc., which the construction units and building enterprises had had with the Bank of Communications were transferred to the People's Construction Bank of China.[87]

3. The Agricultural Bank of China

This bank started business on the 12th of November, 1963, with its head office in Peking. It is a state specialized bank, and is considered to be directly dependent on the State Council.

The main duties of the Agricultural Bank of China are those of making disbursements and loans to agriculture on behalf of the state in accordance with state plans, budgets, policies and institutions, and of exercising unified supervision over these transactions. In recent years the funds which have been disbursed by the state for the support of agriculture have amounted to several billion *yüan* annually, and they have had an important effect in strengthening and developing the collective economy of the people's

---

[86] "Decisions Regarding the People's Construction Bank of China" passed by the 224th Administrative Conference of the Administrative Council on the 9th of September, 1954.

[87] *Jenmin Shouts'e,* 1955 Edition, p. 441.

communes. It is probable that the state will continue to increase its disbursements of funds for the support of agriculture, and will make great efforts to support agriculture. The Agricultural Bank of China was established with a view to enabling these funds to be used to good effect and promoting to an even greater degree the modernization of agricultural production and agriculture.

Hereafter, the Agricultural Bank of China will be responsible for overseeing disbursements and loans in accordance with the plans and the institutions fixed by the state and in accordance with the policies of the Party and the state in respect to disbursements of state funds invested in capital construction in the fields of agriculture, forestry, pastoral industries, water conservancies (not including investment in large and medium-scale water conservancies), etc., working funds supplied by the state to working units in these fields, state disbursements and loans to such state enterprises as state farms, state forests, state stock farms, state fishing grounds, tractor stations, drainage and irrigation stations, etc., state disbursements and relief funds to people's communes and production teams, and state loans to basic economic accounting units of people's communes and enterprises operated by them.

The Agricultural Bank of China must also co-operate with the state agricultural departments in giving guidance to people's communes and production teams in respect to financial administration and accounting, and give assistance for the suitable use of funds accumulated by the collective economies of these bodies.

Other important duties of the Agricultural Bank of China are those of directing the rural credit co-operatives, absorbing idle funds in the rural areas and giving them out as loans, and causing assistance to be given for the relief of financial distress in regard to the production and livelihood of poor peasants and the lower-middle peasants.

The Agricultural Bank of China must also co-operate with the People's Bank of China in overseeing the payment of earnest money for the purchase of agricultural products by advance order in the rural areas by the state commercial departments and act as agent for the People's Bank of China in deposit business, cash control business and other work in the rural areas.

The following is a description of the management supervision organization of the Agricultural Bank of China. At the centre there is the Head Office of the Agricultural Bank of China, while Branch Banks are established in the Provinces, Cities, and Autonomous Regions, Central Sub-Branch Banks in the Special Districts, Sub-Branch Banks in *hsien*, and Business Offices in the Districts, or people's communes equivalent to Districts. This dendritic structure was to be established all over China by January, 1964.

We must also add that a state bank of the same name, " The Agricultural Bank of China," started business on the 25th of March, 1955, with its head office in Peking, and was abolished in April, 1957, upon which the operation of agricultural finance was returned to the People's Bank of China which carried on agricultural finance in the original monistic condition. The duties of the then Agricultural Bank of China were those of directing the credit co-operatives' organization in the rural areas, mobilizing surplus funds in the rural areas over a wide area and rationally applying state loans to agriculture, thereby assisting the development of agricultural production and promoting the socialist transformation of agriculture. The then Agricultural Bank of China, on the basis of the agricultural credit plans approved by the state, was to make long-term and short-term loans to state agriculture, state animal husbandry, producers' mutual-aid co-operative organization in agriculture, animal husbandry, fisheries, forestry, etc., carried on by the masses and individual producers, and was to be responsible for overseeing disbursements of state-budgeted investments in capital construction in the fields of agriculture, forestry, and water conservancies (while the subordinate structure of the Agricultural Bank of China was as yet not fully developed these duties would be performed by the People's Construction Bank of China), directing and assisting the credit co-operative organization for the masses, and receiving savings and ordinary deposits from the rural population, the producers' mutual-aid co-operative organization, the collective farms, and from state-operated agricultural and water-conservancy enterprises and organs. Further, this Agricultural Bank of China was to be subject to the direction from the head office of the People's Bank of China, and its branches were to be subject to the direction from the People's Committees of the Provinces, the Party Committees of the Provinces, as well as from the Provincial Branches of the People's Bank of China.[88] The following

---

[88] *Jenmin Jihpao* (27 March, 1955).

two reasons are given for the abolition of the Agricultural Bank of China and the amalgamation of its structure and functions with the People's Bank of China in April, 1957. The first is that it was extremely difficult to distinguish between the functions of the People's Bank and the Agricultural Bank, and the second is that the establishment of two distinct banks had made it necessary to make a large-scale increase in structure and cadres, and to increase disbursements for capital construction.[89]

The later Agricultural Bank of China, like the People's Bank of China, is an institution directly dependent on the State Council. Consequently the two banks are of equal status in relation to one another, and the present Agricultural Bank of China differs fundamentally from the previous institution of the same name in that the latter was subject to direction from the People's Bank of China. Again, a distinct division of activities between the two Banks is laid down in regard to the disbursement to state funds and agricultural finance.

4. The Overseas Chinese Investment Company

This is a state investment company which absorbs foreign exchange from the Chinese abroad, and organizes its investment in local industries and in other enterprises which will be of benefit to economic construction. By investing in this company overseas Chinese can enjoy the following preferential treatment. (1) The invested funds remain the property of the investor even after the completion of socialist construction in China, and the invested funds can be recouped after 12 years. (2) The dividend paid on the investment is 8% per annum. This should be compared with the 5% dividend paid on privately-owned shares in joint state-private enterprises. (3) Dividends can be sent out of China with the permission of the exchange control organs. These remittances, however, must not exceed 50% of the dividend paid in the year in question. (4) If the investor seeks work in China his application will be given priority, consideration being given to the requirements of the work of the company and the actual circumstances of the applicant. These provisions were set out in the notice entitled " Regulations for the Preferential Treatment for

---

[89] State Council, "Communication Concerning the Abolition of the Agricultural Bank of China," in CFH, 1957 Edition, pp. 87–88.

Investment by Overseas Chinese in the Overseas Chinese Investment Company " published by the State Council on the 2nd of August, 1957. Before this notice was published, the Fukien Province Overseas Chinese Investment Company had been established in 1952 in Fuchow, the Kwangtung Province Overseas Chinese Investment Company had been established in Canton in 1955 as a result of an amalgamation and reorganization of the Overseas Chinese Industrial Construction Company and the South China Industrial Company, and the Shanghai Overseas Chinese Investment Company had been established in Shanghai in 1956. These were all joint state-private companies, and had been reorganized into state companies at the time of the publication of the notice referred to above. In addition to the companies already mentioned, there are at present state Overseas Chinese Investment Companies in Yünnan Province (Kunming), Chekiang Province (Ningpo), Kwangsi Province (Nanning), and Shantung Province. We may also note that the authorities in the government of New China assured an annual dividend of 8% on overseas Chinese capital invested in these joint state-private Overseas Chinese Investment Companies, and that they made bonus payments depending on the state of profits. We may add further that a number of changes have been made in the Regulations governing investment by overseas Chinese in the state Overseas Chinese Investment Company as set out in the notice mentioned above.[90]

5.   *The People's Insurance Company of China*

This insurance company is a state insurance company established in Peking on the 20th of October, 1949. It carries on the following types of insurance business.

(1) Agricultural Insurance. Livestock insurance, crop and harvest insurance.

(2) Fire Insurance. Fire insurance for factories, warehouses, houses, raw materials, manufactured goods, clothes and personal belongings, furniture, etc.

(3) Personal Insurance. Passenger insurance against accident, collective personal insurance, collective insurance for seamen, individual life insurance.

(4) Transport Insurance and War Insurance. Marine insurance,

---

[90]   See T. Miyashita, *The Economic System of New China* (Tokyo, 1964), p. 126.

insurance for transportation by rail, road, air, and by vehicles driven by human or animal power.

(5) Transport Vehicles Insurance. Shipping insurance (including fishing vessels), automobile insurance.

In 1951 the Administrative Council of the Central People's Government introduced compulsory insurance for the property of state organs, state enterprises and co-operatives, and compulsory passenger insurance was also put into effect. The People's Insurance Company of China has a network of branches throughout China and is also represented by the People's Bank of China, the Bank of China, the Bank of Communications, and other industrial and commercial enterprises. The joint state-private Insurance Company of China is a subordinate organization of the People's Insurance Company of China (see below).

6. *Gold and Silver Jewellery Shops*

When the Chinese Communist régime came to power the silver shops were permitted, at least in the following sense. For example, according to Article 8 of the Provisional Regulations for Gold and Silver in the North China Region issued by the North China People's Government on the 27th of April, 1949, silver shops might sell ornamental articles made of gold or silver. However, they were not permitted to buy or sell gold or silver as such, or to buy gold and silver jewellery. They were further obliged to report the materials and manufactured articles in their possession and their sales from day to day to the People's Bank of China. In consequence of these Regulations some thinning of the numbers of silver shops took place. The state Gold and Silver Jewellery Shops were established as an accompaniment to the disappearance of these silver shops and were designed to satisfy the people's love of ornamental articles in gold and silver and, at the same time, to prevent them buying these articles on the black market. The Gold and Silver Jewellery Shops carry on the sale of ornamental articles in gold and silver, the exchange of old ornamental articles in gold or silver for new ornamental articles, the execution of orders for badges and medals, and the undertaking of processing-work on materials provided. It was laid down as the general rule that these shops should only sell, and should not buy. As far as could be traced by the Hong Kong *Ta*

Kung Pao, these state Gold and Silver Jewellery Shops were first established at Tientsin (in May, 1951), and thereafter, up to the end of June, 1952, at Wuhan, Shanghai, Peking, Canton, Chungking, Shenyang, Harbin and Sian. On the 19th of July 1959 the same paper carried a news report on the work of the gold and silver ornament processing department of the state-operated Shihshih Overseas Chinese Store in Chinchiang *Hsien,* Fukien Province. It is said that this processing department was established in the autumn of 1956. From this we may infer that the state Gold and Silver Jewellery Shops were established not only in the great cities but also over a large part of China.

II. Joint State-Private Financial Organs

In New China joint state-private operation is considered to be one of the advanced forms of state capitalism, to be a semi-socialist form of economic organization, and to be the intermediate stage through which private capitalist economy or capitalist commerce and industry must move to the system of whole-people ownership (the state economy). It was in 1956 that " joint state-private operations by whole trades "—that is, joint state-private operations of all trades in a certain city—were put into effect, but in the case of the banking business all private enterprises in China had been brought under joint state-private operation by 1952. Let us now take a brief look at the financial organs operated under joint state-private management.

1. The Bank of China

The Bank of China has a long history. Its origins go back to the Hupu Bank, established in the latter years of the Ch'ing Dynasty as the central bank of the Ch'ing Court, and later reorganized first as the Tuchihpu Bank and again as the Ta Ch'ing Bank. The name " The Bank of China " dates from the establishment of the bank as the central bank of the new republic when the Republic of China was set up in Peking in 1912. When the Kuomintang government was established in 1928 the bank became an international exchange bank chartered by the government, and in the spring of 1935, as a result of the Kuomintang government's bank control policy, the government's control over the personnel and capital of the bank was strengthened, and together with the Central Bank of China, the Bank of Communications and the China Farmers Bank, the bank became one of the four government banks.

When the Communist régime came to power the bank had its bureaucrat capital confiscated, and it was made into a joint state-private bank specializing in foreign exchange and overseas Chinese remittances. The bank thus became a specialized bank. In the "Order Concerning the Strengthening of the Direction and Supervision of the Bank of China," issued by the Administrative Council of the Central People's Government on the 22nd of March, 1950, it is declared that the Bank of China is a joint state-private bank, that one-third of its shares were held by private shareholders and two-thirds took the form of state investment, and that the latter should be considered to have reverted to the ownership of the Central People's Government. The names of 13 directors and auditors newly sent by the government are given. On the 9th of April, 1950, Nan Han-chen, at that time the Head of the People's Bank of China, was appointed chairman of the board of directors of the Bank of China. According to an advertisement published in the Hong Kong *Ta Kung Pao* of the 6th of September, 1951, by the Directorate of the Bank of China, the board of directors of the above-named bank had provisionally fixed the total amount of capital of the bank at 198,000,000,000 *yüan* (330,000 *yüan* in People's Currency per share). The first general meeting of shareholders to take place after the liberation was held in Peking on the 26th of November, 1954. On this occasion the number of private shareholders amounted to 1,262. At the meeting 12 private directors and 4 private auditors were re-elected.

The business carried on by the Bank of China differs to some degree at home and abroad.[91] The domestic business of the bank included (1) banking transactions connected with the import and export trades, (2) remittance exchange business, (3) the receipt of deposits in People's Currency and in foreign currencies, (4) the buying and selling of foreign currencies, (5) offering facilities of of all kinds to overseas Chinese, and (6) other types of foreign ex-

---

[91] The Hong Kong Ta Kung Pao Company, *Trade with China, A Practical Guide* (Hong Kong, 1957), pp. 55–56.

change business. Abroad, the business of the bank is said to have included (1) banking transactions connected with the import and export trades, (2) the receipt of deposits and the making of loans, (3) offering facilities of all kinds to overseas Chinese, and (4) other types of banking business. The Bank of China thus carries on deposit, loan and general banking business abroad, but in China it confines its activities to banking business connected with foreign trade and foreign exchange.

The address of the Directorate of the Bank of China is 28, Tungchiaomin-hsiang, Peking, and the bank has domestic branches at Tientsin, Shanghai, Tsingtao, Chefoo, Hankow, Changsha, Amoy, Fuchow, Ch'üanchou, Canton, Shenchün, Swatow, Haikow, Nanning, Wuchou, Kunming, Wantang, Talien and elsewhere. Abroad, the bank has branches at Hong Kong, Karachi, Chittagong, Rangoon, Singapore, Djakarta, Surabaya, Medan, London and elsewhere. There were branches at Kuala Lumpur and Penang, but since it was enacted under the revision of the Bank Act which took place in the Federation of Malaya in December, 1958, that banks operating in the Federation of Malaya 50% or more of whose capital was owned by foreign governments, or a majority of whose directors was appointed by foreign governments or their representative organs, should cease business within three months after the coming into effect of the new act, these branches ceased business with effect from the 1st of April, 1959. Again, in November, 1962, the Indian government sealed-off and confiscated the Calcutta Branch of the Bank of China and its offices in Bombay. Further, since December, 1962, the deposits and all other assets of the Indian agencies of the Directorate of the Bank of China and other organs of that bank have been frozen. All these events resulted from the Sino-Indian frontier dispute. The Bank of China also has agents and correspondents among banks in England, France, Western Germany, Holland, Switzerland, Austria, Belgium, Italy and other countries.[92]

The organs of the Bank of China associated with the Kuomintang government in Taiwan are still in existence, and the bank has business offices in Tokyo, New York, Washington, Saigon and elsewhere.

---

[92] Ts'ao Chü-ju, op. cit.

2. *The Bank of Communications*

The Bank of Communications, founded in the latter years of the Ch'ing Dynasty, is another bank with a long history. In the period of the Peking Republican Government it ranked with the Bank of China as one of the state banks, but when the Kuomintang government was set up in Nanking the bank was charged with the development of industry under special charter from the government, and as a result of the bank-control measures introduced by the Kuomintang government in the spring of 1934 government control over the personnel and capital of the bank was strengthened, as in the case of the Bank of China, and the bank became one of the four government banks.

When the People's Republic of China was established the Bank of Communications had its holdings of bureaucrat capital confiscated, and it became a joint state-private bank specializing in long-term credit business. According to an advertisement published by the Directorate of the Bank of Communications in the Hong Kong *Ta Kung Pao* on the 9th of October, 1951, a general meeting of the directors and auditors of the bank had fixed the total amount of capital of the bank at 180,000,000,000 *yüan*, or 300,000 *yüan* per share. In the spring of that year a reorganization of the Bank of Communications had been carried out, and since then the bank had been charged with (1) investment in state capital construction, (2) clearing and supervising shareholders' accounts in joint state-private enterprises, and (3) the organization and direction of the long-term money market. The short-term credit business of the bank was transferred to the People's Bank of China.[93] Later, as we have already noted, the People's Construction Bank of China was established in October, 1954, and the business connected with disbursements of funds in respect to capital construction and their supervision which had hitherto been carried on by the Bank of Communications was transferred to the People's Construction Bank of China. Again, joint state-private operation by whole trades was realized in the capitalist commerce and industry in 1956, and with the introduction of fixed rates of interest for the joint state-private enterprises the duties of the Bank of Communications in regard to the joint state-private enterprises lapsed. This may be supposed to have

---

[93] *H-TKP* (19 Apr., 1951).

had a fundamental effect on the bank's position, but as yet there is no news of its being closed down.

3. Investment Companies

These are investment companies which were established in large numbers all over China about 1951 with the participation of the People's Bank of China, such as the Tientsin Investment Company, the Peking Industrial Investment Company, the Wuhan Industrial Investment Company, the Canton Investment Company, the South China Enterprises Company Limited and the South China Industrial Construction Company Limited. Of these, the Canton Investment Company and the two which follow it were set up with capital contributed jointly by the overseas Chinese and the state.[94] As an example we may consider the case of the Tientsin Investment Company which started business on the 10th of June, 1951. The capital and scope of business of this company were as follows (the Hong Kong *Ta Kung Pao,* 9 June, 1951).

The share capital of the company was 30,000,000,000 *yüan,* of which privately-owned (non-official) shares amounted to more than 79%. The scope of its business included (1) investment in works beneficial to the national economy, (2) undertaking the issue of debenture bonds for companies in the fields of industry, mining and public utilities, (3) acting as agents selling, or undertaking to sell, the shares or debentures of the above enterprises, (4) the holding of redemption funds and making of payments of dividends and interest on behalf of the above enterprises, (5) the issue of investment bonds and the undertaking of trust investments, (6) acting as agents buying and selling negotiable securities with government permission, (7) planning investments on behalf of clients, and (8) investing in other related economic works with the permission of the government. Since that time, however, great changes have come about in economic works in China, and it is to be imagined that the existence of investment companies possessing these characteristics and functions must now be precarious.

4. The Insurance Company of China

This insurance company is a subordinate organization of the

---

[94] On the Canton Investment Company and the two companies which follow it, see *Jenmin Shouts'e,* 1955 Edition, p. 442 ff.

People's Insurance Company of China, and is run on a joint state-private basis. The company's capital is 3,000,000 *yüan*, of which 2,000,000 *yüan* is subscribed by the People's Insurance Company of China. The relation between these two Insurance Companies is similar to that between the People's Bank of China and the Bank of China, and while abroad the Insurance Company of China assists the People's Insurance Company of China and undertakes some of the insurance business connected with foreign trade and transportation, it also has branches established in China through which it carries on international transport insurance and insurance business in general. The head office of the company is in Peking, and it has branches at Hong Kong, Macao, Singapore, Penang, Kuala Lumpur, Djakarta, Surabaya and London.[95]

5. Joint State-Private Bank Operating Under the Federated Directorate

Before the Liberation, Shanghai was the economic and financial centre of China. The Chinese banks in Shanghai which could be described as the great banks or influential banks in that city, even although they might be private banks, had close personal and capital connections with leading figures associated with the Chiang Kai-shek régime. Since they had their holdings of bureaucrat capital confiscated after the Liberation, many of these influential banks were transformed into joint state-private banks. There were also certain banks which, being faced by a new environment, requested the government to provide them with capital, and thus became joint state-private banks. In due course, from May, 1951 to September of the same year, these banks were organized into three groups under federated supervision. And in September, 1951, the remainder of the medium- and small-scale banks, native banks and trust companies were organized into two groups under federally operated supervision. However, in the last eleven days of October, 1952, five such groups were combined to form a joint state-private bank, and as an accompaniment to this a unified directorate called the Federated General Supervisory Office for the Joint State-Private Bank was set up, and a Federated Board

---

[95] The accounts of the People's Insurance Company of China and the Insurance Company of China are derived from the Research Committee of Financial Institutions, *The Financial System of China* (Tokyo, 1960), pp. 274–277. (The relevant passage is written by Hideo Yonezawa.)

of Directors for the Joint State-Private Bank was organized. In this way sixty units of banks, native banks and trust companies in Shanghai were concentrated into a single joint state-private bank, and there were also private financial organs outside Shanghai which joined the single joint state-private bank in the course of similar processes of development. The financial organs which did not take part in this process of organization were obliged to give up business, and by 1952, that is, by the end of the period of economic rehabilitation and the beginning of the period of economic construction, all private financial business in China had been brought under joint state-private management. Chapter VI is devoted to a closer examination of these developments.

iii.   The Credit Co-operatives

The credit co-operatives are financial mutual-aid organizations for the working peasantry, but in the realm of rural finance they act as assistants of the People's Bank of China. The credit co-operative organizations had two important tasks in socialist China. The first was to promote the development of agricultural production and to act as an important instrument for carrying out the socialist transformation of the small-peasant economy. The " Decisions on the Development of Agricultural Producers' Co-operatives " which were adopted by the Central Committee of the Chinese Communist Party on the 16th of December, 1953, make reference to this aspect when they state that " agricultural producers' mutual-aid co-operation, agricultural supply and marketing co-operation and agricultural credit co-operation are the three forms in which co-operation is introduced into the rural areas. These three types of co-operation observe a due division of labour among themselves, form interconnections among themselves, and mutually promote their several activities, with the consequence that they gradually link up economic activity in the rural areas with the economic construction plans of the state, and gradually transform the small-peasant economy on the basis of the producers' co-operatives." The second task of the credit co-operatives is that of assisting the productive activities and livelihood of the peasantry by means of loans at low rates of interest, and of striking a blow at the exploitation of usury with a view to eventually overthrowing them altogether. The above-mentioned " Decisions on the Development of Agricultural Producers' Co-operatives " refer to this aspect in the words, " The principal forms of the capitalist element in rural society at present are commercial exploitation, the engrossing of foodstuffs, speculation and usury. An even greater responsibility is thus placed upon the supply and marketing co-operatives and credit co-operatives, and their efforts are directed under the guidance of the state economy towards helping the peasant masses to break free from these forms of exploitation, assisting the completion of the duties involved in state purchases of foodstuffs and other agricultural products, supplying the rural areas with consumption goods and production goods, promoting rural savings and low-interest loans, serving the interests of production in the rural areas, and making efforts to promote the development of the agricultural producers' mutual-aid co-operatives." It is clear from the above that the rural credit co-operatives were a part of the movement for introducing co-operation into rural society.

The history of credit co-operatives organized by the Chinese Communist Party begins in the Shan-Kan-Ning Border Area about 1944. After the advent of the People's Republic of China, experimental work was begun on the establishment of credit co-operatives in 1950, after prices had been stabilized. By the end of 1950, 103 credit co-operatives had been organized in Hopei, Shansi and other Provinces, and credit departments had been established in 439 of the supply and marketing co-operatives. In June, 1951, the People's Bank of China called the First National Rural Finance Conference at which it clearly declared that credit co-operative work was one of the important forms of rural financial work, and when the bank had extended its network of branches down to District and Town level it embarked on the experimental establishment of credit co-operatives on a priority principle. By the end of 1952, the year in which the period of economic rehabilitation ended, there were 2,271 credit co-operatives distributed over the whole of China.

In 1953 when China entered the stage of economic construction and work was begun on the implementation of the First Five-Year Plan, a further development of agricultural co-operation took place. It was in the second half of 1955 that the high tide of the development of co-operation in the Chinese countryside was reached. As an accompaniment to the development of this situation there was also a marked development of rural credit co-operative work in rural China. Restricting our view for the moment to the development of the credit co-operatives, we find that the number of credit co-operatives showed a sudden increase from 9,418 in 1953 to 124,068 in 1954, and in 1955 they further increased to 159,363. After 1956, however, the figures declined. In 1956 there were 102,558 credit co-operatives, and in 1957, 88,368. What we must note here is that this decline in the number of credit co-operatives after 1956 was due to the amalgamation of credit co-operatives as an accompaniment to amalgamations of *Hsiang*, and that this led to an enlargement of the scale of operation of the credit co-operatives. This enables us to understand the fact that in spite of the decline in the numbers of credit co-operatives the total subscribed funds of the credit co-operatives increased from 204,520,000 *yüan* in 1955 to 280,080,000 *yüan* in 1956, as well as the fact that during the same period the total of deposits with the credit co-operatives increased from 606,700,000 *yüan* to 1,078,690,000 *yüan*, and the total of loans from 281,540,000 *yüan* to 500,520,000 *yüan*. (For a detailed account, see Table VIII-3 in Chapter VIII.) When the movement for the introduction of the people's communes began in the Chinese countryside in August, 1958, the credit co-operatives were for a time incorporated in the organization of the people's communes, but at length they again came to exist as entities separate from the people's communes. We will undertake an examination of this point in Chapter VIII, Section 2.

In the National Programme for the Development of Agriculture (Draft) presented to the Supreme State Council by the Central Politburo of the Chinese Communist Party in January, 1956, it was stated that " it is required that by the end of 1957 rural credit co-operatives should be established in each *Hsiang*, and should carry on loan and savings business in the rural areas in a positive manner," but this target was finally reached by the end of 1956, with the exception of a few areas in the outlying parts of China.[96] Again, in 1956 more than 200,000 persons were involved in credit co-operative work.[97]

The most important functions performed by the credit co-operatives hitherto have been (1) the promotion of the socialist transformation of the small-peasant economy, and (2) the elimination of exploitation by usurious money-lenders. However, socialist transformation in rural China reached its peak in the period dating from the second half of 1955, and by 1956 the introduction of co-operation into Chinese agriculture had been basically attained. Hereupon there appeared a few people who judged that the credit co-operatives had fulfilled their function, and opinions were expressed by them to the effect that there was no longer any need for their existence, or that credit departments should be established in the agricultural producers' co-operatives, or that the credit co-operatives should be amalgamated with the Agricultural Bank of China. Teng Tzu-hui, a Vice-Premier of the State Council and Head of the Department of Rural Work of the Central Committee of the Chinese Communist Party, was strongly opposed to these opinions. According to Teng, the superiority of the credit co-operatives consisted in the fact that they transacted deposits and loans in a simple manner which was convenient for the masses, and were able to draw up suitable deposit and loan plans on the basis of their knowledge of local conditions. The credit co-operatives would be needed for some considerable time to come as the assistants of the state banks, and would develop their potentialities to an even greater degree. As reasons for the basic necessity for credit co-operatives in the future, Teng specified the promotion of production in agriculture and agricultural side-occupations, the carrying through of deposit and loan work, the final elimination of exploitation by usurious money-lenders, and the promotion of non-cash transactions (transfer of accounts through the banks) into the rural areas as the basic task of credit co-operatives hereafter.[98]

---

[96] As stated in the speech of Ch'en Hsi-yü, Vice-Head of the People's Bank of China, at the National Congress of Heads of Branch Banks. *T-TKP* (10 March, 1957).

[97] As distinct from these there were more than 100,000 persons engaged in rural financial work. This is reported in an article on the National Congress of the Delegates of the Leading Workers in Rural Finance in the Tientsin *Ta Kung Pao* (26 July, 1956).

[98] *T-TKP* (25 July, 1956).

In the spring of 1958 the establishment of credit departments in the agricultural producers' co-operatives was begun in Annan *Hsien*, Fukien Province. The practice spread throughout the Province, and at length was also adopted in Hopei, Honan, Hupei, Anhui, Kwangsi and other Provinces.[99] The establishment of these departments was the forerunner of the establishment of credit departments of the people's communes. At the middle of August, 1958, was seen the development of the people's communes in the rural areas all over China, its aim attained by the end of the same year, and as an accompaniment to this measure the credit co-operatives were amalgamated with local people's communes. In this way credit departments came to be established in the people's communes, with credit sub-departments attached to production brigades. Before the development of the people's communes, the credit co-operatives possessed an independent organization (general meeting of members' representatives, board of directors, board of auditors, members' small groups, etc.), but after the development of the people's communes the credit departments of the people's communes and the credit sub-departments of the production brigades functioned under the direction of the people's communes or production brigades, and lost their independent organization.[100]

However, from 1962 the credit co-operatives came to exist as entities independent of the people's communes.

In addition to the above we must also make special mention of the functions of the credit co-operatives in absorbing rural savings. The collection of rural savings in China was begun in 1950 by the People's Bank of China. After the development of the rural credit co-operatives between the autumn of 1954 and the spring of 1955 the collection of rural savings was taken over by these co-operatives. Further, while it is true that the state banks gave financial support to the credit co-operatives, there was an increasing volume of redeposits by the credit co-operatives with the state banks. The amount redeposited by the credit co-operatives with the state banks was 190,000,000 *yüan* in 1954, 590,000,000 *yüan* in 1955, and 780,000,000 *yüan* in 1956.[101]

---

[99] Articles in *P-TKP* (23 May, 1958 and 7 Aug., 1958).

[100] "How Should We Arrange the Credit Departments and Credit Sub-Departments in the People's Communes? -II-" *P-TKP* (2 Nov., 1959).

IV. Cash Control and Currency Control

Currency control was instituted in December, 1950, and was a development from the cash control which had been instituted between March and April of the same year. Our account of currency control must therefore start from an account of cash control. Further, a description of cash control must start from the halting of inflation in New China.

The People's Republic of China was established on the 1st of October, 1949, but although the Chinese Communist armies had by then gained overall military hegemony in mainland China, fierce battles were still taking place in the South-West. It was in March, 1950, that the civil war in mainland China was more or less brought to a conclusion by the subjugation of Yünnan Province. We may therefore say that by this time the political revolution constituted by the seizure of political power by the Chinese Communist Party was decisively completed. The time had now arrived for beginning work on the economic revolution which must follow the political revolution. The first step to be taken in the economic revolution was the halting of runaway inflation, the stabilization of the currency. In the course of 1949 prices in China rose by some tens of times. The decisive victories in the civil war helped to stem the tide of steeply rising prices, but the most important factor was the Unified Policy for State Financial and Economic Work passed by the Administrative Council on the 3rd of March, 1950. This Policy was popularly called the San p'ing (Three Balances) policy. This was because the policy had the principal aim of bringing about balance on a national and unified scale in the realms of (1) state financial receipts and disbursements, (2) supply and demand in regard to important material resources, and (3) cash receipts and disbursements. Cash control was introduced in order to attain a balance in cash receipts and disbursements, one of the elements of the San P'ing policy. This measure was first applied to the foreign trade

---

101 Yung Sheng, "An Essay on the Functions of Rural Credit Co-operatives under a Socialist System," T-TKP (7 Apr., 1957).

cash depository of the Ministry of Foreign Trade in March, and in April it was extended to all state organs. The People's Bank of China was charged with the responsibility of carrying out the measure.

The main provisions for cash control were as follows.[102]

(1) The aims of cash control were those of adjusting the circulation of cash, and of economizing in the use of cash. Cash control would be applied first to state organs (all state enterprises, state organs, military units, co-operatives, etc.).

(2) The People's Bank of China would be the organ responsible for carrying out cash control.

(3) All cash and bills held by state organs in excess of a certain limit would be deposited with the local branches of the People's Bank of China or with organizations to which this function had been delegated by the Bank, and state organs would be forbidden to make deposits with private banks or native banks. The balance of cash which state organs would be permitted to have on hand was not to exceed the equivalent of three days' running expenses in places where there were branches of the People's Bank of China, and in places where branches of the People's Bank of China had not been established this balance would in general not exceed the equivalent of one month's running expenses.

(4) Transfer cheques would be employed in making payments between state organs. These cheques would be cleared through the People's Bank of China, and exchange remittances would be made through the People's Bank of China in the case of transactions with other districts.

(5) The state organs would always make payments by means of cheques of the People's Bank of China and not in cash, except in such cases where the use of cash was unavoidable, as in paying out wages, making purchases in the rural areas, making petty disbursements in the cities, etc.

(6) The state organs would adopt the system of economic accounting, and would draw up plans for maintaining a balance

---

[102] Administrative Council of the Central People's Government, "Decisions Relating to the Implementation of Cash Control in State Organs" (passed by the 27th Session of the Administrative Council of the Central People's Government on the 7th of April, 1950), in *CTCFH*, I, pp. 237-238.

between cash receipts and disbursements in each half-year, quarter or month. After being approved by the local Financial Commission, these plans would be handed over to the People's Bank of China and put into effect. In carrying out these plans the Bank would be required to give assistance to the enterprises in order to ensure that they should be able to connect the settlement of their accounts with the state of their loans. In order to attain this aim the Bank would draw up a plan for cash receipts and disbursements, and would circulate copies to the organs concerned for reference.

On the 25th of November, 1950, these provisions for cash control were further enlarged and strengthened, and " currency control" was put into effect. Previous to this, in October of the same year, some danger of inflation had arisen as a result of the participation of the People's Republic of China in the Korean war, a plentiful harvest of agricultural products, an increased rate of activity in exchanges of material resources between town and country, etc., and the Financial and Economic Commission of the Central People's Government had ordered the temporary freezing of the deposits of the state organs.[103]

The following are the main points at which the system was enlarged and extended in the form of currency control, as opposed to cash control.[104]

(1) Hitherto cash control had been obligatory for state enterprises, state organs, military units, and co-operatives, but bodies were now added to the list of those which were brought under currency control. It also became possible for joint state-private enterprises to participate in currency control if they should desire to do so.

(2) Currency control included the following measures in addition to the system of cash control and book transfer settlement then in force.

(a) Borrowing, lending or other commercial credit relations

---

[103] Head Office of the People's Bank of China, " The Work of the State Banks in 1950," in *CTCFH*, III, p. 187.

[104] Financial and Economic Commission of the Administrative Council of the Central People's Government, "Directive Concerning the Instructions for Implementing Currency Control and the Instructions for Drawing up Plans for Currency Receipts and Disbursements," in *CTCFH*, II, pp. 549–576.

must not be allowed to come into being between individual economic units. When a need for short-term loans was felt, these must be obtained from the People's Bank of China.

(b) In respect to investment of funds in capital construction undertaken by the state, the People's Bank of China would delegate this work to a specialized bank to be specified by the People's Bank of China, and would cause it to oversee the investment of these funds on its own responsibility. At first the Bank of Communications was designated as the specialized bank responsible for these investments, but later this function was transferred to the People's Construction Bank of China.

(3) The People's Bank of China would carry on currency control on the basis of the plans for currency receipts and disbursements drawn up by the individual economic units and passed by each controlling department, and would also draw up comprehensive plans for currency receipts and disbursements. Such comprehensive plans for currency receipts and disbursements would be drawn up by the branches of the People's Bank of China at all levels, and these would be sent to the head office of the Bank where they would serve as the basis for drawing up an all-China comprehensive plan for currency receipts and disbursements. For this purpose, Regulations on the Drawing up of Plans for Currency Receipts and Disbursements were issued on the 15th of December, 1950.

By November, 1950, 94% of the economic units which were obliged by law to have accounts with the People's Bank of China had accounts with that Bank, the upper limits of permitted cash holdings had been fixed for two-thirds of the total number of economic units, and nearly half of the economic units had entered into debit and credit relations and book transfer settlement relations with the People's Bank of China. Further between 1950 and September, 1952, the amount of deposits at the People's Bank of China from state enterprises increased by about 60 times.[105]

The cash control and currency control systems placed limits to the amounts of cash which could be held by state organs and other units, and at the same time introduced rationality and planning into the currency receipts and disbursements of these economic units. As need hardly be said, this made some contribu-

---

[105] Hsü Kuang, op. cit.

tion to the stabilization of prices, but there is another point which is of importance as one of the factors stopping the runaway inflation of this period. This is the fact that, with the help of the large amount of cash collected by the People's Bank of China, state commerce was able, with a newly-equipped structure, to obtain possession of large quantities of material resources, and thus to acquire ample real ability for leading the market at that time.

After this period other units joined in the mechanisms for cash control and currency control. It was laid down that, when the state economy sub-contracted processing of goods or placed orders for goods to be carried out by capitalist industry and commerce, payments were to be made by means of book transfer of accounts through the People's Bank of China, and that the Bank would be responsible for overseeing the use of the funds thus deposited by private firms, acting on the basis of the business agreements signed by the state and private companies.[106] The progress of socialist transformation and its basic completion also led to a widening of the sphere of participation in these mechanisms. It need hardly be said that the joint state-private enterprises participated in them. In the period of the agricultural producers' co-operatives, neither the People's Bank of China nor the credit co-operatives were allowed to exercise cash control in relation to the agricultural producers' co-operatives.[107] In regard to the people's communes, Huang Ya-kuang states that the Central Committee of the Chinese Communist Party had decided to apply the system of cash control, and to press forward with non-cash settlements (book transfer settlements). It was laid down that the cash in the hands of the basic economic accounting units among the people's communes (at that time the production brigade) and its subordinate enterprises would in principle be deposited with

[106] Huang Ya-kuang, "Non-Cash Settlements in Chinese Banks," *HC*, No. 16, 1960, p. 17.

[107] An editorial commentary entitled "Activize Rural Finance!" in the Tientsin *Ta Kung Pao* (28 June, 1956) states, "The banks and the credit co-operatives must not exercise cash control in relation to the agricultural co-operatives, the amounts of cash to be kept on hand by the agricultural co-operatives must not be fixed, and the agricultural co-operatives must not be asked to send in plans of their future deposits and withdrawals." Matter to the same effect is found in the directive from the State Council, published in the same paper on the 9th of July, 1956, on the subject of compulsory orders given by banks and credit co-operatives.

the People's Bank of China and the credit departments of the people's communes, with the exception of small amounts of cash retained for incidental expenses. The wages of the members of the communes and other disbursements of a similar nature were to be made in cash, but economic transactions between economic units within the commune and between the communes and the state enterprises were to be carried out through the People's Bank of China and the credit departments of the communes by means of non-cash settlements.[108] However, Huang Ya-kuang was speaking of the situation prevailing in 1960. Concerning the people's communes in the period since 1962, when the basic economic accounting unit of the people's communes became the production team, Kao Hsiang states, "Cash control in relation to the agricultural producing unit under the system of collective ownership is comparatively lax. All that is required by the regulations is that the cash on hand in excess of a certain limit should be deposited with the Bank [the People's Bank of China] or with a credit co-operative designated by the Bank, and in general the cash receipts and disbursements of the production teams of the people's communes are not subject to limitations. When the state buys agricultural produce and agricultural by-products from the production teams payment is made entirely in cash."[109]

We can discern the following successive changes in the methods used in making payments when state commerce or the supply and marketing co-operatives made purchases of agricultural produce in the rural areas.

(1) In the period of the agricultural producers' co-operatives

---

[108] Huang Ya-kuang, pp. 20–21. We believe that Huang Ya-kuang's argument is related to the following decision in regard to the credit departments of the people's communes included in the "Decisions Regarding the Improvement of the System for the Supervision of Financial Administration and Trade in the Rural Areas in Response to the Situation Created by the Establishment of the People's Communes," promulgated by the Central Committee of the Chinese Communist Party and the State Council on the 20th of December, 1958. "The credit departments of the people's communes are at the same time business offices of the local branches of the People's Bank of China. The credit departments of the people's communes must see to it that they implement the state regulations for cash control. Surplus cash held by the economic units subordinate to the communes must be deposited with the higher banks in conformity with the regulation. In this way a unified adjustment of cash throughout the whole country will be assured."

[109] Kao Hsiang, p. 21.

non-cash settlements were made only in the case of large purchases and at the request of the agricultural producers' co-operatives.[110]

(2) In the autumn of 1961, in the period of the people's communes, it was the general rule that the non-cash settlements should be made for purchases of agricultural produce from the collective organizations in the rural areas (principally the production brigades), but payments were made in cash when this was specially requested by the collective organizations.[111]

(3) Since the autumn of 1962, likewise during the period of the people's communes, it has been the general rule that payments for purchases of agricultural produce should in principle be made in cash, and not by means of book transfer settlements, but payments may be made by book transfer settlements if this is specially requested by the production teams.[112]

As reasons for the changes which took place during the period of the people's communes as set out above, we may point to such facts as the transfer of the basic economic accounting unit in the people's communes from the production brigade to the production team which began about the beginning of 1962, and the fact that it was thought necessary to make payments for agricultural produce in cash in order to give a production incentive to the production teams.

We may add that since June, 1963, it appears that it has been left to the seller to decide whether payment for agricultural produce shall be made by book transfer settlements or in cash.[113]

---

110 Editorial commentary, cited in Note 107. *T-TKP* (28 June, 1956).

111 See Editorial, "Improving the Supply of Funds for the Purchase of Agricultural Produce and the Settlement of Payments," *P-TKP* (19 Oct., 1961). Matter of similar import is found in the notice published in the same paper (27 June, 1962): Ministry of Food & the People's Bank of China, "Directive on the Improvement of the Supply of Funds for the Purchase of Grains and Oils in the Summer Quarter."

112 Editorial, "Make Positive Improvements in the Supply of Funds for the Purchase of the Products of Agriculture and Agricultural By-products," *P-TKP* (22 Sept., 1962), and the article on the support for the purchase of agricultural products given by the banks in Liaoning Province published in the same paper (24 Nov., 1962), and the editorial staff's article in the same issue entitled "Improving the Settlement of Payments for Purchases of the Products of Agriculture and Agricultural By-products."

113 See Ministry of Food & the People's Bank of China, "Directive on the

Further, it is the general rule that when purchases of agricultural produce are made from individuals payments are made in cash.

According to the statistics for receipts and disbursements in the year 1959 issued by the People's Bank of China, about 85% of the total receipts and disbursements of the Bank took the form of non-cash settlements (book transfer settlements). Again, more than 80% of the payments made in respect to purchases of agricultural produce in the rural areas at the same period were made in the form of non-cash settlements.[114]

CONCLUSION

The above account has enabled us to get a general view of the socialist financial organization of China centred on the People's Bank of China. By way of conclusion we shall briefly notice one or two questions which we were unable to deal with in the above sections.

The first question is the fate of the foreign banks established

Improvement of the Supply of Funds for the Purchase of Grains and Oils in the Summer Quarter," *P-TKP* (2 June, 1963), and Ch'iao P'eih-sin, " Improving the Supply of Funds and the Settlement of Payments for Purchases of the Products of Agriculture and the Agricultural By-products during the Marketing Season," *P-TKP* (9 Oct., 1963).

114 Huang Ya-kuang, p. 17. In connexion with this point we may add the following supplementary material. After the autumn of 1957, more than 70% of the payments for purchases of the products of agriculture and agricultural by-products in a certain number of areas were made by means of book transfer settlements [Ko Chih-ta & Yang Che-sheng, "An Accurate Treatment of the Problem of Equilibrium in State Finance and Credit Provision," *P-TKP* (17 Aug., 1958)]. More than 90% of the payments made for purchases of agricultural produce in the Special Districts, Cities, and *Hsien* in Honan Province were made by means of book transfer settlements [*P-TKP* (17 Nov., 1958)]. More than 90% of payments for purchases over the whole of Heilungkiang Province were made by means of book transfer settlements [*P-TKP* (19 Nov., 1959)]. According to an article in the Peking *Ta Kung Pao* (7 Nov., 1963), up to the 19th of October 74.1% of the payments made for purchases of raw cotton in the area covered by the Chifengchen Business Office of the Lint'ung *Hsien* Branch of the People's Bank of China, Shensi Province, were made by means of book transfer settlements. According to an article in the Peking *Ta Kung Pao* (10 Oct., 1963), more than 90% of the payments for purchases of foodstuffs from the production teams of the people's communes in Huit'ingch'ü, Chingshan *Hsien,* Hupei Province, were made by means of book transfer settlements.

in mainland China. Foreign banks remained in mainland China for some time, even after the establishment of the new government. However, because of the rise in wages and prices accompanying the development of inflation, the taxes imposed by the new government, labour problems with the Chinese staff and a shrinkage in the volume of transactions, it was no easy matter for these banks to carry on business. Then the Korean War broke out, and in December, 1950, the banks associated with the United States (such as the American Express Co., the Underwriters Savings Bank for the Far East, the Chase Bank, the National City Bank of New York) had their assets frozen on the orders of the new government, and their accounts were cleared and the banks were placed under supervision of the Chinese authorities. Among the foreign banks which remained in China about March, 1953, we may notice the names of the Chartered Bank of India, Australia, and China (now the Chartered Bank), the Hong Kong and Shanghai Banking Corporation, the E. D. Sassoon Banking Company, associated with England, the Banque de L'Indochine, associated with France, the Banque Belge Pour L'Etranger, S.A., associated with Belgium, the Nederlandsche Handel-Maatschappiji, N.V., associated with Holland, etc.[115] In May, 1952, when the question of evacuating British commercial companies from China arose, the Hong Kong and Shanghai Banking Corporation had three branches in China (as opposed to 10 before the war), the Chartered Bank of India, Australia, and China had two (as opposed to 6 before the war), and the Mercantile Bank of India and the E.D. Sassoon Banking Company each had one branch.[116] At present the Hong Kong and Shanghai Banking Corporation and the Chartered Bank of India have branches in mainland China.

The next question is that of the banks associated with the overseas Chinese. The Overseas Chinese Banking Corporation, the Bank of East Asia, and the Chiyu Banking Corporation are all overseas Chinese banks which have their head offices outside China, but they have branches in mainland China and carry on remittance business for the overseas Chinese.

---

[115] According to a notice published in the Hong Kong *Ta Kung Pao* (17 March, 1953) regarding registration in respect to the liquidation of deposits and the remittances uncleared before the Liberation.

[116] *H-TKP* (23 May, 1952).

Leaving aside the overseas Chinese banks, we are truly struck with a sense of history when we recall the former prosperous condition of the foreign banks.

CHAPTER VI

THE SOCIALIST TRANSFORMATION OF PRIVATE
BANKING IN SHANGHAI

INTRODUCTION

IT IS principally in the case of Shanghai that we have source material which enables us to see how the Chinese private banks, native banks and trust companies proceeded along the way of socialist transformation, for only the most fragmentary information is available from other cities. Nevertheless, since Shanghai has been the economic and financial centre of China in the past, an elucidation of the process of socialist transformation in private banking in Shanghai will undoubtedly be of no small advantage in gaining an understanding of the socialist transformation of private banking over the whole of China. In the following sections we shall examine the socialist transformation of private banking in Shanghai from this point of view.

We may also draw attention to our other publications on the subject of the socialist transformation in China.[117]

---

117 T. Miyashita, "The Socialist Transformation of Handicrafts in China," *Kokumin Keizai Zasshi*, Vol. C, No. 5 (Nov., 1959); "Some Problems in the Co-operative Organization of the Chinese Handicrafts," in *Kōbe University International Economic Review* (Kōbe, 1960), Tenth Issue; "The Development of Socialist Transformation," in Aziya Seikei Gakkai, *A Handbook of Chinese Politics and Economics*, 1960 Edition, Part 6, Chap. 2, Sect. 4; *China's Foreign Trade Machinery* (Tokyo, 1961), Chaps. 4 and 5; "The Development of the Organization of the Chinese Enterprises Engaged in China's Foreign Trade," *Kokumin Keizai Zasshi*, Vol. CV, No. 1 (Jan., 1962); *The Economic System of New China* (Tokyo, 1964), Chap. 3.

I. From the Federated Lending Groups to the Federally
   Operated Groups

Since the opening of the five seaports to foreign trade after
the Opium War, Shanghai has developed as the centre of the
Chinese economy, and the most conspicuous development of
Chinese national capital took place in this city. The predominant
position in the national capital of Shanghai was occupied by the
national bank capital of Shanghai. The material basis for the
genesis and development of the Chiang Kai-shek régime was none
other than the national capital of Shanghai, of which the national
bank capital of Shanghai was the nucleus. However, after the
institution of bank control in 1935 and the currency reform in
November, 1935, the position of the state bank capital of the Chiang
Kai-shek régime in the Chinese banking world in Shanghai was
suddenly raised, so that it eventually stood superior to the national
bank capital and acquired the power of controlling the latter.
According to *The All-China Banking Yearbook, 1936,* the Chinese
financial institutions operating in Shanghai after the currency
reform of 1935 included 88 banks, 48 native banks, 11 trust companies, 4 savings societies and 1 finance corporation, comprising
a total of 152. Among the 88 banks, 3 were central and chartered
banks (viz., the Central Bank of China, the Bank of China and
the Bank of Communications), 8 were banks established by provincial or municipal administrations (the City Bank of Greater
Shanghai and the Kiangsu Bank had their head offices in the
city of Shanghai, but the rest had their head offices elsewhere),
and of the remaining 77 banks, 55 had their head offices in
Shanghai and 22 had their head offices elsewhere.[118]
A total of ten banks were singled out as being of particular
importance in the Chinese banking world. The ten comprised
three government banks—the Central Bank of China, the Bank
of China and the Bank of Communications (known as the Three

[118] Economic Research Department of the Directorate, the Bank of China, *The
All-China Banking Yearbook, 1936* (Shanghai, 1936), Chap. 11, pp. 2–12, 74–78, 109–111
and 115–116.

Great Banks: 大三行), three commercial banks—the Shanghai Commercial and Savings Bank, the National Commercial Bank, and the Chekiang Industrial Bank (known as the Three Medium Banks: 中三行), and four commercial banks—the Yien Yieh Commercial Bank, the Kincheng Banking Corporation, the China and South Sea Bank, and the Continental Bank (known as the Four Northern Banks: 北四行). These banks were popularly known by the collective name of "Three-Three-Four: 「三・三・四」."[119] According to Wang Tsung-p'ei, the Three Great Banks represented state capital, the Three Medium Banks represented national capital, and the Four Northern Banks represented feudal capital. However, we interpret the term 'national capital' as meaning nationally-conscious Chinese capital, and in the present case we regard the Four Northern Banks as representing the national capital also. The Three Medium Banks were also known as the Southern Group (南派). The appellation is probably derived from the fact that they were banks established by the co-operation of capitalist families long established in the Provinces of Kiangsu and Chekiang. Before the Bank of China became a government bank as a result of the increase in government shareholdings consequent upon the institution of bank control in 1935 it ranked alongside the Three Medium Banks and the four were known as the Four Southern Banks (南四行). The Four Northern Banks were also known as the Northern Group (北派). The name is probably due to the fact that these four banks started business in Peking and Tientsin. The Four Northern Banks had a Joint Trust Department and a Joint Savings Society, and before the currency reform of 1935 they had a Joint Reserve Vault. Among the Three Great Banks, the Central Bank of China set up the Central Trust of China, and the Central Trust of China set up the Central Savings Society. Under the bank controls instituted in 1934 the Three Great Banks brought other three banks—the Commercial Bank of China, the Ningpo Commercial and Savings Bank, and the National Industrial Bank of China—under their management. Thereafter these three banks were popularly known as the

---

[119] T. Miyashita, *On the Chinese Banking System* (Tokyo, 1941), pp. 169–174 ; Wang Tsung-p'ei, " Chinese Banking Displayed," *Shenpao Yüehk'an*, Vol. IV, No. 8 (Aug., 1935) ; "Chinese Banking at the Present Stage," *Chingchi-hsüeh Chik'an*, Vol. VII, No. 4 (Feb., 1937).

Three Little Banks (小三行). Included among the banks which were dependent on state capital, in addition to the Three Great Banks and the Three Little Banks, were the Farmers Bank of China and some 2 or 3 other banks, and as financial institutions other than banks in which state capital was invested we may mention the Postal Remittances and Savings Banks and the China Development Finance Corporation.

In July, 1937, the war with Japan began, and the periphery of the International Settlement at Shanghai was occupied by the Japanese Army. Later the Chiang Kai-shek régime moved its capital from Nanking to Hankow and then from Hankow to Chungking, and in December, 1941, the Japanese Army entered and occupied the International Settlement. Chinese financial circles in Shanghai underwent great changes in the course of these events.[120] With the recovery of peace in August, 1945 the Chiang Kai-shek régime at length moved its capital back to Nanking, and Chinese financial circles in Shanghai were again confronted by a new situation. The details of this situation are not clear, but we may have little difficulty in imagining that the structure of Chinese banking in Shanghai in about 1935 or 1936 which we have sketched above was restored to a fair degree. We may also suppose that this structure persisted through the troubled times of the Legal Tender Note inflation and the Gold Yüan Note inflation which followed.

Shanghai was liberated by the Chinese Communist armies on the 25th of May, 1949, and it is said that immediately before this date there were 220 Chinese banks, native banks and trust companies in Shanghai. Of these, 17 were state banks, provincial banks or municipal banks associated with the Chiang Kai-shek régime, 118 were private banks, 80 were native banks, and 5 were trust companies.[121] As an accompaniment to the Liberation

---

[120] After the occupation by the Japanese Army on the 8th of December, 1941, there were 54 Chinese banks which were members of the Bankers' Guild, and when the banks which were not members of the Guild were added to these the total was in the region of 100. There were approximately 50 native banks. On the state of banking in Shanghai immediately after the occupation of the International Settlement by the Japanese Army, see the appendix entitled " Problems of the New Financial Order in Shanghai," in T. Miyashita, *A General View of War-time Currency Problems in China* (Tokyo, 1943).

[121] See the number of banking institutions in Shanghai before and after the

of Shanghai the greater part of the state banks, provincial banks and municipal banks associated with the Chiang Kai-shek régime were taken over *en bloc* by the Chinese Communist authorities as being "bureaucrat capital," and we may suppose that the assets of these banks were employed in developing and expanding the People's Bank of China. After the Liberation the Bank of China and the Bank of Communications had their "bureaucrat capital" confiscated and these banks became specialized banks operating under joint state-private management. The Bank of China has come to specialize in foreign exchange and overseas Chinese remittance business, while the Bank of Communications has come to engage in long-term credit business. We may suppose that the Three Little Banks—the Commercial Bank of China, the Ningpo Commercial and Savings Bank and the National Industrial Bank of China—were also made into joint state-private banks as an accompaniment to the confiscation of "bureaucrat capital." Further, the East China Military Region Headquarters of the Chinese People's Liberation Army took over the supervision of the 203 ordinary private banking institutions, issuing Provisional Regulations for the Supervision of Private Banking in the East China Region on the 21st of August, 1949.

The privately-operated banking institutions subject to the Provisional Regulations for the Supervision of Private Banking in the East China Region comprised banks, trust companies and native banks (Article 2). The organ responsible for the supervision of private banking was the Financial and Economic Commission of the East China Region, and the organ appointed to carry out the supervision and inspection of banking institutions in this Region was the People's Bank of China (Article 3). These Regulations laid down rules for private banking governing the sphere of business, registration and the issue of permits for carrying on business, legal fixing of capital funds, the composition of capital, the employment of funds, deposit reserve funds, the obligation of sending in reports, the carrying out of inspection, and penal provisions. In connection with these Regulations the East China

---

Liberation, as shown in Table VI-1. According to the Table there were 220 such institutions in Shanghai immediately before the Liberation, but of these 203 were private banks or native banks (See the editor's note on p. 436 of *SCCS*). We may therefore conclude that the remaining 17 were state, provincial or municipal banks.

Regional Branch of the People's Bank of China issued Regulations for Applications for Registration and Inspection of Capital by Private Banking Institutions in the East China Region on the 1st of September, 1949. By the 20th of September, the closing date for applications for registration and inspection of capital holdings under these two sets of Regulations, 172 banking institutions had gone through the application procedure. In addition to these there were 6 banking institutions whose head offices were located outside Shanghai, and which applied for registration in the places in which their head offices were located. The Provisional Regulations for the Supervision of Private Banking in the East China Region fixed the capital funds of banking institutions in Shanghai at 100,000,000 to 200,000,000 *yüan* (in Old People's Currency) for banks and trust companies, and 60,000,000 to 120,000,000 *yüan* for native banks, and required that the cash capital funds held by banking institutions should exceed the minimum figure thus prescribed, that is, in the case of Shanghai, that they should exceed 100,000,000 *yüan* in the case of banks and trust companies, and 60,000,000 *yüan* in the case of native banks (Articles 9 and 10). Under the circumstances of the time, this situation proved a fairly heavy burden for private banking in Shanghai. The total capital in Gold Yüan Notes held by the 220 banks, native banks and trust companies in Shanghai amounted to no more than 9 *yüan* when converted into People's Currency, and the average capital held by each banking institution was less than 5 *fen* in People's Currency. After these banking institutions had registered themselves with increased capital funds, the total capital funds were raised to more than 20,542,000,000 *yüan* from 9 *yüan*, and the average capital funds per banking institution was more than 115,400,000 *yüan*.[122]

---

[122] *SCCS*, p. 402. On pages 400–402 of the same source a table is given showing the names and capital assets of the native banks immediately after they had increased their capital funds. The total capital held by the 77 Shanghai native banks at this time was 5,623,500,000 *yüan*, an average of 73,020,000 *yüan* per institution. It is not clear at what rates of exchange the capital assets in Gold Yüan Notes held by the banks and native banks were converted into People's Currency. The exchange rate laid down when the Gold Yüan Notes were called in after the Liberation of Shanghai was 100,000 *yüan* in Gold Yüan Notes for 1 *yüan* in People's Currency, but it is certain that this rate of exchange was not applied in the conversion of the capital assets of the banks and native banks. This is at once clear

The following suppositions have been put forward as to the manner in which these banking institutions produced cash for the minimum capital funds prescribed by law.[123]

(1) The cash capital produced by the greater part of the banking institutions, especially the comparatively large banks and native banks, was derived from the disposal of assets kept on secret ledgers. There is record of the People's Bank of China undertaking the conversion of around 4,000 taels of gold as a result of applications made by more than 40 banks and native banks which had transferred these assets from secret ledgers to their formal ledgers. One tael of gold being equivalent to 75 *yüan*, the total value of these assets would amount to approximately 500,000,000 *yüan* in People's Currency. Estimates by many circles indicated that at the least around 150 banks and native banks had transferred assets from secret ledgers to their formal ledgers in accordance with the instructions of the People's Bank of China.[124] Consequently, the greater part of the cash capital put up by the banking institutions in Shanghai came from the secret ledgers kept by the banks and native banks.

(2) Some of the banks and native banks realized assets on their formal ledgers, such as land, buildings, or negotiable securities, and thus provided themselves with cash capital.

(3) Banks and native banks which were unable to raise cash by the above two methods called upon their former shareholders to pay up new shares.

(4) Banks and native banks which were unable to raise cash by the above three methods sought new shareholders to pay up their shares.

(5) In the case of a certain number of banks and native banks,

from the statistical table given on p. 387 of *SCCS*, in which it is stated that in 1948 the total capital assets of the 75 native banks in Shanghai consisted of 19,550,000 *yüan* in Gold Yüan Notes, or an average of 260,700 *yüan* per institution. Unless a much higher rate than that of 100,000 *yüan* in Gold Yüan Notes for 1 *yüan* in People's Currency were applied, the total capital assets of the 220 banking institutions in Shanghai would not have amounted to 9 *yüan* in People's Currency, or an average of 5 *fen* per institution.

[123] *SCCS*, p. 404.

[124] On the 19th of September, 1949, "Instructions for Consolidating Secret and Formal Ledgers in Private Banking in the East China Region" were issued. The complete text is given in *SCCS*, pp. 398–399.

staff and workers employed by them subscribed part of the share capital.

(6) Some branch banks and branch native banks (those whose head offices were located in areas as yet unliberated or in areas other than the East China Region) had their cash capital provided by their head offices.

Because of this situation, there were 20 banks and native banks which did not register when the greater part of banking institutions registered with increased capital funds.[125] Again, among the banks and native banks which registered with increased capital funds, 56 were subjected to punishment for infringements

TABLE VI-1

Number of Banking Institutions which had Their Head Office or Branches in Shanghai Before and After Liberation

	Banks		Trust Companies		Native Banks		Total
	Head Offices	Branches	Head Offices	Branches	Head Offices	Branches	
Before Liberation	84	51	4	1	75	5	220
Ceased Business	15	23	1	0	2	1	42
28 October, 1949	69	28	3	1	73	4	178

Note: The figures for the numbers of banking institutions immediately before the Liberation (which took place on the 25th of May, 1949) include state banks, provincial banks and municipal banks associated with the Chiang Kai-shek régime, but those for the 28th of October, 1949, are for private banking institutions only. Further, branches and sub-branches of institutions having their head offices in Shanghai are not included in the figures given in the Table.

Source: *SCCS*, p. 399.

---

[125] On the question of changes in the number of banking institutions in Shanghai between the Liberation and the time of their registration with increased assets, we have the following statement. "Twenty-six of the private banks and native banks in Shanghai ceased business after the Liberation, among which 3 ceased business on receipt of orders, and 23 ceased business voluntarily. Six ceased business before the increase in the capital funds of these institutions, and 20 ceased business at the time of the increase in capital funds. Among these institutions which ceased business, 22 were banks, 1 was a trust company, and 3 were native banks, and 9 of these institutions had their head offices in Shanghai while 17 had branches in Shanghai " (*SCCS*, pp. 402–403). However, there is a difference of 25 between the 203 private banks and native banks operating in Shanghai at the time of its Liberation and the 178 which later registered. This leaves 1 institution unaccounted for as compared to the 26 which ceased business after the Liberation mentioned in the above source.

of the law.[126]

In connexion with the above account we may consider the numbers of banking institutions in Shanghai before and after the Liberation, as shown in Table VI-1. In the Table, the figure of 178 banking institutions in Shanghai on the 28th of October, 1949, includes 172 registered in Shanghai by the 20th of September, 1949 as mentioned above, and 6 institutions registered outside Shanghai.

The capital funds held by the 178 Shanghai banking institutions given in the above Table under the date 28th of October, 1949 are shown in Table VI-2.

Shanghai banking institutions continued to go out of business after this date. Fifteen of them ceased business between the closing date for registration (20 September, 1949) and the 5th of February, 1950, and between the 6th of February and the 23rd of May, 1950, 83 ceased business. On the 6th of February, Shanghai was bombed by the Chiang Kai-shek régime, and because electrical installations were destroyed and industrial production disrupted, loans made to industry by private banking institutions remained unrepaid, and under the influence of this situation these institutions found it difficult to manipulate their funds, in addition to which they sustained losses amounting to a vast sum. Further, in March the *San P'ing* policy—the Unified Policy for State Financial and Economic Work—was put into effect and prices were stabilized, and many of the Shanghai merchants, industrialists and bankers who had been taking advantage of the runaway inflation and running their business along speculative lines sustained a severe blow. On the 25th of May, 1950, there were still 80 Chinese banking institutions left in Shanghai. Of these, 4 were joint state-private banks, 39 were private banks, 34 were native banks and 3 were trust companies, in addition to which there were 11 foreign banks.[127] That is to say, the numbers of these banking institutions had declined to less than half of the total of 178 in existence on the 28th of October,

---

[126] *SCCS*, p. 408.

[127] *SCCS*, p. 408. On page 421 of the same source there is a Table of Profit and Loss in the Shanghai Joint State-Private and Private Banking Institutions for the First Half of 1950 (1 Jan., 1950 to 30 June, 1950). The Table lists 4 joint state-private banks, 35 Chinese private banks, 30 native banks and 3 trust companies, making a total of 72 institutions. In addition, 10 foreign banks are listed.

1949. According to an editorial in the *Jenmin Jihpao* of the 24th of August, 1950, entitled "A New Direction for Banking," there were 446 private banking institutions in the seven cities of Peking, Tientsin, Shanghai, Hankow, Canton, Chungking and Sian at the end of 1949, but only 213 of them were left by the end of June, 1950. This indicates that the situation in Shanghai was very similar to that prevailing in the country at large.

TABLE VI-2

Capital in Banking Institutions which had Their Head Offices and Branches in Shanghai, 1949

Capital Funds (10,000 *yüan*)	Total Number of Institutions	Banks		Trust Companies		Native Banks	
		Head Offices	Branches	Head Offices	Branches	Head Offices	Branches
2,400	1	—	—	—	—	—	1
3,600–5,000	5	—	2	—	—	—	3
6,000	65	—	15	—	—	50	—
6,200–8,000	12	1	4	—	—	7	—
10,000	28	23	3	1	—	1	—
10,150–11,600	8	7	—	—	—	1	—
12,000	17	2	3	—	1	11	—
12,400–19,000	10	8	—	—	—	2	—
20,000	13	10	1	1	—	1	—
21,000–27,000	11	10	—	1	—	—	—
30,000–34,400	7	7	—	—	—	—	—
80,000	1	1	—	—	—	—	—
Total	178	69	28	3	1	73	4

Source: *SCCS*, p. 403.

The above is an outline account of the process of adjustment which took place in private banking in Shanghai after the Liberation, but it was also during this period that "federated lending" was instituted in the banking business as a means of leading idle capital into productive uses.[128]

On the 24th of September, 1949, an institution styled the Shanghai Banking and Trust Federated Loan Office was formed. This body was organized for the purpose of enabling the private banking institutions of Shanghai, with the assistance of the People's Bank of China, to lead idle capital into productive uses through the banks, native banks and trust companies, and at the same time to co-operate in making purchases of raw cotton for privately-

---

[128] *SCCS*, pp. 411–416.

operated textile companies.   172 banks and native banks are said
to have joined this body, a number which coincides with the
number of banking institutions which had applied for registration
by the 20th of September, 1949.   Among these institutions 93
banks headed by the National Commercial Bank undertook to
lend 2,970,000,000 *yüan*, 76 native banks headed by the Pao Feng
Ch'ien Chuang undertook to lend 1,000,000,000 *yüan*, and 3 trust
companies headed by the First Trust Company of China undertook to lend 30,000,000 *yüan*.   The recipients of the loans were
the Shanghai Private Textile Factories Federated Cotton Purchasing Loan Agency.   The limit of loan was 4,000,000,000 *yüan*, and
the Agency borrowed the money in two instalments.   The first
instalment of 2,000,000,000 *yüan* was borrowed on the 26th of
September, and the second instalment of 2,000,000,000 *yüan* on
the 3rd of October.   The period of the loan was 60 days, the
rate of interest was calculated, after negotiation between the two
parties, at between 80% (minimum) and 90% (maximum) of the
official interest-rates for loans officially published daily by the
Bank Rate Commission of Chinese Banking, and the interest was
paid half-monthly.   The money borrowed could be used only as
funds for participating in the Federated Cotton Purchasing Agency,
and the first item of security for the loans was the receipt for
the shares of paid-up funds of the Federated Cotton Purchasing
Agency by the individual factories, while the second item was the
warehouse bonds for cotton yarn and cloth owned by the individual
factories.   The Loan Office organized communally a Loan Office
Committee, choosing nine persons to represent the banks, native
banks and trust companies participating in the loan (six representing the banks, two the native banks and one the trust companies).
The Committee represented the Loan Office in dealings with outside
persons and bodies, and were also charged with the duties of
sealing contracts concluded on security, making and receiving loans,
the valuation, insurance and investigation of security, liaison within
the individual banks, native banks and trust companies, and
other matters.   The office of the Loan Office was located at the
address of the Bankers' Guild, 59, Hong Kong Road.   In order to
assist the private banking institutions in investing funds in productive uses, the People's Bank of China permitted the banks,
native banks and trust companies participating in the Loan Office

to ask short-term call loans to the People's Bank of China when the money market was stringent. The amounts of such call loans were limited to sums undertaken to loan, and these call loans might be made on three occasions in each month, the duration of each call loan being three days.

Next, the Shanghai Joint State-Private Banking Federated Loan Office was formed on the 14th of December in the same year. This was organized for the purpose of enabling the Shanghai state and private banks, native banks and trust companies to lead idle capital into productive uses, and the Office made loans of funds for productive purposes in response to demands of the factories and merchants of Shanghai. The participators in this Federated Loan Office comprised 41 banks headed by the People's Bank of China, 28 native banks headed by the Pao Feng Ch'ien Chuang and 3 trust companies headed by the First Trust Company of China. The limit of loans was provisionally set at 12,000,000,000 *yüan*, of which the Shanghai branches of the People's Bank of China, the Bank of China, and the Bank of Communications undertook to provide 2,000,000,000 *yüan*, and the private banks, native banks and trust companies undertook to provide 10,000,000,000 *yüan*. No special sphere of business was designated as the intended recipient of loans, but it was laid down that the loans must be made for productive purposes. The period of each loan was limited to 60 days, and the minimum rate of interest was to be 90% of the average of the official rates of interest for loans published daily by the Bank Rate Commission of Chinese Banking. The rate of interest was to be negotiated between the parties, and the interest was to be paid every ten days. Fifteen persons were put forward on the part of the Federated Loan Office as representatives of the banks, native banks, and trust companies participating in making such loans, and they formed a committee (including the Shanghai branch of the People's Bank of China as an *ex-officio* member) which dealt with decisions regarding the principles to be followed in making loans, liaison between the individual banks, native banks and trust companies, and other matters. The People's Bank of China, the Bank of China and the Bank of Communications participated in this Federated Loan Office, and as a result the funds available for federated lending were greatly increased. The People's Bank of China gave special permission to the private banks, native banks and trust companies participating in the Federated Loan Office to ask short-term call loans to the People's Bank of China when the money market was stringent. Four such call loans might be made in each month, and the duration of each call loan was limited to three days.

As we have already noted above, in the course of the development of this organization for federated lending and in the following few months the number of private banking institutions in Shanghai declined from 178 to 98, and by the 23rd of May, 1950, only 80 were left. However, by June of that year the stabilization crisis based on the *San P'ing* policy came to an end, and financial and economic conditions over the whole of China took a turn for the better. As a part of this tendency banking business in Shanghai, too, was able to free itself from the worst conditions of depression. Further, after May of that year the government pressed forward with a programme for making adjustments in private commerce and industry, aiming at developing production and introducing a progressively greater measure of planning into the market, and we may suppose that these measures were one of the principal reasons for the revival of business in the Shanghai banking world. It was against this background that "federated operation" was put into effect in the Shanghai banking world. Under the positive leadership and encouragement of the People's Bank of China, 45 private banks and native banks formed four Federally Operated Groups about the middle of July, 1950, seeking to promote efficiency and economy in working, closer liaison with commerce and industry, the implementation of financial planning, the smartening-up of methods of work, and thus strove to set their business on the correct lines.[129]

It appears that the formation of the Federally Operated Groups of private banking institutions took place through the following process. Combination for the purposes of "federated operation" had been advocated by certain members of the Shanghai banking world at the time of the stabilization crisis implemented under the *San P'ing* policy in March, 1950, as a result of which many banking institutions went into liquidation. In April the bankers of Tientsin set about organizing a Credit

---

[129]   *SCCS,* pp. 424–432.

Federal Reserve Association in an attempt to avoid liquidations. By means of this organization they proposed to strengthen their credit in relation to outside persons and bodies, to carry out mutual aid among themselves, to plan their work on a communal basis, to improve and investigate loans, and to progress step by step towards federated operation or amalgamation. This news from Tientsin had a most stimulating effect on the demands of banking in Shanghai—demands which coincided with those of the bankers of Tientsin.

In May the Shanghai banking world spoke as follows in a general report of discussion on the question of its own transformation. "We regard federated operation of the business of persons engaged in the same line of business to be an accurate direction in which to proceed, and a good road upon which to embark. Our fellow bankers in Tientsin have already established a precedent in this regard, and we bankers of Shanghai should hasten to follow them and should put into effect a plan carried one step further. We request the financial authorities to give us much cooperation and guidance in the inaugural period, and to give us suitable consideration after the mechanisms of federated operation have been established."

This general report firmly established the possibility of federated operation in the banking world in Shanghai, and at the same time expressed the realization that federated operation was the only road along which the banks and native banks could proceed. Yet we may say that the intentions of the Shanghai banking world in regard to "federated operation," in so far as they were revealed in expressions of opinion such as the above, were of a conservative or defensive nature. However, after the holding of the Third Shanghai People's Congress a certain section of the private banks and native banks was engaged in transformation, and because a gradual improvement took place in the state finances and in economic conditions at the same time there was a revival of business in commerce and industry, as a result of which both capital and labour acquired the faith to go forward and overcome their difficulties. For this reason, some degree of progressive spirit was discerned when the Federally Operated Groups were formed on the 1st of July.

The following four Federally Operated Groups were formed

among the private banking institutions of Shanghai.

(1) The First Federally Operated Group, established on the 1st of July, 1950. This comprised 12 institutions, including 7 banks (the Chung Foo Union Bank, the Chung Hsin Bank, the China Development Bank, the Land Bank of China, the Chinese Industrial Bank, the Ho Ch'eng Bank and the Mao Hua Bank), 4 native banks (Ts'un Ch'eng, Chin Yüan, Fu Yüan and Pao Feng), and 1 trust company (the First Trust Company of China). The total number of employees was 1,154.

(2) The Second Federally Operated Group, established on the 1st of July, 1950. At first this comprised 12 institutions, including 5 banks, 6 native banks, and 1 trust company, but on the 4th of September, 1950 these were joined by 2 more banks and 1 more native bank. The Group then comprised 15 institutions, including 7 banks (the Teng-Hsu Commercial and Savings Bank, the Yung Heng Commercial and Savings Bank, the Cheng Ming Commercial and Savings Bank, the Shanghai Citizen's Commercial and Savings Bank, the Shanghai Women's Commercial and Savings Bank, and the later participants in the Group, the China United Commercial and Savings Bank and the Wai Chung Commercial and Savings Bank), 7 native banks (Hung Hsiang, Fu K'ang, Shan K'ang, Shen T'ai, Heng Feng, Yüan Ch'eng, and a later participant, Chien Ch'ang) and 1 trust company (the China Trust Company). The employees numbered 786.

(3) The Third Federally Operated Group, established on the 16th of July, 1950. This comprised 12 institutions, including 1 bank (the Ho T'ai Bank) and 11 native banks (Jen Ch'ang, Wu Feng, Yung Lung, Ts'un Te, Hung Ch'ang, Chih Yu, Ch'un Yüan Yung, Hsin Yu T'ai, Ch'ing Ch'eng, Chen Hsing and Pao Ch'eng). The employees numbered 363.

(4) The Fourth Federally Operated Group, established on the 23rd of July, 1950. This comprised 6 native banks (T'ung Jun, Ch'un Mao, T'ai Lai, Chih Ch'ang, Hui Ch'ang Yüan and Chü K'ang Hsing). The employees numbered 218.

These four Federally Operated Groups comprised 15 banks, 28 native banks and 2 trust companies—a total of 45 institutions employing 2,521 persons. At this time there were 65 institutions in the private banking business in Shanghai.[130] These 45 institutions, therefore, represent 70% of the total number.

As to the meaning or nature of "federated operation" we may refer to the Fifth Article of the Provisional Regulations for Private Enterprises, passed by the 65th Session of the Administrative Council on the 29th of December, 1950. "In the case of enterprises engaged in the same kind of business, or of enterprises which, though not engaged in the same kind of business, are linked in production or in working processes, a part or several parts of their working processes may be managed under federated operation, this being done under the voluntary principle and on the basis of preserving the pre-existing organization, and these enterprises may draw up rules for "federated operation" for the working of which they may receive permission from the local supervisory organs. State enterprises and joint state-private enterprises may also participate in such federally-operated organizations. After permission has been given for the working of such federally operated organizations, they can receive protection in law, and the state economy must extend co-operation to these federally operated organizations."

In the following we propose to examine the general nature and organization of the Federally Operated Groups in the private banking business in Shanghai, using the First Federally Operated Group's articles.

First, the aim in forming the Group is stated to be that of "strengthening the links between those engaged in the same business, manipulating the collective power of the members, carrying on business in a planned manner, assisting commerce and industry, and by so doing fitting in with the economic policies of New Democracy" (Article 1).

---

130 If it is assumed that there were 65 banking institutions in Shanghai in the first ten days of September, 1950, there was a decrease of 7 institutions in the space of somewhat more than two months since the end of June of that year, when there were 72 such institutions. There were 30 native banks at the end of June, 1950, among which 27 had participated in the Federally Operated Groups from the first (the non-participants being the Chien Ch'ang, Chih Hsiang and Wan Hsiang T'ai native banks). Chien Ch'ang joined the Second Federally Operated Group on the 4th of September, 1950, Chih Hsiang notified cessation of business on the 1st of August, 1950, and Wan Hsiang T'ai notified cessation of business on the 9th of September, 1950 (the editor's note in SCCS, p. 429).

There were five conditions for membership, (1) that the proposed member should have own profit, or should be the owner of considerable property (or funds) which would be able to cover losses and leave a surplus, (2) that the proposed member should be effecting co-operation between capital and labour, (3) that the proposed member should have produced concrete results in promoting efficiency and economy in working, (4) that the proposed member's outstanding debts should not exceed 20% of his total deposits, and (5) that the proposed member should have fulfilled his duties in regard to the People's Victory Commodity-Unit Bonds within the stipulated period. After investigation of these matters by the Group Committee, those fulfilling the requirements of these conditions might become members of the Group on receiving the approval of all the members of the Committee (Article 4).

Each member would be responsible for the internal organization, business, and profit and loss of his own enterprise (Article 6).

Each member was charged with the fulfilment of the following six duties, required for the purpose of increasing his own strength and that of the collectivity (Article 9).

(1) Carrying out business operations in a positive manner, making funds readily available, and carrying out the provisions of the economic accounting system.

(2) Members must subscribe 10% of their deposits each month in order to make up the minimum sum required for federated loans. This proportion would be gradually increased. The percentage would be applied to deposit balances at the end of each month.

(3) Members must assume the responsibility of gradually reducing the proportion occupied by their outstanding debts.

(4) Members must send in returns and reports as required and in due time, and must always exchange reference materials dealing with credit enquiries and information relating to the objects for which loans were made and the limits of such loans, as well as other matters. As a measure designed to ensure safety in the manipulation of funds, members would be required to ask the Committee to look into the matter before they undertook the lending of comparatively large sums.

(5) The members would undertake commissioned work as representatives of the state banks in all lines of business.

(6)   The members of the Group would faithfully carry out the decisions of the Committee. Further, when it was considered necessary in consequence of the decisions of the Committee for members to put up property as security, either as individuals or collectively, members must make available to the Group such property as might be thought fit by the Committee (Article 13).

The duties to be performed by the Group itself were set out in the following three provisions.

(1)   The Group, in co-operation with the members, must carry out the work required under the provisions for federated operation (Article 10).

(2)   The Group could represent the members in concluding contracts linking the Group with the state banks (Article 11).

(3)   The Group must co-operate in adjusting the funds of the members, and when necessary requests could be made for re-mortgage loans or re-discounts from the People's Bank of China in the name of the Group (Article 12).

The organization of the Group employs the democratic committee system.   One person was put forward as a representative by every enterprise taking part in the Group, and these representatives formed the Committee. From the Committee a Chairman and two Vice-Chairmen were elected (both offices being held for periods of half a year, with no bar to re-election). (Article 14.) Besides establishing secretarial, accounting, business, planning, credit enquiry and study departments and allotting duties to them, the Committee appointed an inspectorate of 3 members who investigated the business, expenses, etc., of the members (Articles 16 and 17). All members were to be present at the meetings of the Committee, and decisions must receive the approval of two-thirds of the members present. If for some reason a member was unable to be present, he could send a delegate to the meeting to represent him (Article 18). When Committee meetings were held, responsible persons from the trade unions of the members' employees must be required to attend, and to take part in the deliberations (Article 19).

Such was the general aspect of the First Federally Operated Group, and from it we may be able to infer the nature and organization of the other Federally Operated Groups.

We may add that the fact that co-operation between capital and labour is mentioned in one of the conditions for membership of the Federally Operated Group and the fact that the Group is obliged to require the attendance of responsible persons from the trade unions at the Committee meetings of the Federally Operated Group probably has some connexion with the fact that at this time it was being proposed that the working class should exercise supervisory functions in private enterprises. In this connexion we may also note that in June, 1950, the Financial Workers' Trade Union of Shanghai and the Provident Committee of the Shanghai Banking Guild laid down Regulations Governing the Organization of the Joint Capital and Labour Conference in Banking Enterprises in Shanghai.[131]

As an accompaniment to the formation of the Federally Operated Groups the deposits and loans of the Groups showed a marked increase. The two Tables which follow (Tables VI-3 and VI-4) show the courses taken by deposits and loans in the Federally Operated Groups in the space of barely a month between the end of June and the 29th of July, 1950. From these Tables we may see (1) that the balances of deposits and loans in each of the Federally Operated Groups were increasing, and, furthermore, that the rate of increase was more rapid than that obtaining among the banks and native banks as a whole, and consequently was more rapid

TABLE VI-3

Deposits and Loans of the Four Federally Operated Groups (1)

(June, 1950–29th July, 1950)

(Unit: 10,000 *yüan* in People's Currency)

Period	Deposits			Loans		
	(1) Institutions Participating in Federated Operation	(2) All Institutions	(1) as Percentage of (2)	(1) Institutions Participating in Federated Operation	(2) All Institutions	(1) as Percentage of (2)
End of June	9,403,379	55,357,349	16.8	6,777,448	29,176,057	23.2
15 July	10,557,343	55,845,788	18.9	8,382,014	35,092,280	23.9
22 July	11,091,550	56,662,760	19.6	8,616,143	35,275,487	24.4
29 July	11,537,499	57,517,801	20.1	9,334,157	36,839,211	25.3

Source: *SCCS*, p. 434.

131 The complete text of these Regulations, together with that of the Brief Rules Governing the Organization of Joint Capital and Labour Conference in the Fu Yüan Ch'ien Chuang, is given in *SCCS*, pp. 416–420.

TABLE VI-4

Deposits and Loans of the Four Federally Operated Groups (2)

(June,1950–29th July, 1950)

(Unit : 10,000 *yüan* in People's Currency)

Period	Deposits				Loans			
	First	Second	Third	Fourth	First	Second	Third	Fourth
End of June	5,015,143	3,239,169	834,735	314,332	3,661,340	2,260,519	660,046	195,543
15 July	5,550,014	3,540,633	1,093,009	373,687	4,440,165	2,838,625	817,398	285,829
22 July	5,571,110	3,856,861	1,204,189	459,390	4,367,842	2,933,590	986,374	328,337
29 July	5,996,328	3,883,375	1,235,491	422,305	4,846,411	3,090,768	1,035,480	361,498
Percentage Increase during Month	+19.6	+19.9	+48.0	+34.3	+22.4	+36.7	+56.9	+84.9

Source : *SCCS*, p. 434.

than that obtaining among banks and native banks which were not participating in federated operation, and (2) that the increases in the figures for deposits and loans in the cases of the Third and Fourth Federally Operated Groups were greater than those in the cases of the First and Second Federally Operated Groups, and consequently that participation in the Federally Operated Groups was particularly profitable for the small-scale banks and native banks. We must, of course, give full consideration to the fact that these observations cover a very short period.

II. From the Federated or Federally Operated General Supervisory Office to the Unified Joint State-Private Bank

The Federally Operated Groups of which we have given an outline description in the previous section were formed from the comparatively small banks, native banks and trust companies. This being the case, what was the fate of the comparatively large-scale banks ?

At this point it is necessary for us to make reference to the National Congress of Bankers held in Peking between the 1st and the 10th of August, 1950. This Congress presented the following requests to the People's Bank of China on behalf of the banking world. (1) The medium and small banks and native banks requested that the People's Bank of China should give them assistance in the carrying on of their business, and while declaring their desire to progress from federated operation to amalgamation, requested the assistance of the state bank in connexion with this matter also. (2) The larger banks called for the co-operation of the state bank in the adjustment of outstanding debts (there were 40,000,000,000 *yüan* of outstanding debts in Shanghai alone). (3) The Shanghai Commercial and Savings Bank, the National Commercial Bank, and the Kincheng Banking Corporation, the Continental Bank, the China and South Sea Bank, the China State Bank, Ho Ch'eng Bank and the Young Brothers Banking Corporation requested that the state should confiscate those of their shares which were to be confiscated as " enemy " (Chiang Kai-shek régime) shares, and should appoint to their boards Public Share Directors (representing the interests of state capital).[132]

In this way the great banks of Shanghai were made into joint state-private banks because they were not only confronted by difficulties in running their business as a result of the increase in outstanding debts, but they also had harboured " bureaucrat capital." It was because the great banks of Shanghai had originally had close personal ties with important figures associated with the Chiang Kai-shek régime that " bureaucrat capital " was found to have been invested in them. An important point to be noticed here is the decline which took place in the strength of these banks. While the greater part of the generality of the medium and small banks and native banks showed a profit at the year-end closing of accounts in 1950, six banks—the China and South Sea Bank, the Shanghai Commercial and Savings Bank, the Kincheng Banking Corporation and three others—showed comparatively great losses, these being due to large accumulated deficits, unpaid outstanding debts, and loan obligations towards federated institutions.[133]

It was against this background that in 1951 the comparatively large-scale banks in Shanghai formed the following three groups.[134]

---

[132] Nan Han-chen, " Concerning the Report of the National Congress of Bankers," in *CTCFH*, II, pp. 538–539.

[133] *SCCS*, p. 437.

[134] The description is mainly derived from the following articles and accounts in the Hong Kong *Ta Kung Pao*: Chang Liu, " Federated Operation in the Joint State-Private Banks " (1 June, 1951); Chang Shu-chung, " News from Shanghai " (7 Oct., 1951), and accounts on the 8th and 15th of September, on the 3rd of November, and on the 13th of December, 1951.

On the 27th of May, 1951, five joint state-private banks, the Hsin Hua Trust and Savings Bank, the Ningpo Commercial and Savings Bank, the National Industrial Bank of China, the Commercial Bank of China and the Chien Yeh Commercial and Savings Bank established a Federated General Supervisory Office. These five banks were known as "The Five Southern Banks" (南五行), but after this reorganization they came to be known as "The New Five Banks" (新五行). On the 1st of September, the China State Bank, the National Commercial Bank, the China Development Bank and the Ho Ch'eng Bank joined in this institution, and on the 1st of November they were joined by the Young Brothers Banking Corporation, the Yüan Yüan Ch'ang Bank and the Chekiang First Bank (originally the Chekiang Industrial Bank). There were then 12 members of this group.

At the end of July, 1951, the Shanghai Commercial and Savings Bank (Chief Director Ch'en Kuang-pu) was reorganized as a joint state-private bank, with the state bank holding 34% of its 100,000 shares.

On the 1st of September, 1951, the Kingcheng Banking Corporation, the Continental Bank, the Yien Yieh Commercial Bank, the China and South Sea Bank and the Joint Bank established a Federated General Supervisory Office, applying to the People's Bank of China for public investment (state shareholding), and at the same time these banks were reorganized as joint state-private banks. These five banks were known as "The Five Northern Banks" (北五行).

In this way 18 of the great Shanghai banks were organized in three groups—a group centred on the Five Southern Banks or the New Five Banks, the Five Northern Banks and the Shanghai Commercial and Savings Bank.

The majority of the banks participating in these groups were great Shanghai banks with many branches in all parts of China. With the participation of the China State Bank and the other three banks, the number of units subordinate to the Federated General Supervisory Office of the New Five Banks increased from 118 to 164 by September, 1951. These units were distributed over 32 areas, including Peking, Tientsin, Canton, Shanghai, Hong Kong and Macao, etc., and they employed more than 6,000 persons. At that time the Shanghai Commercial and Savings

Bank had 34 branches and sub-branches in Peking, Tientsin, Shanghai, etc., employing more than 1,750 persons. The Five Northern Banks had 78 branches and sub-branches in 16 areas, including Peking, Tientsin, Shanghai, Hankow, Canton, Chungking and Hong Kong, etc., and employed more than 3,500 persons.

On the subject of the meaning and effects of "Federated Supervision," Chang Liu gives the following explanation in connexion with the organization for federated supervision in the New Five Banks group. Under federated supervision the identity of each of the banks is preserved, but business and personnel administration are centralized, and the centralized distribution system is employed in calculating profit and loss. For this purpose a Federated General Supervisory Office is established as an organ superior to the individual banks. The federated supervision system among the joint state-private banks was brought into being on the basis of a decision to "establish federated supervision mechanisms among the joint state-private banks, and to carry these one step further to the centralization of direction" reached at the Second National Congress of Bankers, and the system was brought into operation among the five joint state-private banks with the approval of their boards of directors. Two general principles were embodied in the above-mentioned decision. The first included the centralization of supervision, the strengthening of the organization, a unified supervision of business and a unified control over financial operations, and the second included the principle of giving equal consideration to the rights and interests of public and private shareholders. On the basis of these general principles the joint state-private banks drew up a Summary of Agreements among the Joint State-Private Banks in Connection with the Organization of the Federated General Supervisory Office. According to this Summary, federated supervision among the five banks was to be established and operated under the following assumptions.

(1) A Federated Board of Directors would be organized, 3 to 5 directors being recommended by the individual banks. The Federated Board of Directors would organize the Federated General Supervisory Office, and this would be the highest executive mechanism in the centralized supervision and running of the five banks.

(2) The Federated General Supervisory Office would be in direct control over the head offices, branches and sub-branches of the individual banks, and would send directions to them directly. However, the status of each of the banks as defined by law would be preserved.

(3) The financial operations performed by the individual banks would be dealt with in accordance with the nature of the business in question. The individual banks would deal in their own ways with the fixed assets, securities, investment, spot foreign exchange, outstanding debts and pre-war deposits and bank-staff savings business which they had carried on before the establishment of the general supervisory mechanism. Profits and losses in these forms of business would appertain to the individual banks, and the general supervisory mechanism would exercise unified direction and supervision in regard to such business. Except for the forms of business listed in the above provision, all assets and debts resulting from the deposit, loan, exchange, agency and foreign exchange business carried on by the individual banks would be subject to the centralized management of the general supervisory mechanism, and profits and losses in these forms of business would be calculated by means of the centralized distribution system.

(4) The general supervisory mechanism would exercise unified control over personnel administration in the individual banks. A Chairman and a Vice-Chairman would be appointed to the general supervisory mechanism, and Secretarial, Planning, Inspection, Accounting, Business, Personnel Administration and Working Offices would be set up. A separate Shanghai Area Business Committee would also be set up, and would ensure accuracy in the performance of business.

By these measures federated supervision would seek to make adjustments of excess personnel in overlapped branches and sub-branches, to make economies in running expenses, and to promote efficiency.[135]

From Chang Liu's account it is clear that federated supervision was a preparatory measure for the amalgamation of the participating banks, and that the participating banks were already virtually amalgamated. However, Chang Liu's account makes no

---

[135] Chang Liu, op. cit.

mention of the relations between the organization for federated supervision and the People's Bank of China. In other words, he says nothing at all on the subject of whether representatives of the interests of public shareholdings were members of the Federated Board of Directors or not. However, since the participating banks were joint state-private banks and would have directors representing the interests of public shareholdings, it is possible to infer that these directors would be chosen as members of the Federated Board of Directors.

After the great banks in Shanghai had been reorganized into three groups in this way, the First Federated Group in the Shanghai private banking business formed the First Federally Operated General Supervisory Office in the last ten days of September, 1951, and at the same time the Second Federated Group formed the Second Federally Operated General Supervisory Office. The banks and native banks participating in the First Federally Operated General Supervisory Office showed some changes as compared with those which had participated in the First Federated Group. As we have already noted, the China Development Bank and the Ho Ch'eng Bank had joined the Federated General Supervisory Office of the New Five Banks, and so they did not participate in the First Federally Operated General Supervisory Office. On the other hand, two new banks joined this Office—the Tung Lai Bank and the Tung Nan Bank. The Office was later joined by the Fu K'ang Ch'ien Chuang (originally a member of the Second Federally Operated Group) and the Kuo An Bank. Thus the banks and native banks participating in the First Federally Operated General Supervisory Office at first numbered 12, and later 14. The banks and native banks which had participated in the Second Federally Operated Group all joined the Second Federally Operated General Supervisory Office at its inception, with the exception of the Fu K'ang Ch'ien Chuang, and accordingly there were 14 participants in that Office. However, on the 1st of November, 1951, the total of 12 institutions in the Third Federally Operated Group together with the T'ung Jun, Ch'un Mao and T'ai Lai native banks from the Fourth Federally Operated Group joined the Second Federally Operated General Supervisory Office, and the number of banks

---

186 *SCCS*, pp. 441–444.

and native banks participating in that Office was raised to 29.[136]

It is clear from the following passage in the Report of the Work of the First Federally Operated Group of Private Banking Institutions, Shanghai, dated July, 1951, that the formation of the Federally Operated General Supervisory Offices was a preparatory measure for the amalgamation of private banking institutions in Shanghai, and that shortly before this date conditions had become ripe for the transition from federated operation to amalgamation. " The questions of what is the accurate direction in which private banking should proceed, and of how private banking should fit in with the establishment of the government's overall financial system were treated as follows in the general report of the National Congress of Bankers of August, 1950. ' The conducting of business under federated operation must be advanced step by step, and the conditions created for amalgamation.' Again, the report says, ' Through federated operation we proceed step by step towards amalgamation.' This sets before us the way which we should tread, and the tasks, now one step advanced, which await us. In the past year our Federally Operated Group has brought to fulfilment certain conditions bearing on the question of amalgamation. The time is now ripe for amalgamation, and since it appears that the members of the Group have an accurate appreciation of the significance of this fact, the Group and its members have, during the present month, eagerly looked into the question of carrying out amalgamation, and have made positive efforts to devise plans for this purpose. After repeated deliberations in committee, general principles governing amalgamation have been decided upon, and a draft policy plan has been to be drawn up by the three Sub-Committees of Organization, Business, and Assets and Liabilities, in preparation for the organization of ' the First Federally Operated Bank.' The Organization Sub-Committee has met twice, and has discussed the questions of whether the newly established bank should adopt the general supervisory system and whether the second-class direct supervision system should be adopted in organizing branches and sub-branches, as well as the organization of a general supervisory office, the number of members and organization of the boards of directors and auditors, and also the question of how the early realization of amalgamation may be expedited. The Sub-Committee has also given consideration to the question of the simultaneous advance of federated supervision and preparation (i.e., of the Federally Operated General Supervisory Office and preparations for amalgamation—Miyashita). The Business Sub-Committee has met twice, and has discussed the questions of how communally organized business may be strengthened and improved before amalgamation, how to prevent effects which may appear in the performance of business during the transition period, and how the unified handling of business after amalgamation should be planned. The Assets and Liabilities Sub-Committee has met twice, and has discussed all items relating to the valuation of assets and liabilities, making inquiries into the unified forms of reports and tables. At meetings of the Committee, and also at other times, the question of amalgamation has been put on the agenda and discussed. The question of amalgamation is one which concerns the future of all the members of our Group, as well as concerning the future of the banking business throughout China. There is much work to be done and serious responsibilities to be undertaken. We must see to it that we band ourselves together and unite in co-operation for the forwarding of this task.... Preparing the way for amalgamation and providing the conditions which will make it possible have been the principal occupations of our Group during the present month. After repeated discussions, it had been decided by the time this report was drawn up that federated supervision should be put into effect during the preparatory period. With a view to accomplishing amalgamation at an early date, the business, financial operations and personnel administration have been subjected to overall management, thus building firm foundations for amalgamation, while on the other hand the revaluation of property has also been carried out in a positive manner."[137]

We can get a general view of the nature and organization of the Federally Operated General Supervisory Office from the Summary of Agreements of the First Federally Operated General Supervisory Office.[138]

Let us now examine this point.

First, the intentions lying behind the establishment of the Federally Operated General Supervisory Office are clarified in the

---

[137] *SCCS*, pp. 438-439.

[138] *SCCS*, pp. 439-441, where the complete text is given.

section entitled General Provisions. " The Chung Foo Union Bank, the Chung Hsin Bank, the Land Bank of China, the Chinese Industrial Bank, the Mao Hua Bank, the Ts'un Ch'eng Ch'ien Chuang, the Chin Yüan Ch'ien Chuang, the Fu Yüan Ch'ien Chuang, the Pao Feng Ch'ien Chuang, the First Trust Company of China, the Tung Lai Bank and the Tung Nan Bank (hereinafter referred to as ' the units '), having passed through the stage of federated operation have deliberated among themselves and have drawn up plans for amalgamation to form ' the First Federally Operated Bank' under the direction of the People's Bank of China, to the end that they may advance one step forward and centralize supervision, strengthen their organization, subject business to overall management, bring financial operations under unified control, and may the better fulfil their tasks in the introduction of planning into the financial, economic and banking policies of the state. During the preparatory period each unit will retain its original status as defined by law, and, under the principle of according equal consideration to public and private shareholders, a Federated Board of Directors will first be set up, the First Federally Operated General Supervisory Office for Banking Institutions will be organized, and this Summary of Agreements will be laid down and adhered to by those concerned" (Article 1).

These General Provisions, while making it clear that the establishment of the Federally Operated General Supervisory Office was a provisional measure for the preparatory period preceding amalgamation, also show us that the Office was of the same nature as the Federated General Supervisory Office formed among the great banks, in that the participating units would retain their original status as defined by law and would act on the basis of the principle of giving equal consideration to the rights and interests of public and private shareholders. We may go one step further, and say that there is practically no doubt whatever that federated supervision among the great banks was as much a preparatory measure for the amalgamation of the units as the federally operated supervision proposed here. We may be sure that the move towards federally operated supervision progressed simultaneously with the actual development of federated supervision, and that the former was greatly influenced by the vision embodied in the latter.

In the sphere of organization, the People's Bank of China was to appoint two directors representing the interests of public shareholdings, the Board of Directors of each unit was to. recommend one of its members as a plenipotentiary delegate, and these persons were to constitute a Federated Board of Directors. Under the direction of the People's Bank of China, this Federated Board of Directors was to be the supreme directing and policy-making mechanism in the centralized supervision and management of the individual units. It was to organize a General Supervisory Office, and to act as the supreme executive mechanism in the centralized supervision and management of the individual units. It would also be responsible for making preparations for the establishment of a Federally Operated Bank (Articles 2 and 3). We should note that although the People's Bank of China was to appoint two members of the Federated Board of Directors as representatives of the interests of public shareholdings, it did not have shareholdings in either the General Supervisory Office or the individual units. This is made clear by an editor's comment in the *Source Material Relating to Native Banks of Shanghai (SCCS)*. " The General Supervisory Offices in these two Federated Groups only have members of their boards of directors representing the interests of public shareholdings on behalf of the state bank, and have not yet progressed to the stage of joint state-private operation. They are a form belonging to the elementary stage of state capitalism. However, they have advanced one step from the period of the Federally Operated Groups."[139] Thus, while federated supervision was put into effect among the great banks on the basis of joint state-private operation, the federally operated supervision instituted among the medium and small banks, native banks and trust companies had no such basis in joint state-private operation, but in spite of this fact there were directors appointed as representatives of the interests of public shareholdings, and we must not fail to observe this important difference between the two.

The following was laid down as to what changes would be undergone by the individual units after the establishment of the General Supervisory Office.

(1) After the establishment of the General Supervisory Office the head offices of the units and their branch and sub-branch

---

[139] *SCCS*, p. 392.

mechanisms in Shanghai and elsewhere would all come under the direction and control of the General Supervisory Office. Each unit would retain its status as defined by law, but the supervisory departments in the head offices of the units would be amalgamated in the General Supervisory Office (Article 4).

(2) Plans must be drawn up for the unified management of business in the units after the General Supervisory Office had been set up. In the case of the branch and sub-branch mechanisms located outside Shanghai, these plans could be put into effect over a period of time, taking local conditions into consideration (Article 5).

(3) Until the General Supervisory Office was set up, each unit would be able to dispose of the items of assets and liabilities listed in the Appended Items (I), and the resulting profits and losses would appertain to the units in question. The General Supervisory Office would direct and oversee this work in a unified manner (Article 6). Apart from the items listed in the above-mentioned Appended Items (I), all assets and liabilities in the deposit, loan, exchange, warehousing, custody, agency and foreign exchange business carried on by each of the units would be managed centrally by the General Supervisory Office, and profits and losses resulting from these forms of business would be distributed centrally by the General Supervisory Office (Article 7). After the General Supervisory Office had been set up, all such funds as might be loaned or borrowed by the individual units became deposits with or lendings to the General Supervisory Office (Article 8). The Appended Items (I), mentioned in the above passage is missing from the text, but on this point it may be of some use to refer to the third paragraph in Chang Liu's account of the organization for federated supervision among the New Five Banks. Whatever the truth may be in this matter, federated supervision and federally operated supervision had in common the fact that the various forms of business which constituted the work of the units were to be brought under the unified and centralized control of the new mechanism.

(4) Personnel administration in the individual units was to be controlled by the General Supervisory Office on a unified basis (Article 9). The institutional aspects of personnel ad-

ministration and the remuneration and welfare facilities for staff and workers must be gradually unified (Article 10).

(5) Under the direction of the Federated Board of Directors, positive efforts would be made in preparing for the establishment of the First Federally Operated Bank (Article 11). The General Supervisory Office would be responsible for carrying out the revaluation of the assets and liabilities of the individual units, and so contribute to the carrying through of amalgamation (Article 12).

The above is the gist of the Summary of the Agreements of the First Federally Operated General Supervisory Office, and it is said that the Summary of Agreements of the Second Federally Operated General Supervisory Office is basically similar.[140]

In this way, between May, 1951 and November of the same year a total of 61 Shanghai banking institutions comprising 34 banks, 25 native banks and 2 trust companies (these constituting practically the whole of the Chinese banking business in Shanghai at that time) were organized into groups under the control of five General Supervisory Offices.

By the last eleven days of October, 1952, however, these five groups had combined, and had formed a single joint state-private bank, and at the same time a unified supervisory office called the Federated General Supervisory Office for the Joint State-Private Bank had been set up, and the Federated Board of Directors for the Joint State-Private Bank formed. On the 30th of October the boards of directors for the five groups—the Federated Board of Directors for Eleven Joint State-Private Banks,[141] the Federated Board of Directors for the Five Northern Joint State-Private Banks, the Board of Directors for the State-Private Shanghai Commercial and Savings Bank, the Federated Board of Directors for the First Federally Operated Group, and the Federated Board of Directors for the Second Federally Operated Group—applied to the People's Bank of China for the organization of the unified Federated General Supervisory Office for the Joint State-Private Bank, and on the same day the first general

---

140 *SCCS*, p. 441, editor's note.

141 As has been noted above, 12 banks were members of these Joint State-Private Banks. They are probably spoken of as the " Eleven Joint State-Private Banks " because one of the members joined the group by amalgamation.

meeting of the unified Federated Board of Directors for the Joint State-Private Bank was held. At the second general meeting of the unified Federated Board of Directors for the Joint State-Private Bank, held on the 18th of December, 1952, a list of the names of the members of the Federated Board of Directors, consisting of a total of 103 persons, was made public, and decisions were reached on matters of internal organization and personnel. Of the 103 directors, 27 were appointed as representatives of the interests of public shareholdings, and 76 as representatives of the interests of private shareholders. The Chairman of the Board was Hu Ching-yün, and there were five Vice-Chairmen (of whom three represented private interests) and 27 Managing Directors (of whom 18 represented private interests).[142]

The following statement is made in the Agreed Articles laid down at the time of the establishment of the Federated General Supervisory Office for the Joint State-Private Bank. " In order to fit in with the financial policies of the state and, under the direction of the People's Bank of China, to contribute more fully to state economic construction, the banking business, after consultation among the Federated Board of Directors for the Eleven Joint State-Private Banks, the Federated Board of Directors for the Five Northern Banks, the Board of Directors for the Shanghai Commercial and Savings Bank, the Federated Board of Directors for the First Federally Operated Group and the Federated Board of Directors for the Second Federally Operated Group, will carry out a radical reorganization and will establish a Joint State-Private Bank on the principles of giving equal consideration to the interests of public and private shareholders, maintaining and protecting the interests of the staff and workers, and retaining branches and sub-branches abroad. It has been agreed to abide by the following Articles, to which the participants have affixed their seals." After this preface, the document goes on to make the following points.[143]

---

[142] SCCS, pp. 447–448. The account follows the article in the Hong Kong Ta Kung Pao (1 Jan., 1953). In this article the date of the establishment of the Federated Board of Directors for the Joint State-Private Bank and the Federated General Supervisory Office for the Joint State-Private Bank is given as the 1st of December, 1952.

[143] The complete text of the Agreed Articles drawn up on the establishment of the Federated General Supervisory Office for the Joint State-Private Banks is given in the SCCS, pp. 445–446.

(1)   The several original Federated Boards of Directors and Boards of Directors will put forward representatives endowed with full powers who will organize a Federated Board of Directors for the Joint State-Private Bank (hereafter referred to as the "Federated Board of Directors"), and will exercise the functions of a Board of Directors under the direction of the People's Bank of China.

(2)   The Federated Board of Directors will organize a General Supervisory Office for the Joint State-Private Bank, and will be the supreme mechanism for the supervision and management of the Joint State-Private Bank, under the direction of the People's Bank of China.

(3)   After the Federated Board of Directors has been set up, the original Federated Boards of Directors and Board of Directors will be responsible, under its direction and supervision, for liquidating the assets and liabilities of the units in co-operation with each of their subordinate units. The Federated Board of Directors may send personnel to take part in this work.

(4)   After the assets and liabilities of all the participating units have been liquidated, the Federated Board of Directors will investigate and make decisions regarding shareholders' rights, and will call a general meeting of shareholders at which directors and auditors will be elected, and will formally constitute the Board of Directors.

(5)   After the establishment of the State-Private Bank, profits and losses will be distributed in accordance with the rights of shareholders as investigated and decided upon by the Federated Board of Directors.

In connexion with the liquidation of the assets and liabilities of the subordinate units mentioned in paragraph (3) above, a Liquidation and Valuation Committee of the Joint State-Private Bank was set up. There were 29 members of this Committee, of whom 6 came from the Federated Board of Directors, 7 came from the Eleven Joint State-Private Banks, 5 came from the Five Northern Joint State-Private Banks, 2 came from the Joint State-Private Shanghai Commercial and Savings Bank, 4 came from the First Federally Operated General Supervisory Office, and 5 came from the Second Federally Operated General Supervisory Office (Provisions for the Organization of the above committee,

Article 2). The duties of the Committee were (1) deciding upon plans for carrying out liquidation and valuation work, and seeing that these plans were carried out, (2) laying down principles for the valuation of each property, and investigating and deciding upon concrete standards of valuation for each property, (3) negotiating the value of each valued property, and making decisions in regard to the same, and (4) drawing up schedules for capital accounts and the rights of shareholders (Provisions for the Organization, Article 4).[144]

The general meeting held on the establishment of the Federated General Supervisory Office for the Joint State-Private Bank took place in Shanghai on the 11th of January, 1953. The meeting was held under the chairmanship of Wang Chih-hsin, the Vice-Chairman of the General Supervisory Office. The Chairman of the General Supervisory Office, Ch'en Mu, presented a detailed report on the questions of the nature and business policy of the Joint State-Private Bank, and its relations with the commercial and industrial world.[145]

As an accompaniment to the establishment of the Federated General Supervisory Office the branch and sub-branch mechanisms in large- and medium-size towns in all parts of China were amalgamated. The Office then had 14 branch banks in Peking, Shanghai, Tientsin, Sian, Hankow, Changsha, Canton, Chungking, Chengtu, Kunming, Tsingtao, Nanking, Hangchow and Amoy.[146]

It was at this stage that the principles of "a division of business and a division of clients" or "a division of business among branch banks, and one bank per client" were put into effect. Under these principles a division of labour was put into effect among the Shanghai branch of the People's Bank of China

---

[144] The complete text of the Provisions for the Organization of the Liquidation and Valuation Committee of the Joint State-Private Bank is given in the *SCCS*, pp. 448–449.

[145] *H-TKP* (19 Jan., 1953).

[146] *H-TKP* (7 Feb., 1953). The article states, "The Joint State-Private Bank has fourteen branches in all parts of the country, and at present there are four business departments in its Shanghai branch, namely the Business, Foreign Exchange, Warehousing, and Land and Buildings Departments, as well as twenty-two Business Offices and fourteen Sub-offices. Since the foundation of the Bank within one month ago it has been gradually getting its business under way, under the direction of the People's Bank of China."

and the Shanghai branch of the Federated General Supervisory Office, and at the same time each business or businessman in commerce or industry was caused to have an account with only one bank. In this way a large number of overlapped accounts were reduced, and in addition to this the following points were mentioned as the chief advantages conferred by these principles.[147]

(1)   After the introduction of a division of business among the branch banks the book-keeping work of the banks could be simplified, resulting in a saving of labour, and enabling the directing personnel in the banks to specialize and to devote a greater part of their time and attention to study, so that the efficiency of working could be improved. The book-keeping work of businessmen in commerce and industry would also be simplified, and this would be extremely advantageous for the running of their own enterprises.

(2)   Closer links could be established between the banks and businessmen in commerce and industry, so that in future the banks would understand the situation in commerce and industry in regard to production, trade and movements of funds, would make suitable arrangements for the grouping together of related forms of business, and would adjust the supply of funds on a planned basis, thus contributing to the attainment of the aims of developing production and promoting the circulation of commodities as provided for in the state economic plans.

(3)   Under the conditions of a division of business among the branch banks the relations between the banks and businessmen in commerce and industry would not be confined to business transactions, but could be further developed into close personal links which would make mutual aid and co-operation possible. The banks would be able to promote improvements in the running of commerce and industry by means of business relations, particularly by means of loan relations, and could cause a development of production by introducing greater speediness into the provision of funds, and by accumulating funds.

---

147   The account is based on the article in the "Replies to Queries" column in the Hong Kong *Ta Kung Pao* (9 Feb., 1953) entitled "Rules for the Effecting of Division of Work in the Joint State-Private Banks of Shanghai."

(4) After the implementation of a division of business among the branch banks the payment of taxes by businessmen in commerce and industry would be rendered more convenient. Article 9 of the Trial Regulations for the Commodity Circulation Tax provides that " those who are under the obligation of paying commodity circulation tax will in accordance with the provisions calculate the tax themselves and will open an account at the People's Bank of China into which these taxes will be transferred," but since the Joint State-Private Bank was already acting as the part of the organization of the People's Bank of China dealing with private business, the Joint State-Private Bank could be designated by the People's Bank of China as being responsible for opening the accounts into which the commodity circulation tax would be transferred.

The principles of " a division of business among branch banks, and one bank per client " were first put into effect in Shanghai. The Shanghai branch of the Joint State-Private Bank readjusted 14,000 overlapped accounts in the single month of December, 1952, rationalized their methods of management, introduced simplifications of procedure, and penetrated deeply into commerce and industry, strengthening their links. After discussion between the responsible persons representing the Shanghai branch of the People's Bank of China and the Shanghai branch of the Joint State-Private Bank, a number of the principal forms of business in the commercial and industrial world in Shanghai were divided between the People's Bank of China or the Joint State-Private Bank. This method, by means of which a division of labour was introduced into the business functions of the People's Bank of China and the Joint State-Private Bank, was then put into effect in the other great cities of China.

On the 5th of May, 1953, the Federated Board of Directors for the Joint State-Private Bank and the Federated General Supervisory Office for the Joint State-Private Bank moved from Shanghai to Peking (108 Hsichiaomin Hsiang). These mechanisms were now directly subject to the direction of the head office of the People's Bank of China.[148]

It is said that at the beginning of 1952 there were approximately 180 banks and native banks in China.[149] At this time

---

[148] *H-TKP* (24 May, 1953).

there were about 60 banks and native banks in Shanghai. Thus, from the point of view of numbers one-third of the banks in China were located in Shanghai, but since Shanghai had originally been the centre of the Chinese economy there was no small number of great banks in Shanghai which had networks of branches and sub-branches in the cities and towns all over China. Consequently, the development of the socialist transformation of private banking in Shanghai which we have described above necessarily produced effects on a nation-wide scale.

We will now present selected passages from a short piece describing the transition which took place in the banking world in Tientsin in 1950 and 1951, written by an author named Wang Chi.[150] We may be able to see how the development of the situation in Shanghai affected Tientsin.

"In May of this year (1951) a group of banks headed by the Hsin Hua Trust and Savings Bank were the first to organize a General Supervisory Office for the Joint State-Private Banks, and during the last several months they have shown a rapid development in their business, after having set their internal organization in order and having received directions from the state bank. For example, the deposits lodged with 8 banks of this group amounted to more than 60% of the total deposits at the 29 banks and native banks in Tientsin. For this reason, the Yien Yieh Commercial Bank and the remainder of the Five Northern Banks organized a Federated General Supervisory Office in September, and thereafter the state-private Shanghai Commercial and Savings Bank and the Chiu An Bank organized a Federated Supervisory Committee, while the Tung Lai Bank, the Land Bank of China, and Chung Foo Union Bank joined the First Federally Operated General Supervisory Office, Shanghai. Since then all banking institutions in Tientsin have been participating in arrangements for joint state-private operation or federated operation, and the centralized management of banking has entered a new stage. For this reason, under the direction of the state bank the Federated Supervisory Committee for the Tientsin Joint State-Private Banks

---

149 Chih P'ei, "The Correct Direction for the Development of the Private Banks and Native Banks," *Chingchi Taopao*, Vol. VI, No. 1 (Jan., 1952), p. 25.

150 Wang Chi, "The Change-over in the Banking Business in Tientsin," *H-TKP* (14 Jan., 1952).

has been organized, and the unification of financial resources advanced one step further. The power of the state bank has increased without remission, and the business of the Joint State-Private Banks has also continued to expand. Because the speculative element has disappeared from the market, the native banks have recognized their disunion and blindness, and they are making positive efforts to participate in joint state-private operation in their business."

Further, there were some medium- and small-scale local banks and native banks which amalgamated with banks participating in arrangements for federated supervision. For example, " The T'ai Feng Jen and Te Feng Hsiang native banks in Nanch'ang in the Central-South Region amalgamated with the Yüan Yüan Ch'ang Bank of Nanch'ang, a bank participating in a General Supervisory Office, on the 1st of December (1951), having received the approval of the People's Bank of China and the said General Supervisory Office. Again, in Tientsin, Peking, Sian, etc., where there is a fair concentration of private banks and native banks, as well as among individual banks and native banks in Shanghai, there are some who are applying for participation in organizations for federated supervision, and these arrangements are at present in course of negotiation."[151]

Again, the private banks and native banks in Wuhan had passed through the stage of federated operation and had now formed a single bank. " Hitherto the 15 private banks and native banks in Wuhan had been organized in three federally operated groups, but they have now been combined in the Wuhan Federated Commercial Bank. The bank was established on the 1st of October (1951) and was formally opened for business on the 3rd. With the establishment of this bank the native banks have disappeared from Wuhan, and the name 'native banks' has become a term in the history of banking."[152]

It will be clear from our examination of this source that the seizure of control of the Shanghai banks and native banks by the People's Bank of China in accordance with the formula which we have described in the preceding pages was not a local incident peculiar to Shanghai, but was a part of a large-scale move on the

[151] *H-TKP* (13 Dec., 1951).
[152] *H-TKP* (4 Oct., 1951).

part of that bank to gain control over all the banks and native banks in the country.

We have now described the course by which the banking institutions in Shanghai, operating as they did on a nation-wide scale, were brought together in a single Joint State-Private Bank. One question, however, still remains. Why was it that in 1951 when the comparatively large banks had been organized in three groups operating under federated supervision and the comparatively small banks, native banks and trust companies had been organized in two groups operating under federally operated supervision and when all these groups, with the exception of the Shanghai Commercial and Savings Bank group, were proceeding along the road to amalgamation as independent bodies, these five groups were suddenly amalgamated to form a single Joint State-Private Bank at the end of 1952? The first explanation which occurs to us is that since the First Five-Year Plan was scheduled to begin in 1953, the authorities of the People's Government and the People's Bank of China may have considered it necessary to obtain firm control over all banks, native banks and trust companies. The editor of the *Source Material Relating to the Native Banks of Shanghai* has the following to say about the necessity and possibility of the banking business reaching the stage of joint state-private operation by whole trades at an earlier date than in the case of commerce and industry, and his words may serve to clarify this point. "The necessity and possibility of effecting joint state-private operation over the whole range of the banking business at an earlier date than in any other sector of the economy are determined by the nature of the banking business and the historical conditions under which banking developed in old China. The capitalist banks and native banks carrying on credit-provision business differ in character from commerce and industry in general, and they constitute one of the economic threads of life which must be taken over by the state first of all. In socialist society the banks have the important duty of mobilizing the idle capital which is present in society and of distributing funds in a planned manner, and it is required that they should be characterized by strict centralization, unity and planning. This determines the fact that the socialist transformation of the capitalist banks and native banks must take place before that of commerce and industry in general. The banks and native banks of old China were originally characterized by a very high degree of centralization (regional centralization, head-office centralization and concentration of capital), and after the gradual penetration of the work of transformation over a period of several years they were subjected to rules providing for the liquidation of their assets and the determination of shareholders' rights after they had passed through the stages of federated operation, federated supervision and had attained to amalgamation. Thus, with the help of the strength of the political power of the working class and the greatness of the state economy (including the state banks) it was possible for joint state-private operation to be put into effect throughout the whole range of capitalist banks and native banks in China at an earlier date than in any other department of the economy."[153] Secondly, we must point to the results of the *San-fan Wu-fan* (三反五反) movement[154] carried on for approximately six months between the end of 1951 and the end of June, 1952. In this connexion the following remarks of the editor of the *Source Material Relating to the Native Banks of Shanghai* on the subject of the native banks of Shanghai are worthy of our attention. "The *Wu-fan* movement provided a most serious lesson for the capitalists of native banks, as it did for the whole of the national bourgeoisie. If we are to judge by the exposures made and cases reported, there were grievous cases of *Wu-tu* (五毒) conduct among a certain section of the capitalists of native banks, speculation and breaches of the law being universal among them. Under the leadership of the Party and under the pressure of the struggle waged by staff and workers many capitalists of native banks confessed and recognized their crimes. As a result of the *Wu-fan* movement a process of differentiation occurred among the capitalists of native banks, leading to a heightened consciousness on the part of many people, and thus the conditions were created for the introduction of the joint state-private operation throughout the whole banking

---

[153] *SCCS*, p. 17.

[154] *San-fan Wu-fan* movement is a campaign against what were known as the "Three Evils" and "Five Evils." The "Three Evils" are the evils of corruption, waste, and bureaucracy, while the "Five Evils" comprise the bribery of government personnel, tax evasion, theft of state property, cheating on government contracts, and stealing economic information.

business."[155] This " brain-washing " effect may be said to have taken place not only among the capitalists of native banks of Shanghai but also among the capitalists of banks. Thirdly, we must note the fact that because of the great change in the economic and social situation, and especially because of the extension of the power of the state socialist banking organs centred on the People's Bank of China, bankers in general suffered a rapid reduction of their sphere of activity, so that it became difficult for them to carry on business and their economic power was weakened. We have already drawn attention to the weakening of the power of the great Chinese banks in Shanghai after the Liberation, but we may also listen to the testimony of Ts'ao Chü-ju regarding the generality of banks and native banks. " During the *Wu-fan* movement many instances of illegal speculative activities were detected among the private banks and native banks, with the result that an end was made to the false prosperity in the market which had been brought about by the illegal speculative activities with the help of which they had survived. Their functions of absorbing the idle capital and of supplying funds in society were daily reduced to smaller proportions, and at the same time the effects of the leadership of the People's Bank of China in the money market became daily stronger. If we take the example of the amount of savings absorbed and the deposits made by private commerce and industry, we find that in the two and a half years between June, 1950 and December, 1952, the proportion dealt with by the state banks rose from 58.6% to 92.8%, while that dealt with by the private banks and native banks declined from 41.4% to 7.2%. During this period all the private banks and native banks were showing losses, and so difficult was it for them to carry on business that they were scarcely able to survive. In response to this situation the government instituted joint state-private operation throughout the entire banking and native banking business in December, 1952, organizing a Joint State-Private Bank carrying on business under the direction of the People's Bank of China. In this way the socialist transformation of private banking was basically completed and an end made to capitalist banking business in China, while a unified socialist banking system was built up and advantageous

---

[155] *SCCS*, p. 16.

conditions provided for another step to be taken by the state in the socialist transformation of capitalist commerce and industry."[156]

CONCLUSION

The editor of the *Source Material Relating to the Native Banks of Shanghai* regards the groups belonging to the two Federally Operated General Supervisory Offices formed among the native banks and medium- and small-size banks in 1951 as being a form belonging to the elementary stage of state capitalism, and regards the groups belonging to the three Federated General Supervisory Offices formed by the large-scale banks during the same year as being advanced forms of state capitalism. The editor says, " These two are to be distinguished as forms of state capitalism. The Federated General Supervisory Offices organized by the large banks included no small number of banks which changed at once to joint state-private operation after the Liberation, in addition to which the state made some degree of investment in these groups and sent a certain number of personnel to take part in their work, so that these groups are one of the advanced forms of state capitalism. However, the Federally Operated General Supervisory Offices for the two Federally Operated Groups merely had the participation of directors representing the interests of state shareholdings on behalf of the People's Bank of China and had not yet embarked upon joint state-private operation, so that they are a form belonging to the elementary stage of state capitalism. Nevertheless, they have advanced one step from the period of the Federally Operated Groups."[157]

In connexion with the content of this testimony we have already drawn attention to the fact that when the Federally Operated General Supervisory Offices were formed public directors were appointed, although there were no state shareholdings in the banks and native banks in question, and we must think it something of a discovery that these groups are considered to be a form belonging to the elementary stage of state capitalism. To this we

---

[156] Ts'ao Chü-ju, " Banking in the Last Ten Years," in *Ten Glorious Years* (Peking, 1959), Vol. 1, p. 399.
[157] *SCCS*, p. 392.

may add our opinion that advanced forms of state capitalism
were already in existence when individual banks embarked on joint
state-private operation in the period prior to the formation of the
Federated General Supervisory Offices. We do not think that
there will be much dispute over this point, but the question
consists in whether a number of phenomena which we have examined in the preceding pages—the Shanghai Banking and Trust
Federated Loan Office, the Shanghai Joint State-Private Banking
Federated Loan Office, and the four Federally Operated Groups—
include forms belonging to the elementary stage of state capitalism
or not, and, if they do, which of these phenomena constitute such
forms. In the light of the statement in Article 31 of the Common
Programme of the Chinese People's Political Consultative Conference, "An economy in which state capital and private capital
co-operate together is an economy possessing the character of a
state-capitalist economy," we believe that the Shanghai Joint
State-Private Banking Federated Loan Office is certainly to be
regarded as a form belonging to the elementary stage of state
capitalism.

In the Chinese sources the words "state capitalism" and
"joint state-private operation" have been in use since the foundation of the People's Republic, that is, since the time when the
Common Programme was issued, while the words "socialist transformation," together with the words "socialist industrialization,"
came into use after the proclamation of the General Line for the
Transition Period of the State in the autumn of 1953, and it was
after the beginning of the second half of 1955 when "joint
state-private operation by whole trades" began to be spoken of in
contradistinction to "joint state-private operation of individual
enterprises." However, the process by which the banking business
in Shanghai was converted *en bloc* to joint state-private operation
was a process which brought to reality all that was contained in
the term "joint state-private operation by whole trades" and did
so before the term came into use. Further, we can have no doubt
but that the theory and experience of the work of socialist
transformation in the banking business in Shanghai up to 1952
provided valuable lessons for the practice of socialist transformation in capitalist commerce and industry at a later date.

The groups which were formed in the banking world of

Shanghai, like those formed in all other branches of the Chinese economy, were formed naturally along lines of kinship, geographical association and membership of the same line of business. Before the establishment of a unified Joint State-Private Bank the banking business in Shanghai was drawn together into 5 groups, but until this was accomplished the natural ties mentioned above were in operation to a great degree. However, when a unified Joint State-Private Bank was formed these ties were totally negated. Consequently, the process by which a unified Joint State-Private Bank was formed in Shanghai provides a miniature illustration of how non-modern elements pass through the process of modernization.

Nevertheless, we must not overlook the following words of Hsü Ti-hsin. "The principal business carried on by the Joint State-Private Bank is that of receiving savings deposits as agent for the People's Bank of China."[158] That is to say, the unified Joint State-Private Bank in which all the banking institutions of Shanghai were brought together had fallen to the status of a mere savings bank. To one who knew the flourishing condition of national bank capital and national native bank capital in former years this must appear a sad declension indeed.

---

[158] Hsü Ti-hsin, *An Analysis of the National Economy of Our Country in the Transition Period* (Peking, 1957), p. 247. No alteration or addition is made to this passage in the revised edition of this book, *An Analysis of the Chinese National Economy in the Transition Period 1949-1957* (Peking, 1962), p. 202.

CHAPTER VII

SOME PROBLEMS OF FINANCIAL POLICY

INTRODUCTION

In 1960, as a result of criticism of the results produced by the First Five-Year Plan and the blows inflicted by natural disasters, the Chinese government sharply switched its policy of excessive emphasis on heavy industry and took steps to rebuild and adjust economic construction with agriculture as the basis. In accordance with this line it was announced at the Ninth Plenary Session of the Eighth Central Committee of the Chinese Communist Party in January, 1961, that capital construction in heavy industry would be reduced to a suitable scale. At the Third Session of the Second National People's Congress in April, 1962, this reduction of the scale of capital construction was made general throughout the whole economy, and it was made clear that an overall balance between the various sectors of the national economy would be pursued in the order of agriculture, light industry and heavy industry.

What course was followed by financial policy in the midst of the development of this adjustment of the Chinese national economy? This chapter will be devoted to the discussion of a number of problems connected with this question.

1. The Strengthening of Bank Credit Work

"Bank credit" is an abbreviation of the expression "bank credit loans." Further, the words "bank credits" as used in the socialist society of present-day China correspond to what are widely referred to in Japan as "loans," and originally had the meaning of "short-term credit loans, but have not the meaning of unsecured loans." Consequently, strengthening bank credit work means strengthening the loan policies of the banks, and this has become the principal characteristic of financial policy in China in recent years. Let us examine this problem in more detail.

In socialist society the credit loans made by banks are a form of planned redistribution by the state of funds made available under the principle of a loan. These loans are also important instruments in overseeing each enterprise and each sector of the national economy through the form of currency.[159] In present-day China the People's Bank of China (hereafter sometimes simply referred to as 'the Bank') is the centre of bank credit.

Seven sources of funds for bank credit are given: (1) credit funds passed to the Bank from the state exchequer, (2) profits accumulated by the Bank itself, (3) deposits received from state enterprises and collective economic organizations, (4) savings deposited by the inhabitants of town and country, (5) deposits received from the state exchequer (the chief of these being exchequer surplus funds), (6) deposits received from state organs, bodies, army units and enterprise-units, and (7) issues of currency.[160] With these funds the Bank makes principally seasonal or temporary loans of liquid funds to enterprises of all kinds. However, among the loans made by the Bank long-term loans of fixed funds are included in the loans made to agriculture, and a part of the running liquid funds required by the enterprises is supplied by the Bank. On these points the reader should refer to the account of this matter given below. The content and forms of the manipulation of funds as carried on by the People's Bank of China have undergone a number of changes in the course of history and are still in process of change at present, so that we find ourselves unable to make

[159]   Liu Hung-ju, "The Significance and Functions of Strengthening Supervision of Credit Planning," *P-TKP* (1 Aug., 1962).

[160]   Chin Ch'ün, "On the Credit Work of the Banks," *Jenmin Jihpao* (27 Apr., 1962), and Ko Chih-ta, "The Functions of the State Banks in Socialist Construction," *P-TKP* (15 Oct., 1962). It is also said that between 60% and 70% of credit funds are derived from exchequer grants and exchequer deposits. See Ko Chih-ta & Wang Cho, "Some Problems Related to the Work of State Finance and Credit Provision," *P-TKP* (17 Nov., 1961).

a dogmatic characterization of them, but at all events it will serve as a standpoint or standard for the analysis of the activities of the Bank if we regard the Bank as being chiefly concerned with satisfying the demand for seasonal and temporary liquid funds on the part of the enterprises.[161]

The first point made in connexion with the credit policies of the Bank is that a distinction must be made between budget funds and credit funds, and that this distinction must be observed in the supervision and use of these funds. In particular, budget funds and credit funds differ in regard to the following two points. (1) Budget funds are essentially non-repayable, and are used in meeting the demand for running funds required in all sectors of state economic construction, while in contrast to this credit funds are essentially repayable, and are used in satisfying temporary demands for funds on the part of economic units. (2) In the case of state budget funds the procedure is for demands for funds to be made beforehand and statements of accounts presented at a later date, while in the case of credit funds demands for funds take the form of borrowings, followed by repayment when due in accordance with plans. Since budget funds and credit funds differ in nature in this way, they must not be employed together or diverted from one use to the other. The accounts pertaining to these two types of funds must be kept separately, and the distinction between them must be observed in making use of these funds ("division of supervision, and observance of distinction in use").[162] That is to say, credit funds must not be used either directly or in a disguised form in paying any normal running expenses of a non-repayable nature. Funds to be used by enterprises in advancing capital construction, carrying out the technological revolution, increasing fixed capital assets, etc., are to be made up from held-over profits of enterprises and funds allotted under budgetary arrangements. Among the liquid funds used by the enterprises, "fixed-sum liquid funds," that is, the minimum

---

[161] On the question of the changes which have taken place in the credit policies of the People's Bank of China since the Liberation, see Hsü Ti-hsin, *An Analysis of the Chinese National Economy in the Transition Period, 1949-1957* (Peking, 1962), pp. 206-207.

[162] Ko Chih-ta, "Problems of the Supply and Supervision of State Financial Funds and Credit Funds," *Jenmin Jihpao* (31 March, 1961), and Han Po, "On the Problems of Maintaining a Balance between the Budget, Credit, Cash and Material Resources," *P-TKP* (22 June, 1962).

sum of liquid funds which may be diverted and used by an enterprise in normal running expenses required by the advancing of production, may be paid out of budget funds, and each enterprise may use such funds as its own funds, but "excess fixed sum liquid funds," that is, the liquid funds required by enterprises on a temporary basis in the processes of production, supply and marketing for seasonal and other special reasons, must be made up from credit funds. However, as we shall show later, since the 1st of July, 1961, 20% of the "fixed-sum liquid funds" of state industries and state transportation enterprises has been passed to the People's Bank of China out of the budget funds by the Ministry of Finance, and has been made available by the Bank in the form of bank credit loans.

Let us present an example connected with this question. Between 1959 and February, 1961, the Hsiang T'ai Internal Combustion Engine Factory at Harbin broke the provisions of the financial administrative system on several occasions, diverting liquid funds to capital construction and carrying out welfare work on behalf of its staff and workers. The local Bank applied its supervisory powers to the factory, and stopped loans to the factory on four occasions in order to remedy the situation in accordance with the provisions of the financial administrative system, but was unable to produce any effect. In December, 1961, the factory diverted 240,000 *yüan* of liquid funds to install spaceheating apparatus in its premises and to build boats. The local Bank again stopped loans, and decided to require payment of former loans. Hereupon the factory was faced with production difficulties for the first time, and as a measure designed to overcome this situation the directing cadres at the factory recognized the necessity of conducting the factory in accordance with the provisions of the financial administrative system, and eventually devised measures for improving the supervision of the management of the factory. As a result they were able to make good their losses and to show a profit in the first quarter of 1962.[163] This is an example in which credit funds were diverted to purposes for which the enterprise should have used either its own funds or budget funds.

We would add, in connexion with the present question, that

---

[163] *Jenmin Jihpao* (10 May, 1962).

the necessity of maintaining a balance between budget funds and credit funds is recognized, and that steps are taken to secure it. We listed above seven sources of bank credit funds, and there now arises the question of how the balance is to be made up when the demands for funds on the part of industry, commerce, agriculture, etc., cannot be met with the funds accumulated under sources (2)–(6) in that list—accumulated Bank profits and all forms of public and private deposits and savings deposits. One solution in such a case is new issues of currency, but when such issues are not accompanied by a parallel increase in the volume of commodities coming on to the market as a result of the development of production there is a danger that they may be the cause of runaway inflation, and they must be made with care. In order to correct the unbalance between budget funds and credit funds and to bring about a balance between them, it has been the practice since 1957 for the bank credit funds to be passed from the state to the Bank at the beginning of each year, when the budget is drawn up. This comes under the first source of bank credit funds in our list above. Before 1957 no provision had been made for assuring a balance between these two types of funds when the budget was drawn up at the beginning of each year, but when the budget had been put into operation any surplus remaining was passed to the Bank for use as credit funds.

The second point made in regard to the credit policies of the Bank is that the Bank must abide by the " three principles governing bank credit." These are (1) that loans must be made in accordance with plans, (2) that loans must be repaid at the stipulated date, and (3) that there must be material resources as security for loans.

The credit plans of the Bank are an organic part of state economic planning, and during the present period, in which the national economy is in process of adjustment, it is especially necessary that there should be a high degree of centralization and unity in this field. The fundamental basis upon which the Bank conducts its credit activities is the " comprehensive credit plan," an important constituent of the state financial administration plans which form the part of the state economic plans. In these plans the state prescribes the concentration or distribution of funds in greater or lesser sums as well as the sectors to which

funds are to be distributed through the intermediacy of the Bank
and the principles under which distribution is to take place. The
main bases for the credit plans drawn up by the Bank are the
production plans of the various sectors of the national economy,
the commodity circulation plans and the state financial administration plans. The comprehensive credit plan for the whole of
China is drawn up under the unified direction of the People's
Bank of China on the basis of the credit plans of each state
department, region and enterprise. The comprehensive credit plan
is thus a synthesized reflection of the planned and proportional
development of the national economy. In response to the demand
for centralization and unity in credit planning, the rights of fixing
credit ceilings and of giving permission for the granting of credit
are vested in the Centre. No state department, unit or individual
may increase loans one penny above the credit ceilings without
the permission of the Centre (or of a superior organ). Plans for
which permission has been granted must be put into effect without fail. If for some special reason it is found necessary to
contract loans in excess of the duly permitted ceilings, it is possible
to make application under a fixed procedure for the authorization
of increased ceilings. Until permission for such increased ceilings
is received the previously authorized plans must be adhered to.
Further, in the case of enterprises supervised from the Centre, the
ceilings for loans are sent down from the responsible state department at the Centre and the head office of the People's Bank of China
to the enterprises and the local branches of the Bank respectively,
and loans are made by the local Banks within the ceilings laid
down, after each loan has been subjected to individual examination. In the case of enterprises under local supervision, ceilings
for loans are sent down from the head office of the People's
Bank of China to the branches of the Bank in each Province,
City and Autonomous Region, and they send down ceilings within
the general ceilings authorized by the head office of the People's
Bank of China, in consultation with the relevant state departments
and with the permission of the directing state departments on
the spot, to each subordinate unit of the Bank catering for
enterprises supervised at Province, Special District, and *Hsien*
levels, and the supervisory state departments for the enterprises
at these various levels are responsible for controlling the use of

these ceilings.[164]

In order to carry out loans in accordance with the plans drawn up under these basic planning conditions, the borrowing enterprises or units must send in " borrowings plans " to the Bank every quarter, giving a detailed account of the purposes for which money is to be borrowed, the reasons for borrowing, and the period for repayment. The subordinate units of the Bank which make these loans must strive to realize the following three general principles. (1) They must examine the " borrowing plans " of the enterprises with care, and assure themselves of the amount to be borrowed and the purposes for which it is to be used. (2) When loans are made they must be made in accordance with the amounts and purposes prescribed by the plans. (3) When money is lent the Banks must carry out inspection at certain times and see that the plans are being adhered to, that there are material resources as security for the loans, and that the loans are repaid in due time. If any enterprise does not adhere to these general principles the Bank may apply punishments to the enterprises by stopping lending, and by recovering money lent.

It is perhaps unnecessary to explain the obligation to repay loans in due time. The Chinese writers point out (1) that the greater part of credit funds are derived from public and private bank deposits, that most of this money represents funds which are temporarily idle and which may be withdrawn at once whenever they are needed, and that consequently the manipulation of credit funds must be carried out speedily, and (2) that the obligation to repay loans in due time is designed to assure planned operation in lending.[165] The mention of material resources as security for loans may lead us to suppose that these are " secured loans," but in this context the words are not used in that sense. In this context the words refer to the fact that when loans are made the enterprises may use them only in meeting temporary requirements for funds in the fields of production and the circula-

---

[164] This account is based on Yen Fang-wen, " On the Problems of Strengthening the Supervision of Bank Credit," *P-TKP* (7 March, 1962), and the cited articles by Chin Ch'ün and Liu Hung-ju. On the comprehensive plans for financial administration, see Chang T'ing-tung, "A Brief Discussion of the Comprehensive Plans for State Financial Administration," *P-TKP* (11 June, 1962).

[165] Ho P'ei-yü, " The Three General Principles for Bank Credit," *P-TKP* (30 Apr., 1962).

tion of commodities, and may not use them for disbursements of a non-repayable character such as disbursements made by the state financial administration, or for the purposes of commercial credit, as in credit purchases or advance payments for goods.[166]

The third point made in connexion with the credit policies of the Bank is the requirement that, through its supervision of loans the Bank shall conduce to an improvement of the condition of the supervisory systems of the enterprises. In the Peking *Ta Kung Pao* of the 7th of September, 1961, the Industrial and Commercial Loans Supervisory Bureau of the People's Bank of China published a piece entitled "Positive Co-operation in Mobilizing the Hidden Material Resources Held by the Enterprises is the Important Task of the Moment in the Industrial Credit Work of the Banks." From about the same date articles appeared in the press describing how goods in store were being cleared off, not only in industrial enterprises but also in commercial enterprises, and how the mobilization and useful employment of goods left idle was being pushed forward in co-operation with the relevant departments in the fields of state financial administration, banking and the supervision of material resources.[167] As time went on it was noticed in particular that an unhealthy condition in the supervi-

---

[166] Ko Chih-ta, "Problems of...," and Ts'ai Chin, "On the Subject of 'the Security of Material Resources'," *P-TKP* (10 June, 1962). In the above article Ko Chih-ta states that the stoppage of payments of earnest-money for advance contract purchases of agricultural produce was also done with the aim of requiring loans to be made only on the security of material resources, but, as we have explained elsewhere, payments of earnest-money were being made for advance contract purchases of raw cotton in 1963.

[167] In the Peking *Ta Kung Pao* (5 Sept., 1961), there is an article which relates how the commercial, government finance, banking, industrial and other state departments of the economy in the city of Shenyang co-operated in making a thorough survey of the stocks of commodities held by commercial organizations, and the same issue of the paper carried a leading article entitled "A Thorough Stock-taking in the Commercial Warehouses." On the 7th of September, 1961, the paper carried the document, "Positive Co-operation in Mobilizing the Hidden Material Resources Held by the Enterprises Is the Important Task of the Moment in the Industrial Credit Work of the Banks," published by the Industrial and Commercial Loans Supervisory Bureau of the Head Office of the People's Bank of China to which we have referred on this page as well as an article relating how the industries of the city of Chinchou, in co-operation with the state department of the economy dealing with financial administration, banking, and the supervision of material resources, "have made a positive start in the work of stock-taking and the determination of funds, impelled by a spirit of orderliness and centring their efforts on production."

sory systems of the enterprises was one of the causes of material resources being left idle, and it was maintained with emphasis that the Bank should contribute to the improvement of the condition of the supervisory systems in the enterprises and to the strengthening of the economic planning system. The Bank always has close relations with the enterprises through its credit relations, and one of the reasons for it being given the task of exercising a directing function in relation to the running of the enterprises was that in the process of conducing to an improvement of the condition of credit relations and supervising the making of loans the Bank was in a good position to understand the managerial weaknesses of the enterprises.

The original purpose for which the Bank takes part in management and supervision in the enterprises and strengthened its powers of supervising loans is that of maintaining the three general principles governing credit loans, but from another point of view we may say that this is a means of implementing a policy of tightening the money market. Another point which should be noticed in this connexion is the strengthening of cash control by the Bank. As is well known, the use of cash is kept to the minimum in China, and as far as possible transactions are cleared by the book transfer through the Bank. This is called cash control. The following is an outline of the latest state of cash control. Cash is used principally in economic relations between the state (including state enterprises and state organs) and collective bodies on the one hand and individuals on the other. When the state and the collective bodies pay wages to individuals, distribute currency among them in accordance with the number of labour-days, and purchase the products of domestic side-occupations from the members of communes, cash is used. Cash is also used for payments of small sums between state enterprises. In the case of exchanges of commodities between state enterprises and the rural people's communes or production teams, payments may be made in cash at the request of the people's communes or production teams. In the case of commodity exchanges between state enterprises and collective bodies when large sums are paid, the general rule is that book transfer payments should be made through the Bank.[168] Looking at cash control as actually carried on at present,

---

[168]   Chin Ch'ün, op. cit.

we find that the Bank is making efforts to keep the amounts of cash held by the enterprises as small as possible, reducing the number of cash payments and increasing the number of book transfer payments.[169]

The fourth point made in connexion with the credit policies of the Bank is the requirement that the Bank should see to it that its subordinate credit personnel are caused to perform their duties to the full. It is the subordinate credit personnel who are the persons directly responsible for executing the state credit policies in relation to the enterprises within the framework of the state credit system, and the Bank must cause them to perform their duties to the full, improving the quality of such personnel and giving them security in their place of work. For these purposes increased educational and training facilities for these personnel are required, in addition to a sense of responsibility on their own part.[170]

---

[169] Among the chief articles on the subject of cash control published in the Peking *Ta Kung Pao* are: The Nan T'ung Cotton Sheet Factory, Kiangsu Province, and the Minchulumen Branch of the General Stores Company, Wuch'ang District, in Wuhan, Hupei Province (15 Apr., 1962); the Ta *Hsien* Branch of the People's Bank of China, Ssuchuan Province (8 May, 1962), and the Anyang *Hsien* Branch of the People's Bank of China, Honan Province, and the Hsiaolungk'an Business Office of the People's Bank of China, Shapa District, Chungking (27 Apr., 1962). If we may judge by the information contained in these sources it would appear to be general for payments made between localities or in the same locality (apart from payments of wages) to be transacted by book transfer payments through the Bank when the sums exceed 30 *yüan*. The cash in hand at the Minchulumen Branch of the General Stores Company, Wuch'ang District, in Wuhan, Hupei Province is fixed at less than 150 *yüan*.

[170] In the case of enterprises directly subordinated to the Centre, the specialist financial supervisory personnel and the credit personnel of the banks are dispatched by the Ministry of Finance at the Centre and the head office of the People's Bank of China respectively, while in the case of locally-administered enterprises the specialist financial supervisory personnel and the credit personnel of the Bank are dispatched by the local financial administrative authorities and the local Bank authorities respectively. In some cases two such persons were sent to one enterprise, and in some cases they dealt with several enterprises. See Editorial, "Strengthen the Work of the Specialist Financial Supervisory Personnel and Bank Credit Personnel," *P-TKP* (22 Apr., 1962). See also the staff commentator's article "Let the Bank Credit Personnel Perform Their Functions to the Full!" *Jenmin Jihpao* (25 Aug., 1962); the article "How May the Credit Personnel Be Caused to Perform Their Duties to the Best Advantage?" *P-TKP* (from 25 May to 1 June, 1962), and the article in the same paper (29 Oct., 1962) dealing with the methods of training of subordinate credit personnel employed by the Sant'ai *Hsien* Branch of the People's Bank of China, Ssuchuan Province.

The fifth point made in connexion with the credit policies of the Bank is the contention that the Bank should devote efforts to publicizing the credit system. Some deliberate infringements of the provisions of the state financial administrative system and the credit system have occurred, but no small number of such cases have been due to ignorance of these systems. This is the reason for carrying on publicity regarding these systems.[171]

The above are the principal problems connected with the strengthening of the credit policies of the Bank. In connexion with these questions we may add that there have recently been changes in the ways in which the liquid funds of state enterprises are made available. We shall discuss this point in Section III.

II. The Provision of Funds for Agriculture by the State

In China there are the following routes or forms by which the state supplies the funds necessary for the development of agricultural production.[172]

(1) Capital construction investments in agriculture.

These funds are paid out of the state budget for the purposes of such capital construction works in agriculture as the construction of large-scale water conservancy works or small-scale field water conservancy works.

(2) Capital construction investments in industries serving agriculture.

These funds are paid out of the state budget for the purposes of building or expanding factories making or repairing agricultural machinery and factories producing chemical fertilizers and agricultural chemicals.

(3) Agriculture, forestry, and water conservancy works funds.

---

171 Editorial, "The Prospects since the Movement for Strengthening Supervision of State Financial Administration and Credit," *P-TKP* (27 May, 1962).

172 Chin Ming (Vice-Minister of Finance), "Giving the Fullest Support to Agriculture is the Political Task of State Financial Administration," *Jenmin Jihpao* (1 Dec., 1960); Chang Hsiu-min, "On the Subject of the Problems of Support for Agriculture by State Finance and the Banks," *P-TKP* (10 Oct., 1962); Yang Pʻei-hsin, "On the Relation between Credit-Provision and Agriculture," *P-TKP* (17 Dec., 1962), and Sung Hsin-chung, "On the Problems of State Financial Support for Agriculture," *P-TKP* (24 Dec., 1962).

These are paid out of the state budget for the establishment and operation of agricultural machine tractor stations, drainage and irrigation stations, agriculture and forestry technical extension stations, meteorological stations, etc.

(4) Gratuitous investment in the people's communes.

These funds are paid out of the state budget for the purposes of capital construction or production in people's communes or production teams which are labouring under adverse economic conditions, or in people's communes or production teams which have suffered from serious natural disasters, and by this means efforts are made to enable such people's communes or production teams to catch up with the more opulent people's communes and production teams within a short period of time. These payments began in 1959. In 1959 they amounted to 1,000,000,000 *yüan*, and in 1960 to 1,500,000,000 *yüan*.[173]

(5) Long-term interest-free loans.

These funds are paid out of the state budget into special purpose funds and are lent by the Ministry of Finance through the state banks. They are used chiefly for the purposes of enabling the production teams of the people's communes to purchase work-animals, water-wheels, barrows, agricultural boats, fishing nets, drainage and irrigation machinery, as well as ploughs, harrows and other agricultural implements of the middle-size range. The purchase of such resources for use in agricultural production generally possesses the character of capital construction and the loans required amount to very large sums, so that it is very difficult for the production teams to repay the loans within one year. For this reason the state lends these funds without charging interest, and the period for repayment is generally set at from 2 to 3 years up to 5 years, with further provisions for suitable extensions when necessary. The production team may repay all the money at once, or repayment may be made in a number of instalments. The greater part of such loans are made in important commercial foodstuff producing bases, or in areas which have suffered from natural

---

[173] In 1960 direct gratuitous investment in the people's communes accounted for 1,500,000,000 *yüan* in the state budget, and this sum approached half of the amount directly levied from the people's communes in the form of agricultural taxes (Chin Ming, op. cit.).

disasters, and are used in assisting resistance to or defence against natural disasters and the development of agricultural production. These long-term interest-free loans to agriculture were a measure adopted in 1962, and the ceiling for loans of this kind in that year was 700,000,000 *yüan*.[174]

(6) Short-term loans.

These are made by the state banks out of their own funds, and meet the demands of the people's communes and production teams for funds to be used in purchasing chemical fertilizers, agricultural chemicals, seed, and small agricultural implements. The period of these loans is in general one year, and the interest charged is comparatively low. The ceiling for loans to agriculture in 1962 was 2,400,000,000 *yüan*, of which 700,000,000 *yüan* were allotted to long-term loans as stated above, and 1,700,000,000 *yüan* were allotted to short-term loans.[175]

(7) Earnest money paid in respect of advance contract purchases of agricultural products and agricultural by-products.

These are earnest money paid when state commercial departments make purchases of some important agricultural products or agricultural by-products in accordance with state plans from people's communes or production teams which had contracted in advance to sell these goods. This arrangement is devised with a view to relating the production plans of the people's communes and production teams to the state purchasing plans, and to enabling the people's communes and production teams to use these funds in meeting their requirements for funds of all kinds for use in the processes of production. This arrangement also makes it possible to prevent an excessive concentration of payments in respect of purchases at the seasons when agricultural products come on to the market. The recipients of earnest money for advance contract purchases are mainly those people's communes and production teams which supply comparatively large quantities of commercial crops. The advance contract purchase system for

---

174 The account is based on the cited article of Chang Hsiu-min. An article in *Jenmin Jihpao* (22 Oct., 1962) also gives an account of the general character of the long-term interest-free loans to agriculture. According to this article, between July and September of that year 300,000,000 *yüan* had been given out on loan over the whole of China.

175 The account is based on Chang Hsiu-min's article.

agricultural products was established all over China in 1955, when it was used in making purchases of raw cotton and tea. However, there are examples of the use of this system before this date by the supply and marketing co-operatives in China. In these cases it was used on a local or individual basis in arranging purchases of a certain number of agricultural products. Advance contract purchases of raw cotton, as well as of tea, silk and cocoons, ramie, tobacco, and wool were made in 1956. Not only were prescriptions laid down regarding payments of earnest money to be made in respect of advance contract purchases, but the supply of exchange goods or remunerative goods was also considered.[176] We may add that it appears that the making of payments of earnest money in respect of advance contract purchases was stopped at a later date,[177] but these payments were again being made in 1963, at least in the case of purchases of raw cotton.[178]

The funds supplied by the state for the purposes of developing agricultural production may be said to have been supplied in one of the above forms, and, with the exceptions of forms (6) and (7), all these forms involve direct payments out of the state finances.

This being so, to what matters should attention be paid when such funds are to be supplied by the state? The following points in particular are put forward in connexion with this point.[179]

---

[176] For details see the State Council directive on advance contract purchases of raw cotton, 1956, published on the 22nd of December, 1955, and printed in the Tientsin *Ta Kung Pao* (23 Dec., 1955), and the State Council directive on advance contract purchases of tea, silk, ramie, tobacco and wool, published on the 27th of January, 1956, and printed in *Jenmin Jihpao* (1 Feb., 1956).

[177] Ko Chih-ta, " Problems of . . . ." Ko Chih-ta holds that this system of payments of earnest money is undesirable, in that these payments disturb the balance between material resources and currency in the national economy.

[178] For example, a staff commentator's article in the Peking *Ta Kung Pao* (27 Feb., 1963) is devoted to the work of making payments of earnest money for advance contract purchases of raw cotton.

[179] In addition to the sources given in foot-note 172, see also the following editorials in the Peking *Ta Kung Pao*: " Supply Production Funds for Spring Cultivation Successfully " (2 March, 1961); " The Routes by which the Banks Can Give Support to Agricultural Production " (25 Apr., 1961); " Pursue the Agricultural Loan Work in 1962 Successfully " (22 Feb., 1962); " See to It that Production Funds for Agriculture Are Well Supplied and Well Used " (27 June, 1962), and " Disburse Agricultural Loans and Support Autumn Agricultural Production " (15 Aug., 1962). See also the staff commentator's article in the same paper on the 9th of July, 1962,

First, efforts must be made to see that overall consideration is given when arranging distribution, so that a comprehensive balance may be maintained. There are many sources from which the funds used by agriculture are derived—exchequer funds, bank credit loans, and the funds accumulated by the people's communes and production teams themselves. Among the exchequer funds there are basic construction investment funds, agriculture, forestry and water conservancy works funds, and funds for the assistance of the people's communes and production teams. Among the bank credit loan funds there are long-term and short-term loans. Among the funds accumulated by the people's communes and production teams themselves there are expanded reproduction funds and simple reproduction funds. All these funds can be used in agricultural production, but each differs in the uses to which it is put, and consequently efforts must be made to see that consideration is given to a suitable overall distribution which will maintain a comprehensive balance among them.

Secondly, each type of funds must be kept in a separate account and must be supervised separately, while funds must not be diverted from one account to another. This point is clear from the explanation given in the preceding paragraph.

Thirdly, when funds are to be supplied it must be assured that the necessary production materials which are to be purchased with the help of the funds are in fact available. If the combination of material resources and funds is disrupted it will be impossible to attain the aim for which agricultural production funds are supplied. Moreover, it is not the case that all is well provided that the material resources are available ; it is again required that these resources should be necessary for the peasants, and that they should be welcomed by them. It is said that in order to enforce the principle of combining funds and material resources, " Three Combination " meetings are held by supply and marketing co-operatives, Bank and production teams in many areas. In the case of one such type of " Three Combination " meeting a small type of goods exchange meeting is held at which representatives of the production teams, supply and marketing co-operatives and the Bank attend. The supply and marketing co-operatives set out their stock of goods and the production teams choose and

"Disburse Agricultural Loans Accurately and in Time."

purchase the goods they require on the spot. The Bank supplies the required funds and settles the accounts of the transaction on the spot. In another form of this institution state commercial departments combine with the state banking departments to form a "work group." They then present themselves before the production teams, armed with their commodity catalogues, funds, etc., and assist the production teams in purchasing the production materials which they most urgently require at the moment.[180]

Fourthly, the supply of funds must be organized on the assumption that the people's communes and production teams should be self-supporting, and that state aid should occupy a secondary position in their finances. Thus, the funds and material resources in the people's communes and production teams should be used to the greatest possible extent first, and only when these resources are insufficient should the state supply funds. Among the ways in which the state banking departments can assist the people's communes and production teams in augmenting their own funds are the sale of surplus material resources lying unused in the stores of the people's communes and production teams, the recovery of all kinds of debts owing to the people's communes and production teams, and co-operation in introducing diversification into the management of their agricultural production.[181]

Fifthly, the efficiency in the use of funds must be raised by supplying funds at the appropriate time and employing them in a manner calculated to produce the maximum concentrated effect. Agriculture is a form of production which is of a very seasonal character, and funds must be available at the right time. As for the points at which the use of funds should be concentrated, first consideration should be given to the areas which are producing bases of foodstuffs and cotton. Besides raising the efficiency of funds by supplying them at the appropriate time, using them to produce the maximum concentrated effect, and making separate arrangements for the supervision of funds used for different purposes, the supervision of financial administration in the people's

---

180 *P-TKP* (13 Oct., 1962).

181 See Han Pu-kao (Head of the Shensi Provincial Branch of the People's Bank of China), "How Best Can the Banks Assist in Improving Supervision and in Using Funds in the Communes and Production Teams?" *P-TKP* (2 July, 1961), and the example of Su *Hsien*, Hopei Province, in an article in the same paper (17 March, 1962).

commununes and production teams must be strengthened, and the observance of economy, or the management of the people's communes and production teams with industry and thrift, must be enforced.[182]

Sixthly, all plans for the supply of funds must be drawn up on the basis of surveys of the actual condition of demand for funds in the rural areas.[183]

There are two more points which we must discuss in connexion with the above account.

The first point concerns the lowering of the interest rates charged by the People's Bank of China on its loans to agriculture. With effect from the 1st of May, 1961, the rate of interest charged on agricultural loans from the People's Bank of China to the rural people's communes (including production brigades and production teams), the rate of interest charged on loans by the Bank to state farms and individual members of people's communes was lowered from 0.6% per month to 0.48% per month. For loans contracted before the 1st of May and still unrepaid by that date the rate of interest was calculated differently in respect to the two periods. Interest was charged at 0.6% per month in respect to the period before the 1st of May and at 0.48% per month thereafter. In the case of loans from the People's Bank of China to industries carried on under the management of people's communes, the interest-rate charged on transactions between banking institutions as applied between the People's Bank of China and the credit sub-departments remained unchanged. At the same time it was laid down that although there need be no change in the rates of interest charged on loans by the credit sub-departments, if such changes were thought to be necessary or possible

---

[182] As an example of the strengthening of the supervision of financial administration in a people's commune by the Bank, see the article by a correspondent from the Business Office of the People's Bank of China in the Chinnan District, Shansi Province, entitled "The Experience of the Production Brigades of Yüehyang Commune Assisted by the Bank Office in Strengthening Supervision of Financial Administration," *P-TKP* (12 July, 1961).

[183] For examples of drawing up plans for making loans to agriculture from the People's Bank of China on the basis of on-the-spot surveys, see the example of the Sub-branch of the People's Bank of China at Chiangyu *Hsien*, Ssuchuan Province, in the Peking *Ta Kung Pao* (22 Jan., 1962), and the example of the Homuching Business Office of the Sub-branch of the People's Bank of China at Tunglu *Hsien*, Hopei Province in the same paper (3 June, 1962).

by the individual credit sub-departments they might fix their own rates of interest, taking into consideration the standard rates of interest charged by the state bank. They were required to report their proposed new rates of interest to the directing organs in the Provincial (City) or Autonomous Region administrations, and they could bring the new rates of interest into effect on receiving their permission. As need hardly be said, this was a measure designed to promote the development of agricultural production from the economic side. A leading article in the Peking *Ta Kung Pao* of the 30th of April, 1961 is devoted to a discussion of the merits of this measure, part of which reads as follows. " The rate of interest per month on agricultural loans from the People's Bank of China has been gradually lowered from 2% in 1950 to 0.6% in 1960, and the amount loaned to agriculture by the People's Bank of China increased to 6,600,000,000 *yüan* in 1960. The loans made to agriculture by the People's Bank of China in 1960 amounted to more than 50% of the sum levied by the state in agricultural taxes. These large increases in loans to agriculture and the gradual lowering of the rate of interest have given powerful support to the positive development of agricultural production by the people's communes, production teams and the broad masses of the peasantry. When applied to the 6,000,000,000 *yüan* already loaned to agriculture by the People's Bank of China, the lowering of the interest-rate from 0.6% to 0.48% per month makes possible a reduction of more than 86,400,000 *yüan* in the burden of interest paid by the people's communes and production teams. With this sum more than 8,000 standard-type tractors, or more than 300,000 tons of chemical fertilizer, could be bought."[184]

The second point concerns the shift in the destination of the main body of agricultural loans from the production brigades to the production teams in the people's communes. This shift is connected with the fact that whereas the production brigade was originally designated as the basic unit of economic accounting in the three-level system of ownership in the people's communes, the basic unit of economic accounting was later shifted to the production teams. Yen Fangwen says, " Within the sphere of the production brigade, all land, work-animals, agricultural implements and other production

---

[184] Editorial, "An Important Measure for the Support of Agriculture," *P-TKP* (30 Apr., 1961).

materials (except those owned by the production teams or individual members of the communes) are owned by the production
brigade, and all the income of produce handed over by the production teams is also owned by the production brigade in
accordance with the production contract plans together with the
income of produce from agriculture carried on under the direct
management of the production brigade, and the production brigade
carries out unified distribution of whole income throughout the
whole sphere in which it operates. The production brigade is the
basic unit of economic accounting in the people's communes, and
is responsible for organizing the whole of the income of produce
derived from the production brigade, for procuring production
funds, and for entering into direct economic relations with outside
bodies and persons, as well as being responsible for the credits
and debts appertaining to the production brigade. It is for this
reason that the chief recipients of agricultural loans are the production brigades, or, in other words, the loans to agriculture
made by the banks are, in the main, to be made directly to the
production brigades and used by them." And again, "The production teams subordinate to the production brigades may carry
on all kinds of production by side-occupations during the slack
seasons, under the proviso that the fulfilment of production tasks
is assured. Further, the members of the people's communes are
to be encouraged to carry on domestic side-occupations, and to
rear domestic animals and poultry, on the condition that this does
not interfere with the collective production. The enlargement of
production by exploiting the hidden productive resources of the
production teams and positive efforts in organizing domestic side-
occupations among the members of the people's communes are
beneficial for the invigoration of the rural economy, the raising
of the incomes of the members of the people's communes, and the
satisfaction of the economic demands of the inhabitants of town
and country, and at the same time they are wholly beneficial to
the development of a socialist economy. For this reason a serious
view must be taken of the difficulties in the way of obtaining the
funds required in starting production by side-occupations in the
production teams and by domestic side-occupations among the
members of the people's communes, and assistance must be given
to them. In general, loans made to the production teams and the

members of the people's communes should be made by the credit departments of the people's communes. No doubt this arrangement has been made because the loans in question are very small and dispersed, while the credit departments of the people's communes, in their position at the bottom of the administrative structure, are comparatively closely related to the production teams and the members of the people's communes, and are thus readily able to understand their situation and to provide solutions for their problems at appropriate times. When the credit departments of the people's communes suffer from a shortage of funds in making such loans the state bank is to assist them by making available the necessary funds."[185] The above testimony of Yen Fang-wen relates to loans to agriculture in the period when the production brigade was the basic unit of economic accounting. As far as the evidence of the Peking *Ta Kung Pao* is concerned, articles following this line on the subject of agricultural loans were found more or less throughout the year 1961. However, in January, 1962, articles appeared in which agricultural loans from the Bank to the production teams were mentioned. After October, 1962, it became clear that the principal recipients of agricultural loans from the Bank were the production teams. Recently Teng Tzu-hui has written in an article in *Hung Ch'i*: "At the present stage the production teams are the basic units of economic accounting in the people's communes, and the lending activities of the state bank in the rural areas are chiefly carried on in relation to the production teams."[186]

III. The Supply of Liquid Funds by the State to the State Enterprises

Recently there have been a number of changes in the forms in which liquid funds have been supplied by the state to the state enterprises.

First, the fixed-sum liquid funds required by the enterprises

---

[185] Yen Fang-wen, " How Should Bank Credit Work Support Agriculture ? " *P-TKP* (5 May, 1961).

[186] Teng Tzu-hui, " The Historical Mission of the Chinese Credit Co-operatives at the Present Stage," *HC*, No. 23, 1963, p. 23.

in state industrial and transportation undertakings are still passed to the enterprises from the state exchequer through the supervising departments of the enterprises and are then considered to be funds belonging to the enterprises themselves, but with effect from the 1st of July, 1961, only 80% of the fixed-sum liquid funds (minus " fixed-sum debts ") are now passed to the enterprises from the state exchequer through the supervising departments of the enterprises and thereafter considered to be funds belonging to the enterprises, and the remaining 20% is passed from the state exchequer to the People's Bank of China, and the Bank is caused to make these funds available to the enterprises in the form of " fixed-sum loans." Funds in excess of the fixed-sum liquid funds are still provided by short-term loans from the People's Bank of China to the enterprises.

The enterprises have fixed funds and liquid funds. The fixed funds of the state enterprises in China, that is, the funds required on a comparatively long-term basis for use in advancing capital construction, carrying out the technological revolution, increasing the amount of fixed assets, etc., are made up from held-over profits and allocations of funds under the state budget. The fixed-sum liquid funds are the funds required by the enterprises in carrying on production, and are the minimum amount of liquid funds required for normal running expenses, while the funds in excess of fixed-sum liquid funds are liquid funds required by the enterprises on a temporary basis in the processes of production, supply and marketing for seasonal or other special reasons. The specific sums which are regarded as the minimum liquid funds necessary for the normal running of the enterprises are determined by the state financial departments, taking into consideration the conditions under which the enterprises operate, and it is for this reason that these funds are prefixed by the word " fixed-sum."

In China it has been the practice for a distinction between budget funds (or exchequer funds) and credit funds to be made in the funds required by the state enterprises, and these two may not be used together or diverted from one category to the other but must be kept in separate accounts and used in separate ways. These are the principles of " division of supervision, and observance of distinction in use."[187]   In particular, budget funds and credit

---

[187] Cf. the cited articles by Ko Chih-ta and Han Po, respectively.

funds differ on the following two points. (1) While budget funds are of a non-repayable character and are used in meeting the demand for funds to cover long-term normal running expenses in all sectors of state economic construction, the credit funds are of a repayable character and are used in meeting the demand for temporary funds by the economic units. (2) Whereas budget funds are applied for before the compilation of the budget and their statements of accounts are presented after they have been used, credit funds are applied for and received in accordance with plans and are repaid within a stipulated period. Of the funds required by the state industrial and transportation enterprises, the fixed funds and the fixed-sum liquid funds had hitherto been supplied from budget funds, while the funds in excess of fixed-sum liquid funds had been supplied from credit funds. Under the new arrangements, however, 20% of the fixed-sum liquid funds are paid out of the state budget, but these funds are made available in the form of bank credit for the enterprises. The source of the 20% is still the state budget, but these funds have lost the character of state budget funds and have acquired the character of credit funds. We may recall that the long-term interest-free loans to agriculture made by the state bank are of a similar character.

Why is it that it has now been decided to pay over 20% of the fixed-sum liquid funds through the People's Bank of China, when the distinction between fixed-sum liquid funds and funds in excess of fixed-sum liquid funds and their supply by different means had served to maintain the principles of "division of supervision, and observance of distinction in use" between the state budget funds and the credit funds? We would say that this has been done for the purpose of having the People's Bank of China attend not only to the supervision of the funds in excess of the fixed-sum liquid funds, but also to that of the fixed-sum liquid funds. An editorial in the Peking *Ta Kung Pao* answered this question in the following terms. "It is because the fixed-sum liquid funds must first be supervised if one is to supervise suitably the funds in excess of the fixed-sum liquid funds. At the same time it is because the People's Bank of China is the centre of state credit, settlement and cash transactions, and has had close relations with the enterprises since the foundation of the People's

Republic, and more especially since the Great Leap Forward, and the participation of the Bank in its capacity of creditor in the work of supervising a part of the fixed-sum liquid funds will be of advantage in carrying out suitable supervision of the fixed-sum liquid funds and the funds in excess of fixed-sum liquid funds, in co-operating with the supervisory departments in the state financial administration and in the enterprises, and in acting in concert with the enterprises in strengthening the supervision of economic accounting and the manipulation of funds in the enterprises."[188]

Secondly, with effect from the third quarter of 1962, new forms were adopted in regard to the liquid funds for commercial enterprises. Hitherto the organizations subordinate to the Ministry of Commerce (excluding those subordinate to the supply and marketing co-operatives) had received all their liquid funds in the form of loans from the People's Bank of China, but this was now discontinued and replaced in part by payments from the state finances of liquid funds which became part of the assets belonging to the enterprises themselves (described in the original Chinese as 'self-owned funds'). In other words, "commodity funds" are still supplied as before by loans from the People's Bank of China, but "non-commodity funds" are paid out of the state exchequer and became part of the assets owned by the enterprises. We may abstract the main points from the new regulations for the separate supervision of "commodity funds" and "non-commodity funds" as follows.[189]

(1) With effect from the third quarter of 1962 the supply of all liquid funds to the organizations subordinate to the Ministry of Commerce (excluding those subordinate to the supply and marketing co-operatives) by means of bank credit would be discontinued, and in place of this arrangement the state would pay out a portion of "self-owned" liquid funds to the enterprises, and the enterprises would manage their funds under two

---

[188] Editorial "An Important Measure for Strengthening the Supervision of Liquid Funds in the Enterprises," *P-TKP* (30 June, 1961). On the subject of the new measures introduced on the 1st of July, 1961, see Ou Ming-yü, "Why Cannot the Liquid Funds of the Enterprises Be Used in Making State Financial Administration Payments?" *P-TKP* (31 July, 1961), and Yen Fang-wen, "On the Problem of the Supervision of the Fixed-Sum Funds in the Liquid Funds of the Enterprises," *P-TKP* (25 Aug., 1961).

[189] *P-TKP* (3 Aug., 1962).

accounts—" deposit account " and " credit account." Hereafter commodity funds would be supplied chiefly in the form of loans from the Bank, and non-commodity funds would be supplied from the "self-owned" funds paid out by the Ministry of Finance.

(2)   After " separate supply and separate supervision " had been introduced into the liquid funds of the commercial enterprises, deposit accounts would be opened at the Bank for the " self-owned " funds to be paid by the state, and these funds would be used principally in respect to packaged goods, cheap goods liable to deterioration, raw material goods, unpaid expenses, currency funds, prepaid allowances in respect of travel expenses, working funds for the prepayment of wages, working funds required by subordinate non-independent economic accounting units, etc.   As for the sphere to be included in the deposit accounts, it was laid down that this should comprise some of the commodity circulation expenses (such as interest, wages, etc.), non-commodity fixed-sum assets, the funds which had to be paid in to the state exchequers—taxes, profits, depreciation fund, receipts from sales of fixed assets, etc.—as well as some other temporary payments coming under the relevant regulations.   The Bank would open credit accounts in respect to loans from the Bank to the enterprises. The credit accounts were to be used by the enterprises in buying commodities, in entrusting the Bank to make receipts, in making remittances of purchase funds and attendant expenses to outside areas, in making payments in respect to expenses attendant on the purchase of goods incurred together with the purchase of goods, or in respect to the total of direct incurred expenses in such transactions, and also in respect to taxes levied on purchases of goods, etc.

These new measures for the supervision of commercial liquid funds produced the following effects.[190]

(1)   These measures make clear the boundaries between the uses of the different types of funds.   After these measures came into force the Bank made loans only in respect to commodities, and all other non-commodity funds were met out of the "self-

190 Staff commentator's article, "New Measures for the Supervision of Liquid Funds in Commerce," *P-TKP* (3 Aug., 1962).

owned " funds belonging to the enterprises themselves. In this way these measures had the effect of making clear the boundaries between the uses of commodity funds and non-commodity funds, and at the same time ensured that there should be a secure commodity backing for bank loans.

(2) These measures serve to promote the strengthening of planned supervision and economic accounting in the commercial enterprises. In using currency, the enterprises must make advance plans regarding which funds were to be drawn from their own funds and which were to be borrowed from the Bank, and must give careful consideration to this matter in order to make suitable adjustments.

(3) Hitherto only the People's Bank of China had had direct relations with the enterprises, but under these new measures the state financial administration was also brought into direct relations with them, and both the Bank and the state financial administration acquired the power to oversee the enterprises. The Bank was charged with overseeing the day-to-day conditions of commodity circulation in the enterprises, while the state financial administration might strengthen its overseeing work in the consideration and determination of expenditure plans for liquid funds in the enterprises and in ensuring that the enterprises made payments of profits and taxes on time. In this way the Bank and the state financial administration could co-operate in overseeing the enterprises in a more effective manner.

The " Provisions Regarding Some Problems in the Work of Credit Departments of the People's Communes and the Problem of Liquid Funds in the State Enterprises " which passed the 83rd Plenary Session of the State Council on the 20th of December, 1958, laid down the following in regard to the liquid funds of the state enterprises. "All the liquid funds of the state enterprises will be transferred to the unified supervision of the People's Bank of China. The whole of the 'self-owned' funds formerly paid out of the state exchequer to the state enterprises will be made available in the form of loans from the People's Bank of China, and interest will be calculated on these loans on a unified basis. . . . The consideration and determination of liquid funds to be used by the enterprises will continue to be carried out under

214

the current methods. That is to say, the part coming under fixed-sum liquid funds (that is, the part required for normal running expenses) will be considered and determined by the state financial administration on its own responsibility, in co-operation with the People's Bank of China and the relevant departments, while the part coming under funds in excess of fixed-sum liquid funds (that is, the part required for seasonal or temporary purposes) will be met by loans made by the People's Bank of China on the basis of actual conditions."[191] We must add that there is a historical gap between these Provisions and the preceding discussion of the supply of liquid funds to the state enterprises. Source material is lacking in regard to the intervening period. We hope to undertake the work of linking up the two historically at a later date when source material becomes available.

CONCLUSION

We may list below what may be considered to be the basic lines of recent Chinese policies in the realm of state finance, currency and credit, whether discussed or not in this chapter.

(1) State financial and monetary policies are devised and executed in a planned manner from the point of view of the national economy as a whole, and as a natural result the main emphasis is placed on the development of agriculture. This fact is particularly clearly revealed in the policies regulating the supply of state funds and taxation.

(2) The supervision of state finance and credit provision has been concentrated upon the unified control of the Centre to a high degree. After 1958 measures were taken which enlarged the powers of local administrations in the supervision of state finance and tax collection, but recently centralization of measures have again been taken.[192] In the realm of credit-provision the

---

191 State Council, "Provisions Regarding Some Problems in the Work of the Credit Departments of the People's Communes and the Problem of Liquid Funds in the State Enterprises," *Jenmin Jihpao* (23 Dec., 1958).

192 Ko Chih-ta & Wang Cho, op. cit.; Yeh Chin-t'ang, "Centralize Financial Powers, Strengthen Supervision!" *P-TKP* (1 Dec., 1961), and Fan Yeh-chün & Li Te-sheng & Chang Chih-tao, "On the Problems of Centralizing and Unifying State Financial Work," *P-TKP* (25 June, 1962).

powers of permitting credit ceilings and allocating credit ceilings are centralized.

(3) Finer distinctions have come to be observed in regard to the nature of different kinds of funds and their uses, and it is now stressed that distinctions should be made in the supervision and use of funds (" division of supervision, and observance of distinction in use "). Examples of such distinctions are those between capital construction funds and liquid funds, between budget funds and credit funds, and between fixed-sum liquid funds and funds in excess of fixed-sum liquid funds. That is to say, an advance has been made from the quantitative control of funds to the qualitative control of funds.

(4) The execution of state financial and credit-provision policies has been powerfully pressed forward. Taxes due are collected with severity, loans due for repayment are collected on the appointed date with severity, and economy and savings have been pressed forward, while at the same time funds have been supplied without stint for necessary purposes.

(5) The state financial administrative departments and the state banking departments are required to give positive co-operation to the enterprises, people's communes, and production teams in the fields of management supervision, enterprise supervision, and economic accounting.

(6) Progress is made in fitting out the sub-structure and improving its quality (subordinate tax collection mechanisms, the specialist financial supervisory personnel, the bank credit personnel, the credit co-operatives, the subordinate savings mechanisms, etc.).

(7) In regard to the devising and execution of plans and the attitude and manner of work to be employed in business it was required that efforts should always be made to carry out on-the-spot surveys and to listen to the voice of the masses.

CHAPTER VIII

THE DEVELOPMENT OF THE RURAL CREDIT
CO-OPERATIVE ORGANIZATION

INTRODUCTION

THE CREDIT co-operative organization in China is a socialist, collective organization for financial mutal-aid set up by the working masses. Before the introduction of the people's communes there were the following three forms of rural credit co-operative organization in China.[193]

(1) The credit co-operatives.

These represented the most advanced form of credit co-operative organization. They were characterized by having a certain sum of subscribed capital (*kuchin*: 股金), by having a progressive organization for the exercise of democratic supervision (for example, directors' meetings, auditors' meetings, members' small groups, members' representatives, etc.), by having deposits as the main source of their funds, and by using these funds in a manner suited to the supply and demand for funds in the rural areas, solving the difficulties of their members in production and in personal life. In general one credit co-operative was formed in each *Hsiang*, but large credit co-operatives might extend their operations over three or four *Hsiang*.

(2) The credit departments established in the supply and marketing co-operatives.

These co-operatives served the members of the supply and marketing co-operatives, and in general they levied no sub-

---

[193] Ta Wu, "The Development of Credit Co-operation in China and Its Functions," *HH*, No. 2, 1954, pp. 31-32.

scribed capital nor had they any organization for directors' or auditors' meetings, but were operated under the direction of the directors and auditors of the supply and marketing co-operative. Deposits were the principal source of their funds, but in some cases the supply and marketing co-operatives paid over lump sums as endowments at the time of their foundation. In order to facilitate the settling of accounts there was no movement of funds between the supply and marketing co-operatives and the credit departments, and the credit departments kept their books separate from those of the supply and marketing co-operatives.

(3) The credit groups (credit mutual-aid groups, credit mutual-aid small groups).

These were the simplest form of credit organization, and there was some variety in the content of their activities. In their most usual form these groups were organized from between 20 and 30 peasant households. After discussion, the members decided on common agreement to be observed communally among them, and they undertook to make introductions among themselves on a collective basis in regard to borrowing and lending, and to stand surety for one another for the repayment of debts. Others of these groups were brought into being as reorganized forms of the traditional associations for the provision of credit called *piaohui* (標會) and *yaohui* (搖會), and the method of meeting the demand for funds which they generally employed was the following. Taking into consideration the producing seasons in agriculture, a date was fixed by which all the members had to pay in a certain same sum each, and, after discussion, this money was used in solving the comparatively great difficulties faced by one or two of the members, and it was provided that they should repay the money in instalments over a specified period. Further, if the members desired it, these associations might also collect small sums as subscriptions, and might meet the demand for funds by undertaking transactions in the form of deposits and loans. In this regard they were similar to the credit co-operatives, but they were smaller organizations and they had no directors' or auditors' meetings. All these forms were organized on a small scale, and in general they had comparatively few members. It is for this reason that they were called ' credit groups ' or ' credit mutual-aid small groups,' but they were of such a nature that if they were expanded a little they might be made into credit co-operatives.[194]

As effects produced by the credit co-operative organization in China before the introduction of the people's communes we may draw attention to the following three points in particular.

(1) They contributed to the development of agricultural production by linking the agricultural producers' co-operative organization and the agricultural supply and marketing co-operative organization, and were an important instrument in carrying out the socialist transformation of the small peasant economy, that is, in introducing co-operation into agriculture.

(2) By relying on the poor peasants and lower-middle peasants and by solving the problems of lack of funds for use in production and for personal purposes among the broad masses of the labouring peasantry in association with the middle peasants, they beat down the forces of capitalism in the countryside and liberated the peasants from exploitation by usury capital.

(3) They became the assistants of the state bank in the provision of rural credit. In general the mechanisms of the state bank extended down to *Hsien* (縣) and *Ch'ü* (區) level, but the *Hsiang* (鄉) and *Ts'un* (村) had no alternative but to rely on the activities of the credit co-operative organization. For this reason the rural credit co-operative organization was required to assist the state bank in connexion with the absorption of savings and the making of loans at *Hsiang* and *Ts'un* level, and to fulfil the functions of a powerful assistant of the state bank.

In this chapter it is intended first to give an outline account of the development of the rural credit co-operative organization in the period before the introduction of the people's communes, and then to examine the present condition of this organization after the introduction of the people's communes.

---

[194] At the end of June, 1953, the average number of members per credit co-operative was 618. In general the credit small groups had between 6 and 15 members. However, there were some among them which had as many as 200 members (Hua Shu, " The General State of the Development of the Mutual-Aid Co-operative Movement in Rural China," *HH*, No. 1, 1954, p. 17).

I. The Rural Credit Co-operative Organization
Before the Introduction of the People's Communes

As early as 1927 Mao Tse-tung spoke of the importance of developing credit co-operatives in the rural areas. Thus, in his "Report of Observations on the Peasants' Movement in Hunan" (March, 1927) he expressed the following opinion. "The co-operatives, and in particular the consumers' marketing and credit co-operatives, are assuredly necessary for the peasants. When they buy things they are exploited by the merchants, when they sell their agricultural produce they are 'squeezed,' and if they borrow money or rice they are exploited by usurers. They feel a very pressing necessity for solving these three problems."[195] Again, in his report to the Second National Congress of the Chinese Soviets (held between the 22nd of January and the 7th of February, 1934, at Juichin, Kiangsi Province) he made the point that attention must be given to the development of the credit co-operatives in order to ensure that when they had struck down usury capital they would be an ample substitute for it.[196]

However, the actual appearance of a credit co-operative organization in one of the areas under the control of the Chinese Communist régime did not take place until 1944.[197] In that year credit departments were added to the 88 supply and marketing co-operatives in the Shan-Kan-Ning Border Area, and the co-operatives undertook credit business in addition to their major activities. After 1945 credit co-operatives of a specialized character were gradually established in places outside the Shan-Kan-Ning Border Area, namely in the rural parts of T'aihang Area and T'aiyüeh Area. According to a survey made in 1947 the credit co-operatives and credit departments established in supply and marketing co-operatives in the above three areas numbered more

[195] *MTTH*, Vol. 1, p. 42; *MTTS*, Vol. 1, pp. 73-74.
[196] Teng Tzu-hui, "The Historical Mission of the Chinese Credit Co-operatives at the Present Stage," *HC*, No. 23, 1963, p. 21.
[197] The account of the history of the credit co-operatives under the Chinese Communist régime is derived from the cited papers by Hua Shu and Ta Wu.

than 800. However, prices became unstable as a result of the civil war between the Communists and the Kuomintang, and since the interest which these credit co-operatives (or departments) could earn by putting out their funds on loan was not sufficient to compensate for the fall in the value of the currency, by 1949 the greater part of them had ceased operation while the remaining 20 odd co-operatives (or departments) were experiencing difficulty in carrying on their business.

On the 1st of October, 1949, the People's Republic of China was established. At the Second Plenary Session of the Seventh Central Committee of the Chinese Communist Party, held at Hsipop'o *Ts'un*, in P'ingshan *Hsien*, Hopei Province between the 5th and the 13th of March, 1949, more than six months before the establishment of the new state, Mao Tse-tung's report spoke of the basic policies to be adopted on a nation-wide scale after the attainment of total victory. In this report he spoke of the necessity of modernizing and collectivizing agriculture and the handicrafts, and went on to maintain that " we must organize producers', consumers' and credit ' co-operatives,' and organize directing organs for the co-operatives at Central, Provincial, *Hsien* and *Ch'ü* levels."[198] After the new state was established, provisions regarding lines of policy in developing co-operatives (including, by implication, credit co-operatives) were made in Articles 29 and 38 of the Common Programme of the Chinese People's Political Consultative Conference which served as the temporary basic law of the state at that time.

It was after March, 1950, when the civil war had been brought to a conclusion, financial and economic work brought under unified direction, and prices stabilized, that work began on developing the credit co-operative organization. It was at this time that the head office of the People's Bank of China and the federated head office of the All-China Supply and Marketing Co-operatives, on the basis of their experience of running rural credit co-operative organizations in the former Liberated Areas and acting on the basis of the objective development of the situation at that time, set up credit co-operatives experimentally in Ting *Hsien*, Hopei Province, and set up credit departments experimentally in the supply and marketing co-operatives at Ch'ingyüan (Paoting), Hopei

---

[198] *MTTH*, Vol. 4, p. 1433.

Province. With these as the basis the credit co-operative organization was gradually extended to cover the whole of the North China Area and beyond.

The development of the rural co-operative organization after the establishment of the People's Republic of China is revealed in the figures given in the following three Tables.

Table VIII-1 shows that at the end of 1950 there were 103 credit co-operatives, 33 credit small groups, and 439 credit departments in supply and marketing co-operatives in China. More than 80% of them were located in the North China Area.

TABLE VIII-1

Development of Chinese Rural Credit Co-operative Organization (1950-1954)

Year	Credit Co-operatives	Credit Small Groups	Credit Departments in Supply and Marketing Co-operatives
1950	103	33	439
1951	538	542	953
1952	2,271	16,218	1,573
1953	9,418	3,994	2,069
1954	124,068	21,281	2,384

Source: Mo Yüeh-ta, *The Progress of Agricultural Co-operation in China* (Peking, 1957), p. 85.

In June, 1951, the People's Bank of China called the First National Rural Finance Conference and declared before this conference that credit co-operative work was one of the important forms of financial work in the rural areas, and work was begun on establishing credit co-operatives experimentally in selected places in each Province in conformity with the extension of the mechanisms of the Bank down to *Ch'ü* and *Chen* (鎮) level. About this time the federated head office of the All-China Supply and Marketing Co-operatives recommended the cessation of the establishment of new credit co-operatives or credit departments in supply and marketing co-operatives as follows: " The credit loan business by the credit co-operatives and the supply and marketing co-operatives solved a number of problems in production and in personal life among the peasantry because the Bank had not yet come into the rural areas. However, deposits and loans in cash were extremely small, and in general they received deposits and made loans in kind.   Consequently an unbalance was produced, many deposits and few loans being made at harvest time, and few deposits being made at the off-crop season, and at the same time unrepaid loans caused the credit co-operatives to make losses on balance.   This produced a number of serious problems, such as the fact that if interest on deposits was low it was found difficult to get deposits, while if the interest on deposits was high the interest on loans became high and consequently unprofitable to borrowers, and the loan business of the credit co-operatives was directly connected with the question of financial policy in the realm of credit provision.   At present, under conditions in which it has been decided that banking business shall be carried on in the rural areas, it is impossible to fix interest rates in the credit co-operatives.   For this reason credit co-operatives and credit departments should not be established, but the Bank should carry on this business on a unified basis, and we should co-operate with it."[199]   By the end of 1951 there were 538 credit co-operatives, 542 credit small groups, and 953 credit departments in supply and marketing co-operatives (See Table VIII-1).   1952 was the year in which the land reform was basically completed in the new Liberated Areas, and the completion of the land reform gave added impetus to a further development of the credit co-operative organization.   By the end of 1952 the national total of credit co-operatives had reached 2,271, that of the credit small groups 16,218, and that of the credit departments in the supply and marketing co-operatives 1,578.

The above is an outline of the development of the Chinese credit co-operative organization up to the end of the so-called " economic rehabilitation period."   In 1953 China entered the " economic construction period."   In the autumn of that year the General Line for the Transition Period was proclaimed by the Party and the state.   It was made clear that the immediate aim in New China was the building of a socialist society, and that socialist industrialization and socialist transformation were the two great means of attaining this aim.   Further, in connexion with the socialist transformation of agriculture the Central Committee of

---

[199]   Federated Head Office of the All-China Supply and Marketing Co-operatives, " For the Carrying on of the Struggle with the Strengthening and Development of the Co-operative Organization," in *CTCFH*, III, p. 510.

the Chinese Communist Party published Decisions on the Development of Agricultural Producers' Co-operatives on the 16th of December, 1953, and promoted the mutual-aid co-operation movement centred on the agricultural producers' co-operatives. These resolutions contain the following directions in regard to the development of the rural credit co-operative organization.[200]

" The agricultural producers' mutual-aid co-operation, the rural supply and marketing co-operation and the rural credit co-operation are the three forms in which co-operation is introduced

TABLE VIII-2

Development of the Business of Chinese Rural Credit Co-operatives and Credit Departments of Supply and Marketing Co-operatives (1953-1955)

(Unit: 1,000 *yüan*)

Year	Deposits		Loans	
	Total	Balance	Total	Balance
1953	73,885	13,699	75,743	17,210
1954	546,832	163,233	324,968	121,524
1955	2,231,451	608,243	836,180	301,088

Source: Same as in Table VIII-1.

TABLE VIII-3

Development of Chinese Rural Credit Co-operatives (1953-1958)

(Unit: 10,000 *yüan*)

Year	Number of Credit Co-operatives	Subscribed Capital	Balance on Deposits	Balance on Loans
1953	9,418	1,201	1,100	834
1954	124,068	12,877	15,890	9,769
1955	159,363	20,452	60,670	28,154
1956	102,558	28,008	107,869	50,052
1957	88,368	31,018	206,581	56,582
1958	—	41,554	402,608	169,837

Notes: 1. In 1956 and 1957 amalgamations of *Hsiang* took place as a result of which credit co-operatives were also amalgamated. Accordingly the numbers of the credit co-operatives declined.

2. In 1958, after the introduction of the people's communes, the credit co-operatives and the business offices run by the Bank were amalgamated, becoming credit departments of the communes or credit sub-departments of the production brigades, but the statistics are incomplete.

Source: "Great Achievement in Rural Financial Work in the Last Ten Years," *P-TKP* (26 Sept., 1959).

[200] The Financial and Economic Publishing Company, *Collection of Literature on the Socialist Transformation of Agriculture* (Peking, 1955), Vol. 1, p. 35.

into the rural areas. These three types of co-operation observe a due division of labour among themselves, form interconnexions among themselves, and mutually promote their several activities, with the consequence that they gradually link up economic activity in the rural areas with the economic construction plans of the state, and gradually transform the small-peasant economy on the basis of the producers' co-operation."

"The principal forms of the capitalist element in rural society at present are commercial exploitation, the engrossing of foodstuffs, speculation and usury. An even greater responsibility is thus placed on the supply and marketing co-operatives and credit co-operatives, and their efforts are directed towards helping the peasant masses to break free from these forms of exploitation, assisting the completion of the duties involved in state purchases of foodstuffs and other agricultural products, supplying the rural areas with material resources necessary for production and liveli-hood, promoting rural savings and low-interest loans, serving the interests of production in the rural areas, and promoting the development of the agricultural producers' mutual-aid co-operation."

"In regard to the development of rural credit co-operatives, there are at present a number of different forms of these institu-tions, for example the credit small groups, the credit co-operatives, and the credit departments in the supply and marketing co-opera-tives. Credit co-operation of this kind must be extended and improved, and systematic support must be given to the introduc-tion of co-operation into agriculture by causing these forms of credit co-operation to be linked even more closely with agricultural producers' mutual-aid co-operation."

In this way the Chinese credit co-operative organization has developed in mutual connexion with the development of the agricultural producers' mutual-aid co-operative organization and the supply and marketing co-operative organization.

On the subject of the state of the credit co-operatives at the end of June, 1953, we have the statistics given in Table VIII-4.

These credit co-operatives were distributed over the 1,800 *Hsien* in China, which means that such co-operatives had been set up in 44% of the total number of *Hsien*. Apart from Tibet, credit co-operatives came to be established in very out-of-the-way places, such as Hainan Island. The development of

TABLE VIII-4

Development of Chinese Credit Co-operatives at the End of June, 1953

Region	Number of Co-operatives	Number of Members	Subscribed Capital (10,000 *yüan* in Old Currency)
North China	2,303	1,099,615	2,694,782
North-East	279	656,391	1,162,393
North-West	228	46,318	116,162
East China	403	212,076	316,829
Central-South	3,585	2,170,299	4,344,651
South-West	66	59,048	125,381
Total	6,864	4,243,747	8,760,198

Note: Under the currency reform of March, 1955, 10,000 *yüan* of Old People's Currency were exchanged for 1 *yüan* of New People's Currency.

Source: Ta Wu, " The Development of Credit Co-operation in China and Its Functions," *HH*, No. 2, 1954, p. 31.

credit co-operatives was most rapid in Shansi and Kiangsi Provinces, and it is said that only these two Provinces accounted for more than 40% of the total number. Chekiang Province had the smallest number—only two. From the Table we may calculate that the national average number of members per co-operative was 618, and that the average subscribed capital per co-operative was somewhat over 12,760,000 *yüan* in Old People's Currency.[201]

According to Table VIII-1, the number of credit small groups fell markedly to 3,994 at the end of 1953 from 16,218 in the previous year. (This may be thought to be largely due to the reorganization of the credit small groups and their incorporation into the credit co-operatives.) There were 2,069 credit departments in supply and marketing co-operatives, an increase of only 30% over the previous year, but the credit co-operatives numbered

---

[201] There are the following statistics regarding the state of affairs at the end of June, 1953. At this time over the whole of China there were 6,871 credit co-operatives, 14,322 credit small groups, and 2,137 credit departments in supply and marketing co-operatives. The total number of members of rural credit co-operatives was 4,252,375 (an average of 618 members per co-operative), the total of subscribed funds was 87,700,000,000 *yüan* (in Old People's Currency; an average of more than 12,780,000 *yüan* per co-operative. Other figures below also in Old People's Currency), accumulated deposits were more than 170,000,000,000 *yüan* (an average of 24,800,000 *yüan* per co-operative), the balance on deposit was 55,000,000,000 *yüan* (an average of more than 8,000,000 *yüan* per co-operative), and between January and September, 1953, the state lent to the credit co-operatives a total of 188,600,000,000 *yüan*, and received back from them 105,900,000,000 *yüan*, leaving a balance of 82,700,000,000 *yüan* (Hua Shu, p. 17).

9,418, a fourfold increase over the previous year.[202] It is quite certain that after 1953 the credit co-operative was the principal form in the credit co-operative movement. However, this was largely due to the putting into effect in 1954 of General Line for the Transition Period of the Party and State and the Decisions on the Development of Agricultural Producers' Co-operatives produced by the Central Committee of the Chinese Communist Party after the autumn of 1953. Previous to this the main emphasis in developing the credit co-operative organization had been placed on the elementary form, the credit small group.[203] The rapid development of the credit co-operation movement which began in 1953 increased its momentum in 1954. According to an article in the Hong Kong *Ta Kung Pao* of the 23rd of May, 1954, there were in China at that date 26,416 credit co-operatives, 3,608 credit departments in supply and marketing co-operatives, and 23,867 credit mutual-aid groups, and in comparison with the previous year the numbers of the credit co-operatives had increased by a factor of 1.8 and the numbers of the credit mutual-aid groups by a factor of 4.98. According to an article in the Tientsin *Ta Kung Pao* of the 16th of December, 1954, there were in China at the end of the third quarter of that year 71,130 independently operated credit co-operatives, 2,504 credit departments, and 53,409 credit small groups, while the co-operatives' membership numbered 43,000,000 and their subscribed capital funds exceeded 200,000,000 *yüan* in Old People's Currency. On the national average there was one credit co-operative per 3.2 *Hsiang*. According to incomplete statistics credit co-operation had been introduced on a full scale in 48 of the *Hsien*, and in these *Hsien* there was a credit co-operative in each *Hsiang*. At the beginning of a leading article in the

---

202 Editorial, "Develop Positively Rural Credit Co-operation," *Jenmin Jihpao* (12 Sept., 1954) gives statistics of 1953 which state that over the whole of China there were more than 9,400 credit co-operatives with almost 6,000,000 members, in addition to which there were more than 2,000 credit departments attached to supply and marketing co-operatives and a large number of credit mutual-aid groups. The subscribed capital funds of these bodies amounted to more than 120,000,000,000 *yüan* (in Old People's Currency, other figures below also in Old People's Currency), the cumulative total of deposits received was more than 740,000,000,000 *yüan*, and the total of loans made was more than 770,000,000,000 *yüan*.

203 The "Directive for Rural Financial Work in the Second Quarter of 1953" issued by the People's Bank of China states this fact clearly in connexion with the question of credit co-operation (See *CFH*, 1953 Edition, p. 91).

Jenmin Jihpao of the 23rd of November, 1954, entitled "Make Positive Efforts to Develop the Credit Co-operatives!", the writer states, "During the present winter and the coming spring it is planned to develop the 50,000 credit co-operatives throughout China (September figures) into 150,000 credit co-operatives, so that 50%–70% of the *Hsiang* will have one credit co-operative each, and to enlarge the 20,000,000 peasant households at present participating in the various forms of credit organization to more than 70,000,000 households. This plan has been put forward in response to the current demands of socialist transformation in the rural areas." According to Table VIII-1 there were 124,068 credit co-operatives, 21,281 credit small groups and 2,384 credit departments in supply and marketing co-operatives at the end of 1954, but an article in the *Jenmin Jihpao* on the 6th of February, 1955, based on incomplete statistics of the People's Bank of China, stated that at that date there were more than 105,000 credit co-operatives in China and a total of almost 60,000,000 members, in addition to which there were more than 38,000 credit mutual-aid groups and more than 2,200 credit departments attached to supply and marketing co-operatives, and on the national average there was now one credit co-operative to every two *Hsiang*. It was on the 17th of March, 1955, that the Hong Kong *Ta Kung Pao* reported that the rural credit co-operatives throughout China had developed to around 130,000.

It was against this background that the Agricultural Bank of China was opened for business in Peking on the 25th of March, 1955. The duties of the Agricultural Bank of China were those of directing the rural credit co-operative organization and mobilizing idle rural capital on a large scale, as well as making state loans to agriculture in a rational manner, assisting the development of agricultural production, and promoting the socialist transformation of agriculture.[204]

In the draft of the National Programme for the Development of Agriculture in the Period 1956-1967 put before the Supreme State Council by the Central Committee of the Chinese Communist Party on the 25th of January, 1956, the following words appeared. "It is required that during the year 1957 the rural credit co-operatives should be basically established at a density of one co-

---

[204] The bank was caused to close in March, 1957.

operative in every *Hsiang* and that positive efforts should be made to develop rural credit loan business and rural savings business."[205] According to an article published about the same time by Li Shao-yü[206] there were then more than 160,000 credit co-operatives, their cadres numbering more than 300,000, their members more than 70,000,000, and their subscribed capital and deposits amounting to between 7 and 8 hundred million *yüan*, and it was expected that "by the spring of 1956 the establishment of a co-operative in every *Hsiang* will be basically completed." However, the realization of this plan took place a year earlier than the requirement put forward in the (draft) National Programme for the Development of Agriculture, namely, in 1956.[207] At the end of 1956 there were approximately 100,000 rural credit co-operatives, and approximately 20,000 branch and sub-branch mechanisms of the People's Bank of China, and between them the two constituted a vast socialist financial network.[208]

In 1954 the balance of deposits in the rural credit co-operatives and the credit departments of the supply and marketing co-operatives amounted to 45.1% of the rural savings deposited with the state banks, and the balance of loans made by them amounted to almost one-fifth of the balance of loans made to the rural areas by the state banks. In 1955 the balance of deposits in the credit co-operatives and credit departments was 4.6 times the rural savings deposited with the state banks, and loans almost one-third of those made by the state banks. This is the reason why the credit co-operative organization is considered to be the assistant of the state banks.[209] Let us give one example of the overthrow of usury by the credit co-operatives. According to a survey carried

---

[205] This draft late. became the revised draft of October, 1957, which passed the Second Session of the Second National People's Congress in April, 1960. The later proposals regarding credit co-operatives differed from those of the first draft.

[206] Li Shao-yü, "See that Rural Financial Work Supports the Agricultural Co-operation," *HH*, No. 3, 1956, pp. 27-28.

[207] This appears in the speech made before the All-China Conference of Branch Bank Managers by Ch'en Hsi-yü (Vice-Head of the People's Bank of China) published in the Tientsin *Ta Kung Pao* (10 March, 1957). Again, Ts'ao Chü-ju, Head of the People's Bank of China, states, "By the end of 1955, the establishment of a co-operative in each *Hsiang* was basically accomplished" (Ts'ao Chü-ju, "Banking in the Last Ten Years" in *Ten Glorious Years* (Peking, 1959), Vol. 1, p. 401).

[208] *Jenmin Shouts'e*, 1958 Edition, p. 571.

[209] Mo Yüeh-ta, p. 86.

out in the areas covered by the 1,037 credit co-operatives in Fukien Province in the first half of 1955, generally prevailing monthly rates of interest charged on loans among private persons before the institution of the credit co-operatives were between 10% and 15%, but after the credit co-operatives had been set up the activities of usurers were basically liquidated in the majority of the areas surveyed, and monthly rates of interest charged on private loans among the masses were also lowered to between 1.4% and 2.0%.[210]

However, there were still a number of problems to be solved in the rural credit co-operative organization. Li Shao-yü recognizes that the credit co-operatives are a powerful force in rural financial activities, but he points out as being the principal problems still existing in the credit co-operatives the fact that their capital resources are still comparatively weak and not yet sufficient to enable them to assist poor peasants and deliver a blow to usury, that rates of interest on deposits and loans are still a little too high, and that suitable solutions have not been found to certain questions relating to the remuneration and living conditions of the cadres of the co-operatives, with the result that they are being prevented from carrying on their work with quiet minds. At this time the monthly rates of interest charged by the credit co-operatives on their loans ranged between 1.35% and 1.5%, and on occasion were as high as 2.5%. The monthly rates of interest on deposits were between 0.9% and 1%. On the 1st of March, 1956, the head office of the Agricultural Bank of China lowered its rates of interest on agricultural loans, and at the same time directions were given to the Bank to lead the credit co-operatives to lower the rates of interest on loans and deposits by the following margins. Monthly rates of interest on current deposits were to be fixed at 0.24%, on fixed deposits at a maximum of 0.6%, and on loans at a maximum of 0.72%.[211]

---

210 Hsü Ti-hsin, *An Analysis of the Chinese National Economy in the Transtion Period, 1949–1957* (Peking, 1952), p. 210.

211 *H-TKP* (2 March, 1956). We may note that the newly prescribed rates of interest on loans from the Agricultural Bank of China were 0.4% per month in the case of loans to poor peasants' co-operation funds, 0.48% per month in the case of loans to agricultural producers' co-operatives and for the reclamation of land by immigrants (in all the above cases the rates remained unchanged), 0.72% per month in the case of loans to agricultural producers' mutual-aid groups, individual peasants

The directive on agricultural financial work issued by the head office of the Agricultural Bank of China in the second half of 1955 (dated 24th August, 1955) points out that there were credit co-operatives in more than 70% of all the *Hsiang* in the country, and as measures for strengthening the existing credit co-operatives draws attention to (1) the strengthening of the direction of the credit co-operatives, (2) the breeding and training of cadres, (3) thorough carrying out of policies and the development of business, (4) the establishment in the credit co-operatives of democratic systems for supervision and for supervision of financial transactions and the rendering healthy of the same. We may note in particular that in this document it is said that "it is required that the rough proportion of 7 to 3 between poor peasants and middle peasants should be attained in appointments of directors and auditors in the credit co-operatives, and impure elements (from the point of view of class status) must be decisively purged from the co-operatives' membership."

As is well known, the high tide of socialist transformation in rural China was reached in the second half of 1955, and by the end of 1956 the socialist transformation of Chinese agriculture had been basically completed. In 1956 and 1957 the number of credit co-operatives declined in comparison with the previous years, but the subscribed capital and balances of deposits and loans increased (See Table VIII-3). From this fact we may perceive that an enlargement has taken place in the scale of operation of the individual credit co-operative. In the Note to Table VIII-3 it is stated that in 1956 and 1957 amalgamations of *Hsiang* took place as a result of which credit co-operatives were also amalgamated and that accordingly the numbers of credit co-operatives declined, but the amalgamation of credit co-operatives may also have taken place under circumstances other than these.

---

and individual members of agricultural producers' co-operatives (including individual handicraftsmen), 0.51% per month in the case of loans to credit co-operatives and deposits by the credit co-operatives with the Agricultural Bank of China, and 0.7% per month in the case of comparatively long-term low interest loans to credit co-operatives suffering from lack of funds.

II.   The Rural Credit Co-operative Organization
      After the Introduction of the People's Communes

The rural credit co-operative organization was developed as an integral part of the measures for the socialist transformation of rural China. This being the case, did the positive necessity for the development of the credit co-operative organization lapse after the people's communes had been established throughout the countryside ? The Chinese writers reply that this necessity has by no means lapsed. The basis for this assertion would appear to consist in the following points.[212]

(1)   At the present stage the people's communes are a socialist collective organization carrying out the principles of the exchange of equal values and distribution in accordance with labour, and they also permit the members to carry on domestic side-occupations and to operate small holdings of their own as a supplement to the collective economy, under the proviso that these activities shall not interfere with the supply of labour to collective production. At the same time, trade transactions at the free markets take place in the rural areas, and these supplement socialist commerce. Because a commodity economy thus continues to exist in rural China, with the enforcement of the principles of an exchange of equal value and distribution according to labour it is possible for inequalities in the funds held by members of the people's communes to persist in the long term. Therefore, some form of popular financial mutual-aid organization such as the credit co-operative organization is indispensable.

(2)   In the historical period of the proletarian revolution and the dictatorship of the proletariat, that is, in the historical period of the transition from capitalism to communism, there is a class struggle between the proletariat and the bourgeoisie and a struggle between two ways, socialism and capitalism, and of

---

[212]   Feng Ch'un-lin, " Tidy up, Strengthen, and Raise up the Credit Co-operatives!" *P-TKP* (9 Jan., 1963), and Teng Tzu-hui, p. 22.

necessity this struggle is also reflected in the field of rural credit provision. Unless the forces of socialism go forward to occupy the positions of rural finance they will assuredly be occupied by the forces of residual feudalism and of capitalism, and rural usury will raise its head. It is for this reason that at the present stage it is still necessary to develop both the state banks and the credit co-operative organization as the assistants of the state banks.

(3)   Since the introduction of the people's communes the state of the rural areas has taken a turn for the better, and as a result a fair quantity of idle funds has been accumulated by some of the members of the communes and some of the production teams. If, however, the rural areas were to meet with natural disasters or similar misfortunes, some of the members will require funds on a temporary basis for productive purposes or for personal expenditure, and from this point of view also the provision of funds in the rural areas will be indispensable. Further, agricultural production is much subject to seasonal considerations, and it is necessary to adjust the seasonal fluctuations in the demand for funds on the part of the members of the communes. This is one reason why the credit co-operative organization is still necessary.

In sum, at the present stage the credit co-operative organization is still entrusted with the performance of important duties in supporting agricultural production, strengthening the people's communes, solving problems in the personal lives of the members, and in other fields.

As an accompaniment to the introduction of the people's communes into rural China which began in the summer of 1958 the parts of the credit co-operative organization which were located in the areas brought under the jurisdiction of certain communes were amalgamated with business offices of the state bank (the People's Bank of China) and became the " credit departments " of these communes.[213] As subordinate organs of the credit departments of the people's communes, credit sub-departments were

---

[213]   T. Miyashita, *The Economic System of New China* (Tokyo, 1964), pp. 166-169. We may also note that just before the time when the people's communes appeared, that is, in March and April, 1958, it was proposed in some quarters that supply and marketing departments or credit departments should be attached to

established in the production brigades. However, by the autumn of 1961 the term " credit co-operative " (*hsinyung hotso-she*: 信用合作社) and its abbreviation *hsinyung-she* (信用社) began to appear frequently, at least as far as can be determined from the Peking *Ta Kung Pao*. From this it appears that some change had taken place in the form of the credit co-operative organization, and an explanation of the details of this change has recently been given by Teng Tzu-hui.[214]

According to Teng Tzu-hui, on the whole the credit co-operative organization exists at present in the following forms.

(1) The form in which credit co-operative is established in each commune, credit sub-co-operative or credit service station in each production brigade or in one group of several production brigades, and credit co-operative members' small group in each production team. This form is originally suited to the cases in which a people's commune is set up in the area of each large *Hsiang*, and where the four-level structure of the *Hsien*, commune, production brigade, and production team is in force.

(2) The form in which credit co-operative is established in each production brigade or in one group of several production brigades, credit co-operative members' small group in each production team, and federated office of credit co-operatives at commune level. The credit co-operatives established in this form correspond, on the whole, to those established in each *Hsiang* which covered the small area before the introduction of the people's communes.

(3) The form in which a credit co-operative is established in each commune, and credit co-operative members' small groups in each production team. This form is adopted where the commune covers a very small sphere and where no production brigades are established below the commune.

(4) There is also the case of a minority of communes which are run and supervised in amalgamation with fishing areas, pastoral husbandry areas, minority nationalities areas, or state farms. The form of organization of the credit co-operatives in these cases may differ in response to the special situations prevailing

agricultural producers' co-operatives, and in a certain number of areas these were established experimentally (p. 169).

[214] Teng Tzu-hui, p. 26.

in these areas.

It has been stated recently that there are more than 100,000 credit co-operatives in rural China.[215] This figure corresponds to the number of credit co-operatives in existence about the end of 1956. It need hardly be said that credit co-operatives have now probably been established on a much larger scale than at that period. It is said that at the end of 1962 the credit co-operatives had collected 500,000,000 *yüan* in subscribed and accumulated funds, and had received 2,810,000,000 *yüan* on deposit.[216] We may add that since the introduction of the people's communes there has been no mention of the credit small groups or the credit departments of the supply and marketing co-operatives.

As subordinate organs of the credit co-operatives there are credit sub-co-operatives or service stations, and efforts are being made to form a widespread credit network. In the case of the credit co-operative of the Hsiyü Commune, Wensui *Hsien*, Shansi Province, more than 3,400 peasant families were organized in 7 production brigades. Hitherto there had been only one credit co-operative and one service station, and since this was inconvenient for the members of the commune when they made deposits or withdrawals the credit co-operative established two credit sub-co-operatives and two service stations in comparatively distant parts of its area. As a result it was realized that in the commune there was a credit co-operative, in a large village and in a remote part of the area there were credit sub-co-operatives, and in smaller villages there were service stations. This was said to be more convenient for the masses.[217] There are 44 credit co-operatives in Tsunhua *Hsien*, Hopei Province, and each co-operative

---

215 This appears in a leading article in the *Jenmin Jihpao* (28 Jan., 1964), entitled "How the State May Support the Development of Funds for Agriculture." A year before, however, Feng Ch'un-lin said in his cited article that there were between 100,000 and 150,000 credit co-operatives in China. Again, the Editorial, "Carry out a Thorough Tidying up of the Rural Credit Co-operatives," *P-TKP* (23 Oct., 1963) stated that "at present there are several tens of thousands of rural credit co-operative mechanisms in China, and between 100,000 and 150,000 credit co-operative cadres, while their subscribed and accumulated funds amount to several hundred million *yüan*, and the deposits received and loans made have also reached considerable proportions."

216 Hu Li-chiao, "Improve Rural Financial Work and Give Effective Support to the Collective Economy," *Jenmin Jihpao* (11 July, 1963).

217 *P-TKP* (29 Sept., 1961).

has a service station in every production brigade in its area. There are more than 470 such stations in the *Hsien*. Cadres from the production brigades and accountants who are eager to serve the masses are engaged as heads of service stations and service station accountants. Within the sphere of the production brigades .the service stations undertake the work of receiving deposits and making payments in place of the credit co-operatives.[218] We may note that in the time of the credit departments of the people's communes there were credit sub-departments in the production brigades and beneath them savings stations or savings representatives were established.[219]

In the rural credit co-operatives in Shihmen *Hsien*, Hunan Province, there are credit sub-co-operatives in the production brigades while beneath them credit co-operative members' small groups consisting principally of poor peasants and peasants of the lower-middle stratum have been established in each of the production teams. These are made the central force in rural credit and lending activities. The heads of the credit co-operative members' small groups are all members of the co-operative who have been elected democratically, and they are poor peasants or peasants of the lower-middle stratum who carry out their duties impartially and eagerly for the benefit of the masses. These men do not separate themselves from agricultural production, and have the fullest knowledge of the production and state of livelihood of the groups of some 10 households to which each of them belongs. At suitable times they can inform the credit co-operative of the state of affairs in their group, and in co-operation with the credit co-operative they visit the houses of their members and carry on part of the co-operative's loan business.[220]

Feng Ch'un-lin states that the latest duties of the rural credit co-operatives are those of " absorbing temporarily idle funds belonging to commune members and to production teams within the area covered by them, assisting in the solution of a number of

---

[218] *Jenmin Jihpao* (16 Jan., 1963).

[219] In the Peking *Ta Kung Pao* (20 March, 1961) the example of the Hsingnung People's Commune, Paich'üan *Hsien*, Heilungkiang Province, is given, and in the issue of the 1st of April, 1961 the example of the credit department of a production brigade in the Tant'u Commune, Lai *Hsien*, Kilin Province, is given.

[220] *P-TKP* (2 Dec., 1963).

temporary difficulties encountered by members in the provision of funds for the production of side-occupations and for personal purposes, and, when they have sufficient funds, making part of the loans for use in respect to expenses in agricultural production which are of the nature of short-term operations, and, consequently, of dealing a blow to the activities of rural usury, suppressing the spontaneous forces of rural capitalism, and promoting the development of agricultural production and the strengthening of the collective economy of the people's communes."[221] This testimony of Feng Ch'un-lin refers to the latest state of affairs, in which the production team is taken as the basic unit of economic accounting, but even during the period which was considered to be that in which the production brigade was taken as the basic unit of economic accounting it was considered that the main recipients of loans from the state banks were the production brigades and that the main recipients of loans from the credit departments of the communes were the production teams and the commune members.[222] It is thought that the loans made by the credit co-operatives should be used mainly in providing funds for domestic side-occupations carried on by members of the communes or for personal purposes (for example, loans in respect to expenses for small agricultural implements, purchase of foodstuffs, piglets and feeding-stuffs, expenses for repairs to housing, medical expenses, etc.), while loans to the production teams should be made only when there are ample funds, and should be limited to short-term loans.[223]

Examining the state of business of the credit co-operatives, we find that in the majority of these co-operatives the amounts loaned occupy a very small proportion of the total of subscribed, accumulated and deposited funds, and that the greater part of the funds of the credit co-operatives is deposited with the state banks. This fact may be taken as indicating that the credit co-operatives discharge an important function in absorbing the savings of the masses.[224]

---

[221] Feng Ch'un-lin, op. cit.

[222] Yen Fang-wen, "How Should Bank Credit Work Support Agriculture?" *P-TKP* (5 May, 1961).

[223] Staff commentator's article, "The Credit Co-operatives Should Give First Priority to the Service for Their Members," *P-TKP* (12 May, 1963).

[224] For example, in October, 1961, in the 80 credit co-operatives in Ta *Hsien*,

Recently, on the basis of state decisions, the People's Bank of China has set aside, out of the funds allocated to short-term agricultural loans, special fixed sums to be used in making interest-free loans to credit co-operatives, thus assisting the rural credit co-operatives which are in difficulties over the supply of funds in the provision of personal loans to poor peasants and peasants of the lower-middle stratum. Loans made out of these funds to poor peasants and peasants of the lower-middle stratum may be made repayable within one year or within 2–3 years, and rates of interest may be suitably lowered.[225]

Over the country as a whole the greater part of the credit co-operatives are now firmly established, but there are still some which are not in this condition. For this reason the question of measures to strengthen and improve the credit co-operatives has been raised, the principal measures proposed being as follows.[226]

Firstly, democratic supervisory systems must be set up and put into operation. The credit co-operatives can be appropriately run only when they have sunk their roots into the masses, and have received the support, favour, and supervisory control of the masses. The following is the range covered by the democratic supervisory systems in the credit co-operatives. The highest organ of power in the credit co-operative is the general meeting of members' representatives. The rules of the credit co-operative should be passed by the general meeting of members' representatives after democratic debate, and all the important items of business dealt with by the co-operative—for example, work planning, disposal of profits and losses, allocation of cadres, interest rates on loans, etc.—must be decided by debate in the general meeting of members' representatives. The general meeting of members' representatives must be held regularly and at fixed

---

Szechuan Province, there were 306,000 members, subscribed and accumulated funds totalled more than 1,514,000 *yüan*, deposits totalled 12,950,000 *yüan* (comprising 8,320,000 *yüan* of collective deposits by the co-operatives, and 4,730,000 *yüan* of deposits by members), the cumulative total of loans was 4,010,000 *yüan*, and deposits by the credit co-operatives with the state banks totalled 12,660,000 *yüan*. See *P-TKP* (29 Dec., 1961).

[225] Editorial, "Help Poor Peasants and Peasants of the Lower-Middle Stratum to Improve Their Economic Position by Giving Them Financial Assistance," *P-TKP* (12 Sept., 1963).

[226] The account is based chiefly on the cited articles by Feng Ch'un-lin and Teng Tzu-hui.

intervals. The items decided upon at meetings of the general meeting of members' representatives are to be put into effect by a responsible board of directors, while a board of auditors oversees all the business working and financial operations carried on by the co-operative. The directors', auditors', and members' representatives must all be elected from among the masses. The cadres of the credit co-operatives must listen to the expressed opinions of the masses in a spirit of impartiality, and must make it their business to serve the masses.

Secondly, the class line must be firmly adhered to. The policy of depending on the poor peasants and the peasants of the lower-middle stratum is the class line which should be followed in all matters of Party's rural policy, and this class line must also be adhered to in order to bring about appropriate management of the rural credit co-operatives. This means that the leadership of the rural credit co-operatives must be in the hands of the poor peasants and peasants of the lower-middle stratum. Absolute predominance of poor peasants and peasants of the lower-middle stratum must be firmly established in the directing organs of the co-operatives, such as the general meeting of members' representatives, the board of directors and the board of auditors, and poor peasants and peasants of the lower-middle stratum must be appointed to the posts of heads of credit co-operative members' small groups. Landlords, rich peasants, counter-revolutionary elements and malignant elements who have insinuated themselves into the credit co-operative organization must be purged at all costs. When the credit co-operatives lay down lines of business policy, plan lending activities, or put these plans into effect, they must hear the opinions expressed by committees of poor peasants and peasants of the lower-middle stratum and study these matters together with them, and all the kinds of business activity carried on by the credit co-operatives must be placed under the supervisory control of the organizations of the poor peasants and peasants of the lower-middle stratum.

Thirdly, the economic policies of the Party must be put into effect with accuracy. This means that all the business carried on by the credit co-operatives must be carried forward on the basis of the relevant policies of the Party, and, consequently, must be such as to strengthen the collective economy, be advantageous for the development of agricultural production, and accord with socialist principles of credit lending. From this point of view the credit co-operatives must see that their lending activities do not cause the peasants to engage in commerce or other speculative activities, and they must not make loans to individual peasants. Again, when each member of the co-operatives as an individual is to purchase work animals, barrows and agricultural implements in the middle-size range, he should use his own money, and the credit co-operatives are not empowered to make loans for such purposes.

Fourthly, the ideological, policy enforcement, and working levels of the cadres of the credit co-operatives must be raised. Steps must also be taken to reduce the number of transfers among cadres, and to improve their remuneration and conditions.

Fifthly, the organs of the Party and the political administration as well as the state banks must strengthen their direction of the various aspects of the credit co-operatives.

CONCLUSION

On the 12th of November, 1963, the Agricultural Bank of China was established in Peking. This is a specialized bank established by the state, and a mechanism under the direct control of the State Council. The appearance of this bank has a great significance for the development of Chinese agricultural financial policy, and at the same time as the bank was set up an adjustment and strengthening of the credit co-operatives was also put in hand. It is clear that the development of the credit co-operatives is about to be visited by a new stage. This is why it is necessary for us to pay full attention to the Chinese rural credit co-operatives.

POSTSCRIPT

The author was resident in China for 14 years before the outbreak of the war between China and Japan and throughout the duration of the war. He was evacuated from Shanghai at the end of December, 1945, after Japan's defeat. He had had no opportunity of visiting China since that time, but he was able, unexpectedly, to visit Peking, Shanghai, Wuhan and Canton, although only during a period of two weeks, in December, 1964. This visit, after 19 years since being evacuated from Shanghai, produced a vivid impression that some truly astonishing changes had taken place in conditions in China. In this postscript the author wishes to correct and augment a few points in this book on the basis of what he saw and heard during his recent travels in China.

1. Circulatory Notes in the Period of the Hupei Peasants' Movement
During a visit to the Hupei Provincial Museum, Wuhan, the author saw a circulatory note on exhibition issued by a credit co-operative of a peasants' association in the period of the Hupei peasants' movement. In the upper part of this note the inscriptions "Peasants' Association" (農民協會), "Credit Co-operative" (信用合作社), and "Circulatory Note" (流通券) were arranged one below the other, printed horizontally from right to left. Beneath them the vertical inscriptions "One String of Cash" (壹串), "The Sixteenth Year of the Chinese Republic" (民國十六年) and "Huangkang Hsien" (黃岡縣) were arranged from right to left. Huangkang *Hsien* is in Hupei Province.

It appears that this note was one of those issued during the latter period of co-operation between the Kuomintang and the Communists, in 1926 and 1927, at the time when the peasants' movement organized by the Chinese Communist Party was flourishing in the Provinces of Hunan, Kwangtung, Hupei and Kiangsi. If we assume this to be so (and the possibility of its being so is

very great), this note has an important significance in the currency
and financial history of the Chinese Communist Party in respect
to the following points.

(1) It would now appear that circulatory notes of this kind were
the first currency issued by the Chinese Communist Party itself. In the Introduction of Chapter I the author stated,
" We may say that the history of currency and currency
policies among the Chinese Communists begins in 1931," but
at the same time drew attention in Note 2 to the existence
of the opinion that the Chinese Communist Party had issued
currency at Tungku and in the Minhsi Revolutionary Base
in April, 1928, after the engagement at Chingkang-Shan.
However, the circulatory note in question was issued at an
earlier date than either of these.

(2) It would now appear that credit co-operatives had been organized by the Chinese Communist Party at least as early as 1927.
Even if this took place in 1927, the date in question must
have been before the breakdown of co-operation between the
Kuomintang and the Communists. (The Communists withdrew
from the Wuhan government on the 15th of July, 1927.)

In the first Section of Chapter VIII the author has stated
that the first appearance of a credit co-operative organization in
the areas under the control of the Chinese Communist régime
dates from 1944 in the Shan-Kan-Ning Border Area, but it would
now appear that a credit co-operative organization had been
actually formed by the Chinese Communist Party at a much
earlier date. In his " Report of Observations on the Peasants'
Movement in Hunan " (March, 1927), Mao Tse-tung says, " The
peasants must organize co-operatives as a measure for economic
self-defence, and must carry out communal buying and communal
consumption. Further, the government must give support to
these.activities and make it possible for the peasants' associations
to organize credit co-operatives,"[227] and it would appear that ideas
of this kind had been put into effect at once in certain areas.

2. *The Currency of the Chinese Soviet Republic*

We wish to add the following points in connexion with the
currency of the period of the Chinese Soviet Republic (November,

---

[227] *MTTS*, Vol. 1, pp. 67–70.

1931–November, 1934).

(1) In the Chinese Revolutionary Museum, Peking, the author saw the lithographic plates from which the state bank printed several types of the paper currency in the period of the Chinese Soviet Republic. According to the explanation given with them, these plates were lost in Kiangsi in the course of the Long March, and were discovered in Kwangtung Province in 1950. There are plates for the one *yüan*, two *chiao*, five hundred *wen* and ten *wen* notes.

(2) At the same Museum a number of notes from the period of the Chinese Soviet Republic are on exhibition, for example, the five *chiao* note of the North-East Kiangsi Soviet Bank, the one *yüan* note of the Workers' and Peasants' Bank, P'ing-chiang *Hsien* (P'ingchiang *Hsien* is in Hunan Province), the three *chiao* note of the Workers' and Peasants' Bank of the Hsiang-O-Kan Provinces, and the five *ch'uan* note of the Workers' and Peasants' Bank of Southeast Hupei. Although it is not a form of currency, the three *yüan* Economic Construction Bond of the Chinese Soviet Republic is also exhibited.

(3) A number of notes of the Chinese Soviet Republic period are also on exhibition at the Hupei Provincial Museum. Included in this collection are the wooden plate from which the Hofeng *Hsien* Soviet Bank printed a five hundred *wen* note in 1931. In addition there are also the two *chiao* credit note issued by the West Hupei Peasants' Bank in 1931 and the " Water Conservancy Works Loan Note " (one *yüan*) issued by the Hunan and Kwangtung Soviet Government in the same year, as well as silver coins (one *yüan*, two *chiao*) of the same period discovered in Huangan *Hsien*.

(4) At the site of the Peasants' Institute, Canton, photographs of the teaching staff in the years 1924–1925 are exhibited, and among them the name Mao Tse-min appears. According to the explanation given alongside the photographs, Mao Tse-min is the younger brother of Mao Tse-tung, and was head of the state bank and of the Minister of National Economy in the period of the Chinese Soviet Republic. It is said that he was captured by members of the Kuomintang in Sinkiang and was killed by Ch'eng Shih-ts'ai in 1943. According to Kanichi Hatano, Mao Tse-min is the younger brother of Mao

Tse-tung and was born in 1895. He was engaged in liaison work in all parts of China on the orders of his elder brother, and it is said that it was he who first made liaison with Chu Te.[228] It was a discovery for the author to learn that Mao Tse-min had been the head of the state bank in the Chinese Soviet Republic.

3. *The Border Currency of the O-Yü Border Area Construction Bank*

In the Hupei Provincial Museum notes issued by the O-Yü Border Area Construction Bank are on exhibition. The denominations are one *yüan*, ten *yüan*, fifty *yüan*, one hundred *yüan*, five hundred *yüan* and one thousand *yüan*. On the one *yüan* and ten *yüan* notes the inscription " The Thirty-First Year of the Chinese Republic " (民國三十一年) appears, and on the one thousand *yüan* note, " The Thirty-Third Year of the Chinese Republic " (民國三十三年). These notes were thus issued between 1942 and 1944, and, according to the explanation given with them, were issued by the New Fourth Army. It is also said that Li Hsien-nien was a divisional commander in this Border Area. The above-mentioned notes were all printed by lithography, and the lithographic plates are exhibited along with them.

4. *The People's Currency and the People's Bank of China*

(I) The kinds of People's Currency in circulation at present are as follows. These are five *yüan*, two *yüan*, one *yüan*, five *chiao*, two *chiao*, one *chiao*, two *fen* and one *fen* notes, and five *fen*, two *fen* and one *fen* coins (aluminium).

The denominations of one *yüan* and over were issued as follows.

(a) On the occasion of the currency reform of the 1st of March, 1955, a one *yüan* note (bearing a picture of the T'ienan-Men and printed in red), a two *yüan* note (bearing a picture of Paot'a-Shan and printed in deep blue), a three *yüan* note (bearing a picture of Chingkang-Shan and printed in dark green), and a five *yüan* note (bearing a picture representing the solidarity of the nationalities and printed in brownish purple) were issued. These were all printed in 1953.

(b) In December, 1957, a ten *yüan* note (bearing a picture of a worker (male) and peasant (female) and printed in black)

---

[228] Kanichi Hatano, *Mao Tse-tung and the Red Stars of China* (Tokyo, 1946), p. 117.

was issued. This was printed in 1953.

(c) In March, 1961, a one *yüan* note (bearing a picture of the T'ienan-Men and printed in blue-black) was issued. This was printed in 1956.

(d) In April, 1962, a five *yüan* note (bearing a picture representing the solidarity of the nationalities and printed in brown) was issued. This was printed in 1956.

(e) In April, 1964, the ten *yüan* note (bearing a picture of a worker and peasant woman and printed in black), the five *yüan* note (bearing a picture representing the solidarity of the nationalities and printed in brownish purple), and the three *yüan* note (bearing a picture of Chingkang-Shan and printed in dark green) were taken out of circulation. The notes had to be handed within the period of one month between the 15th of April and the 14th of May (no exchange of these notes took place after the 15th of May), and their circulation on the market was stopped with effect from the 15th of April. The two *yüan* note printed in 1960 (bearing a picture of a lathe operator and printed in dark green) was issued at the same time as this measure was put into effect.

Consequently, at present the highest denomination note of People's Currency in circulation is the five *yüan* note.

(II) According to information obtained from the authorities at the Head Office of the People's Bank of China, the branch and sub-branch mechanisms of the People's Bank of China are as follows. Head Office, 1 (Peking); Branches, 28 (a branch is established in each Province, Autonomous Region, and Directly Administered City); Central Sub-Branches, 174 (established in Special Districts); Sub-Branches, 1,961 (established in every *Hsien*); Branch Offices 1,058 (established in street districts in towns); Business Offices, 1,400, and Savings Offices, 6,000. The total number of business premises is 10,622 and the total number of employees 230,000.

5. The Joint State-Private Bank

In Chapter VI the circumstances in which the Shanghai banks, native banks and trust companies were reorganized after the Liberation and eventually made into a state-private bank operating under the control of a Federated General Supervisory Office for Joint State-Private Bank have been discussed in detail, but hitherto the author, whose studies had been confined to the written documents, had been unable to ascertain the exact name of the joint state-private bank which came into being in this way. "Seeing is believing," and this doubt was dispelled when the author arrived in China. The answer is that the name of the bank is The Joint State-Private Bank.

That is to say, the term 'joint state-private bank' has two significations in China at present. The first is that of banks which are of the nature of joint state-private undertakings, and the Joint State-Private Bank under the control of the Federated General Supervisory Office, along with the Bank of China, the Bank of Communications, and other institutions, is included under this denomination. The second is that of the Joint State-Private Bank as a proper noun, and these words are the appellation of the joint state-private bank under the control of the Federated General Supervisory Office.

ABBREVIATIONS

CCYC   經濟研究 *Chingchi Yenchiu* (Economic Research), Peking, Science Publishing Company, Monthly (until 1957, bi-monthly).

CFH   金融法規彙編 *Chinjung Fakuei Huipien* (Collection of Legal Enactments Relating to Finance), compiled every year after 1953 by the Head Office, the People's Bank of China, Peking. 1953–54 Edition was printed by the Financial and Economic Publishing Company in 1955, and 1955 Edition and followings were printed by the Financial Publishing Company.

CTCFH   中央財經政策法令彙編 *Chungyang Ts'aiching Chengts'e Faling Huipien* (Collection of Legal Instructions from Centre Relating to Financial and Economic Policy), edited by the Financial and Economic Commission, Administative Council, Peking, New China Bookshop, (Series I) 1950, (Series II) 1951, (Series III) 1952.

HC   紅旗 *Hung Ch'i* (Red Flag), Peking, Hung Ch'i Magazine Company, Semi-monthly.

HH   學習 *Hsüeh Hsi* (Studying), Peking, Hsüeh Hsi Magazine Company, Semi-monthly.

MCG   滿鐵調查月報 *Mantetsu Chōsa Geppō* (The Monthly Report of the South Manchurian Railway Company), Talien, Monthly (discontinued issuing in 1945).

MTTH   毛澤東選集 *Mao Tse-tung Hsüanchi* (Selected Works of Mao Tse-tung), 4 vols., First edition, Peking, People's Publishing Company, 1960.

MTTS   毛澤東選集 *Mō Taku-tō Senshū* (Selected Works of Mao Tse-tung), 6 vols., edited by Mō Taku-tō Senshū Kankō-kai, Kyōto, Sanichi-shobō, 1952-1953.

SCCS   上海錢莊資料 *Shanghai Ch'ienchuang Shihliao* (Source Material Relating to the Native Banks in Shanghai), edited by the Shanghai City Branch, the People's Bank of China, Shanghai, Shanghai People's Publishing Company, 1960.

H-TKP   香港大公報 *Hong Kong Ta Kung Pao*, Hong Kong, Ta

Kung Pao Company, Daily.

P-TKP   北京大公報 *Peking Ta Kung Pao*, Peking, Ta Kung Pao Company, Daily (Rebirth of the Tientsin *Ta Kung Pao*).

T-TKP   天津大公報 *Tientsin Ta Kung Pao*, Tientsin, Ta Kung Pao Company, Daily (discontinued issuing in 1956).

PERIODICALS

(excluded materials listed in Abbreviation)

IN CHINESE LANGUAGE:

Chingchi-hsüeh Chihk'an   經濟學季刊 (Quarterly Journal of Economics), Shanghai, Chinese Society of Economics, Quarterly.

Chingchi Nienpao   經濟年報 (Economic Yearbook), Hong Kong, Chingchi Taopao Company, Annually.

Chingchi Taopao   經濟導報 (Economic Report), Hong Kong, Chingchi Taopao Company, Weekly.

Hua Shang Pao   華商報 (Chinese Commercial News), Hong Kong, Hua Shang Pao Company, Daily.

Jenmin Jihpao   人民日報 (People's Daily), Peking, Jenmin Jihpao Company, Daily.

Jenmin Shouts'e   人民手冊 (People's Handbook), edited and printed by the Ta Kung Pao Company annually. Published in Shanghai, 1952 Edition; in Tientsin, 1953-1956 Editions; in Peking, 1957 Edition and following issues.

Shehui K'ohsüeh Ts'achih 社會科學雜誌 (Journal of Social Sciences), Peking, Research Institute of Society, Quarterly.

Shenpao Yüehk'an   申報月刊 (Monthly Shenpao), Shanghai, Shenpao Company, Monthly.

IN JAPANESE LANGUAGE:

Ajiya Kenkyū   アジア研究 (Asiatic Studies), Tokyo, Ajiya Seikei Gakkai, Quarterly.

Jinmin Chūgoku 人民中國 (People's China), Japanese edition, Peking, Monthly.

Kokumin Keizai Zasshi 國民經濟雜誌 (Journal of National Economy), Kōbe, Kōbe University, Monthly.

REFERENCES

Administrative Council of the Central People's Government, " Decisions Relating to the Implementation of Cash Control in State Organs " 關於實行國家機關現金管理的決定, in *CTCFH*, I.

Aziya Seikei Gakkai アジア政經學會, *A Handbook of Chinese Politics and Economics* 中國政治經濟綜覽, 1962 Edition, Tokyo, Institute of Domestic and Foreign Political Studies, 1962.

Bank of China (Economic Research Department of the Directorate), *The All-China Banking Yearbook, 1936* 全國銀行年鑑 一九三六, Shanghai, 1936.

Campbell & Tullock Gordon C., " Hyperinflation in China, 1939-49," *Journal of Political Economy*, Vol. LXII, No. 3 (June, 1954), Chicago.

Central Supervisory Bureau of Co-operative Works & People's Bank of China, " Dicisions Concerning State Bank Aid for Co-operatives " 關於國家銀行扶助合作社的決定, in *CTCFH*, II.

Chang Hsiu-min 張秀民, " On the Subject of the Problems of Support for Agriculture by State Finance and the Banks " 談財政銀行支援農業問題, *P-TKP* (10 Oct., 1962).

Chang Liu 章榴, " Federated Operation in the Joint State-Private Banks " 合營銀行的聯合管理, *H-TKP* (1 June, 1951).

Chang Shu-chung 張恕忠, " News from Shanghai " 上海通訊, *H-TKP* (7 Oct., 1951).

Chang T'ing-tung 張廷棟, "A Brief Discussion of the Comprehensive Plans for State Financial Administration " 略論總合財政計劃, *P-TKP* (30 Apr., 1962).

Chang Yü-lan 張郁蘭, *A History of the Development of Banking in China* 中國銀行業發展史, Shanghai, People's Publishing Company, 1957.

Chao Yi 昭毅, " Movements of the Official Foreign Exchange Rates " 外匯牌價的動態, *H-TKP* (26 Jan., 1951).

Ch'en Hsing 陳醒, " The Opening of the Domestic Free Market " 國內自由市場の解放, *Jinmin Chūgoku*, No. 49 (May, 1957).

Ch'en Yang-ch'ing 陳仰青 et al., *Some Theoretical Problems Connected with the People's Currency* 關於人民幣的若干理論問題, Peking, Financial and Economic Publishing Company, 1954.

Cheng Chu-yüan 鄭竹園, *The Financial Institutions of the Chinese Communists* 中共的金融制度, Hong Kong, Union Publishing Company, 1954.

Ch'i Ch'i-sheng 漆琪生, " Financial Policy in the Red Areas of China " 中國赤區の金融政策, *MCG*, Vol. XV, No. 12 (Dec., 1935).

Chiang Chung-ch'uan 蔣仲川, *Illustrated Account of Chinese Gold, Silver and Nickel Coins* 中國金銀鎳幣圖說, Shanghai, Universal Stamp & Coin Company, 1939.

Ch'iao P'ei-hsin 喬培新, " Improving the Supply of Funds and the Settlement of Payments for Purchases of the Products of Agriculture and the Agricultural By-products during the Marketing Season " 做好旺季農副産品收購的資金供應工作, *P-TKP* (9 Oct., 1963).

250

Chih P'ei 至培, "The Correct Direction for the Development of the Private Banks and Native Banks" 私營行莊發展的正確方向, *Chingchi Taopao*, Vol. VI, No.1 (Jan., 1952)

Chin Ch'ün 金群, "On the Credit Work of the Banks" 論銀行的信貸工作, *Jenmin Jihpao* (27 Apr., 1962).

Chin Ming 金明, "Giving the Fullest Support to Agriculture is the Political Task of State Financial Administration" 大力支援農業是財政部門的政治任務, *Jenmin Jihpao* (1 Dec., 1960).

Chou Mo Pao Company 週末報社, *A Handbook of Finance and Trade in the South China Region* 華南區金融貿易手冊, Hong Kong, Chou Mo Pao Company, 1949.

Chu Chien-nung 朱劍農, "The Operation of the Laws of Value in Our Country during the Transition Period" 價值規律在我國過渡時期的作用, *CCYC*, No. 5, 1955.

Fan Yeh-chün 范業駿 & Li Te-sheng 李德盛 & Chang Chih-tao 張之道, "On the Problems of Centralizing and Unifying State Financial Work" 論財政工作中的集中統一問題, *P-TKP* (25 June, 1962).

Federated Head Office of the All-China Supply and Marketing Co-operatives, "For the Carrying of the Struggle with the Strengthening and Development of the Co-operative Organization" 爲鞏固與發展合作社的組織而鬥爭, in *CTCFH*, III.

Feng Ch'un-lin 馮春林, "Tidy up, Strengthen, and Raise up the Credit Co-operatives!" 整頓鞏固提高信用合作社, *P-TKP* (9 Jan., 1963).

Financial and Economic Commission of the Administrative Council of the Central People's Government, "Directive Concerning the Instructions for Implementing Currency Control and Instructions for Drawing up Plans for Currency Receipts and Disbursements" 關於貨幣管理實施辦法及貨幣收支計劃編製辦法的指示, in *CTCFH*, II.

Financial and Economic Commission of the Military Administrative Commission in East China Region, *Collection of Legal Instructions Relating to Financial and Economic Matters in the East China Region* 華東區財政經濟法令彙編, Series I and II, Shanghai, Huatung People's Publishing Company, 1951.

Financial and Economic Publishing Company 財政經濟出版社, *Collection of Literature on the Socialist Transformation of Agriculture* 農業社會主義改造文集, Vol. 1, Peking, Financial and Economic Publishing Company, 1955.

————, *The Significance and Functions of the New People's Currency* 發行新的人民幣的意義與作用, Peking, Financial and Economic Publishing Company, 1955.

Forman, Harrison, *Report from Red China*, London, Robert Hale, 1946.

Government of Japan (Research Bureau, Ministry of Foreign Affairs), *An Outline of Communist China* 中共概論, Tokyo, 1949.

Government of the People's Republic of China (State Council), "Communication Concerning the Abolition of the Agricultural Bank of China" 關於撤銷中國農業銀行的通知, in *CFH*, 1957 Edition.

———— (State Council), "Provisions Regarding Some Problems in the Work of the Credit Departments of the People's Communes and the Problem of Liquid Funds in the State Enterprises" 關於人民公社信用部工作中幾個問題和國營企業流動資金問題的規定, *Jenmin Jihpao* (23 Dec., 1958).

———— (State Statistical Bureau), *Ten Great Years—Statistics of the Economic and Cultural Achievement of the People's Republic of China* 偉大的十年—中華人民共和國經濟和文化建設成就的統計, Peking, People's Publishing Company, 1959.

Government of People's Republic of China & People's Bank of China, "Directive on the Improvement of the Supply of Funds for the Purchase of Grains and Oils in the Summer Quarter" 關於做好夏季糧油收購資金供應工作的指示, *P-TKP* (27 June, 1962).

————, "Directive on the Improvement of the Supply of Funds for the Purchases of Grains and Oils in the Summer Quarter" 關於做好夏季糧油收購資金供應工作的聯合指示, *P-TKP* (2 June, 1963).

————, "Notice Regarding Bonds Issued in Former Soviet Areas and in Liberated Areas which Are to Be Called in by the People's Bank of China" 關於由人民銀行繼續收兌全國解放前蘇區解放區發行的公債的通知, in *Collection of Legal Enactments of the People's Republic of China* 中華人民共和國法規彙編, Series VIII.

Han Po 韓勃, "On the Problems of Maintaining a Balance between the Budget, Credit, Cash, and Material Resources" 論預算信貸現金物資之間的平衡問題, *P-TKP* (22 June, 1962).

Han Pu-kao 韓步高, "How Best can the Banks Assist in Improving Supervision and in Using Funds in the Communes and Production Teams?" 銀行怎樣幫助社隊管好用好資金, *P-TKP* (2 July, 1961).

Hatano, Kanichi 波多野乾一, *Mao Tse-tung and the Red Star of China* 毛澤東と中國の紅星, Tokyo, Teikoku-shoin, 1946.

Himori, Torao 日森虎雄, "The Chinese Red Army and the State of the Development of the Soviet Areas -II-" 支那赤軍及ソヴェート區域の發展情況 -II-, *MCG*, Vol. XII, No. 9 (Sept., 1932).

Ho P'ei-yü 何培煜, "The Three General Principles for Bank Credit" 銀行信貸三原則, *P-TKP* (30 Apr., 1962).

Hong Kong Ta Kung Pao Company, *Trade with China, A Practical Guide*, Hong Kong, Ta Kung Pao Company, 1957.

Hsieh Mu-ch'iao 薛暮橋, *Economic Planning and the Laws of Value* 經濟計劃與價值規律, Peking, Chinese Youth Publishing Company, 1957.

Hsin Yung 辛膺, *Prices under Chinese Communist Rule* 中共治下的物價問題, Hong Kong, Union Publishing Company, 1953.

Hsü Kuang 許光, "The Development and Achievements of Banking in New China in the Past Year" 一年來新中國金融事業的發展與成績, *Chingchi Nienpao*, 1953 Edition, Hong Kong, Chingchi Taopao Company, 1953.

Hsü Ti-hsin 許滌新, *An Analysis of the Chinese National Economy in the Transition Period, 1949-1957* 中國過渡時期國民經濟的分析一九四九～一九五七, Peking, People's Publishing Company, 1962. (Revised edition of *An Analysis of the National Economy of Our Country in the Transition Period.*)

————, *An Analysis of the National Economy of Our Country in the Transition Period* 我國過渡時期國民經濟的分析, Peking, Science Publishing Company, 1957.

Hu Li-chiao 胡立教, "Improve Rural Financial Work and Give Effective Support to the Collective Economy" 做好農村金融工作有效地支援集體經濟, *Jenmin Jihpao* (11 July, 1963).

Hua Shu 華恕, "The General State of the Development of the Mutual-Aid Cooperative Movement in Rural China" 我國農村互助合作運動發展的一般情況, *HH*, No. 1, 1954.

Huang Ta 黃達, *Currency and Currency Circulation in the Socialist Economy of China* 我國社會主義經濟中的貨幣和貨幣流通, Peking, Financial and Economic Publishing Company, 1964.

252

——, " The Principles Governing Bank Loans and Their Relation to Currency Circulation " 銀行信貸原則與貨幣流通, *CCYC*, No. 9, 1962.

Huang Ya-kuang 黃亞光, " Non-Cash Settlements in Chinese Banks." 我國銀行的非現金結算, *HC*, No. 16, 1960.

Institute of Economic Research, Academia Sinica, Shanghai 中國科學院上海經濟研究所 & Economic Research Institute, Shanghai Academy of Social Sciences 上海社會科學院經濟研究所, *Collection of Materials Relating to Prices in Shanghai Before and After Liberation* 上海解放前後物價資料匯編, Shanghai, Shanghai People's Publishing Company, 1958.

Institute of Economic Research, Nank'ai University 南開大學經濟研究所, *Nank'ai Index Materials, 1913-1952* 一九一三年～一九五二年南開指數資料匯編, Peking, Statistical Publishing Company, 1958.

——, *The Nank'ai Collection of Price Index Source Material* 南開指數資料匯編, Peking, Statistical Publishing Company, 1958.

Kann, Eduard, *History of Minting in China* (Bulletin of the Numismatic Society of China, No. 5), Shanghai, Numismatic Society of China, 1939. This work also appears in *The Central Bank of China Bulletin,* Vol. III, No.1 (March, 1937).

——, " Modern Banknotes in China," *Finance & Commerce,* Vol. XXX, No. 12 (Oct., 1937), Shanghai, Finance & Commerce.

Kao Hsiang 高翔, " On the Function of the State Banks in Socialist Construction " 論國家銀行在社會主義建設中的作用, *CCYC*, No. 10, 1962.

Kara Murza, G., " The Economic Policies of the Chinese Soviet Areas " 中國ソヴェートの經濟政策, *MCG*, Vol. XVI, No. 5 (May, 1936). Trans. Shichirō Homma. Original title: Г. С. Кара Мурза, "Экономическая политика Китайских Советов," *Проблемы экономики,* № 3, 1935.

Ko Chih-ta 葛致達, " Problems of the Supply and Supervision of State Financial Funds and Credit Funds " 財政資金與信貸資金的安排和管理問題, *Jenmin Jihpao* (31 March, 1961).

——, " The Functions of the State Banks in Socialist Construction " 國家銀行在社會主義建設中的作用, *P-TKP* (15 Oct., 1962).

Ko Chih-ta 葛致達 & Wang Cho 王啄, " Some Problems Related to the Work of State Finance and Credit Provision " 財政金融工作中的幾個關係問題, *P-TKP* (17 Nov., 1961).

Ko Chih-ta 葛致達 & Yang Che-sheng 楊哲省, " An Accurate Treatment of the Problem of Equilibrium in State Finance and Credit Provision " 正確對待財政金融計劃工作中的平衡問題, *P-TKP* (17 Aug., 1958).

Ko Lin 葛林, *Rural Financial Work* 農村金融工作, Peking, Chunghua Bookstore, 1953.

Li Ch'eng-jui 李成瑞 & Tso Ch'un-t'ai 左春臺, *The Work of the Banks under Socialism* 社會主義的銀行工作, Peking, Financial and Economic Publishing Company, 1964.

Li Hsien-nien 李先念, " Some Problems in the Practical Aspects of Financial Administration and Credit Provision " 財政金融工作中的幾個問題, *HC*, No. 1, 1960.

Li Shao-yü 李紹禹, " See that Rural Financial Work Supports the Agricultural Co-operation " 做好農村金融工作支援農業合作化, *HH*, No. 3, 1956.

Lin Chi-k'en 林繼肯, " On the Operation of the Laws Governing Currency Circulation under Socialist System " 論貨幣流通規律在社會主義制度下的作用, *CCYC*, No. 2, 1963.

——, *Problems of Currency and Circulation under a Socialist System* 社會主義制度下的貨

幣流通問題, Peking, Financial and Economic Publishing Company, 1964.

Liu Hung-ju 劉鴻儒, "The Significance and Functions of Strengthening Supervision of Credit Planning" 加強信貸計劃的意義和作用, *P-TKP* (1 Aug., 1962).

Liu Liu 劉瀏, "The New Bank System in Process of Growth" 新的銀行制度在生長中, *H-TKP* (11 June, 1951).

Lo Keng-mo 駱耕漠, *Problems of the Standard and Functions of the Chinese People's Currency* 我國人民幣底本位和職能問題, Vol. 1, Shanghai, People's Publishing Company, 1958.

Mao Tse-tung 毛澤東, *Economic Problems and Government Financial Problems* 經濟問題與財政問題, Third Edition, Hong Kong, New Democracy Publishing House, 1949.

―――, "On New Democracy" 新民主主義論, in *MTTH*, Vol. 2, 1960.

―――, "On United Government" 論聯合政府, in *MTTH*, Vol. 3, 1960.

―――, "Organize!" 組織起來, in *MTTS*, Vol. 6, 1953.

―――, "Report of Observation on the Peasants' Movement in Hunan Province" 湖南農民運動考察報告, in *MTTH*, Vol. 1, 1960.

―――, "*The Chinese Revolution and the Chinese Communist Party*" 中國革命與中國共產黨, in *MTTH*, Vol. 2, 1960.

Miyashita, Tadao 宮下忠雄, "A Review of Income and Expenditure in the State Finances of the Chinese Communist, and a Consideration of Their Future Prospects" 中共國家財政收支の囘顧と展望, *Aziya Kenkyū*, Vol. III, No. 2 (1957).

―――, *A Specialized Study of the Chinese Currency System—A Study of the Silver Tael System in Modern China* 中國幣制の特殊研究―中國近代銀両制度の研究, Tokyo, Japan Society for Promotion of Sciences, 1952.

―――, "Chiang Kai-shek's Wartime System of Currency Issue" 戰時下蔣政權の貨幣發行制度, *Kokumin Keizai Zasshi*, Vol. LXXVI, No. 4 (1944).

―――, *China's Foreign Trade Machinery* 中國の貿易組織 (Asian Economic Studies Series No. 17), Tokyo, Institute of Asian Economic Affairs, 1961.

―――, "Financial Administration" 財政, in Aziya Seikei Gakkai アジア政經學會, *A Handbook of Chinese Politics and Economics* 中國政治經濟綜覽, 1962 Edition, Tokyo, Institute of Domestic and Foreign Political Studies, 1962.

―――, *Mao Tse-tung's New Democracy* 毛澤東の新民主主義, Kōbe, The Research Institute for Economics and Business Administration, Kōbe University, 1951.

―――, *On the Chinese Banking System* 支那銀行制度論, Tokyo, Ganshō-dō, 1941.

―――, "Problems of the New Financial Order in Shanghai" 上海金融新體制の問題, in *A General View of War-time Currency Problem in China* 支那戰時通貨問題一斑, Tokyo, Nihonhyōron-sha, 1943.

―――"Some Problems in the Co-operative Organization of the Chinese Handicrafts" 中國手工業合作組織の若干問題, *Kōbe University International Economic Review*, Tenth Issue, Kōbe, 1960.

―――, "The Development of Socialist Transformation" 社會主義改造の發展, in Aziya Seikei Gakkai アジア政經學會, *A Handbook of Chinese Politics and Economics* 中國政治經濟綜覽, 1960 Edition, Tokyo, Hitotsubashi-shobō, 1960.

―――, "The Development of the Organization of the Chinese Enterprises Engaged in China's Foreign Trade" 中國對外貿易企業組織の發展, *Kokumin Keizai Zasshi*, Vol. CV, No. 1 (Jan., 1962).

―――, *The Economic System of New China* 新中國の經濟制度, Tokyo, Yūhikaku, 1964.

——, " The Socialist Transformation of Handicrafts in China " 中國手工業の社會主義改造, *Kokumin Keizai Zasshi*, Vol. C, No. 5 (Nov., 1959).

Mo Yüeh-ta 莫日達, *The Progress of Agricultural Co-operation in China* 我國農業合作化的發展, Peking, Statistical Publishing Company, 1957.

Nan Han-chen 南漢宸, " Concerning the Report of the National Congress of Bankers " 關於全國金融業聯席會議的報告, in *CTCFH*, II.

National Government of Kwangtung Province, "Instructions for the Issue of Silver Yüan and Silver Yüan Notes " 銀元及銀元兌換券發行辦法, in Wu Kang 吳岡 ed., *Source Materials Relating to Currency Inflation in Pre-Revolutionary China* 舊中國通貨膨脹資料, Shanghai, People's Publishing Company, 1958.

Ou Ming-yü 歐名昱, " Why Cannot the Liquid Funds of the Enterprises Be Used in Making State Financial Administration Payments? " 企業流動資金爲什麼能用於財政開支, *P-TKP* (31 July, 1961).

P'eng Ti-hsieng 彭廸先 & Ho Kao-chu 何高箸, *Principles of the Theory of Currency and Credit* 貨幣信用論大綱, Peking, Sanlien Bookshop, 1955.

People's Bank of China, " Directive for Rural Financial Work in the Second Quarter of 1953 " 關於一九五三年第二季度農村金融工作的指示, in *CFH*, 1953 Edition.

—— (Correspondent Department, Business Office, Chinan District, Shansi Province), " The Experience of the Production Brigades of Yüehyang Commune Assisted by the Bank Office in Strengthening Supervision of Financial Administration " 岳陽公社銀行營業所帮助大隊加強財務管理的經驗, *P-TKP* (12 July, 1961).

—— (Head Office), *Lending and Settlement for Industry and Commerce* 工商業信貸與結算, Peking, Financial and Economic Publishing Company, 1964.

—— (Head Office), " The Principal Forms of Work Performed by the State Banks in the Year 1951 " 一九五一年國家銀行的主要工作, in *CTCFH*, III.

—— (Head Office), " The Work of the State Banks in 1950 " 一九五〇年國家銀行工作, in *CTCFH*, III.

—— (Industrial and Commercial Loans Supervisory Bureau, Head Office), " Positive Co-operation in Mobilizing the Hidden Material Resources Held by the Enterprises is the Important Task of the Moment in the Industrial Credit Work of the Banks " 積極協助企業調動物資潛力是當前銀行工業信貸工作的重要任務, *P-TKP* (7 Sept., 1961).

People's Publishing Company 人民出版社, *An Outline Account of the State of the Liberated Areas during the War Against Japan* 抗日戰爭時期解放區概況, Peking, People's Publishing Company, 1953.

Raeburn, Duncan, " Chinese Soviet Coins and Notes," *China Journal of Science and Arts*, Vol. XXVI, No. 3 (March, 1937), Hong Kong, China Journal Publishing Company.

Research Committee of Financial Institutions, *The Financial System of China* 中國の金融制度, Tokyo, Nihonhyōron-sha, 1960.

Shang Ming 尚明, " The Achievement of the Chinese Currency Policy " 我國貨幣政策的成就, in *The Significance and Functioning of the New People's Currency* 發行新的人民幣的意義與作用, Peking, Financial and Economic Publishing Company, 1955.

Shih Wu 石武, "An Essay Regarding the Basis of the People's Currency in Marxist Currency Theory " 試論人民幣在馬克思主義貨幣理論上的根據, *CCYC*, No. 2, 1957.

Shoh Chin-wen 壽進文, *Talks about Currency and Credit* 貨幣與信用講話, Shanghai, New Knowledge Publishing Company, 1955.

Snow, Edgar, *Red Star Over China*, London, Victor Gollancz Ltd., 1937.

Stalin, J., *Economic Problems of Socialism in the USSR*, Moscow, 1952. Original title: И. Сталин, *Экономические проблемы социализма в СССР*.

Sun Chih-fang 孫治方, "Let Planning and Statistics Be Set on the Foundation of the Laws of Value" 把計劃和統計放在價值規律的基礎上, *CCYC*, No. 6, 1956.

Sung Hsin-chung 宋新中, "On the Problems of State Financial Support for Agriculture" 論財政支援農業問題, *P-TKP* (24 Dec., 1962).

Ta Wu 大五, "The Development of Credit Co-operation in China and Its Functions" 我國信用合作的發展情況及其作用, *HH*, No. 2, 1954.

Teng Tzu-hui 鄧子恢, "The Historical Mission of the Chinese Credit Co-operatives at the Present Stage" 信用合作社在我國現段階的歷史使命, *HC*, No. 23, 1963.

T'ien Ch'un-sheng 田椿生, *How Should the Fixed Sums of Liquid Capital Funds for Industry Be Determined?* 怎樣制定工業流動資金定額, Peking, Financial and Economic Publishing Company, 1964.

Tōa Keizai Chōsa Kyoku 東亞經濟調查局, *A Study of the Chinese Soviet Movement* 支那ソヴェート運動の研究, Tokyo, 1934.

Tokunaga, Kiyoyuki 德永清行 & Miki, Tsuyoshi 三木毅, *The Financial Mechanisms of New China* 新中國の金融機構, Tokyo, Yūhikaku, 1958.

Ts'ai Chin 蔡金, "On the Subject of 'the Security of Material Resources'" 從「物資保證」談起, *P-TKP* (10 June, 1962).

Ts'ao Chü-ju 曹菊如, "Banking in the Last Ten Years" 十年來的金融事業, *Jenmin Jihpao* (1 Nov., 1959).

———, "Banking in the Last Ten Years" 十年來的金融事業, in *Ten Glorious Years* 輝煌的十年, Vol. 1, Peking, People's Daily Publishing Company, 1959.

Tseng Ling 曾凌, *The Superiority of the Currency System of the People's Republic of China* 中華人民共和國貨幣制度的優越性, Peking, Financial and Economic Publishing Company, 1955.

Tuan Yün 段雲, "On a Number of Problems in the Work of China's Socialist Banks" 論我國社會主義銀行工作的幾個問題, *HC*, No. 1, 1964.

Tseng Ling 曾凌 & Han Lei 韓雷, "The Circulation of Currency in the Liberated Areas, 1948-1949" 一九四八至一九四九年解放區的貨幣流通, *CCYC*, No. 3, 1955.

Wang Chi 王季, "The Change-over in the Banking Business in Tientsin" 天津金融業的變換, *H-TKP* (14 Jan., 1952).

Wang Lan 王蘭 & Liu Hung-ju 劉鴻儒, *Problems of Bank Loans under Socialism* 社會主義的銀行信貸問題, Peking, Financial and Economic Publishing Company, 1964.

Wang Tsung-p'ei 王宗培, "Chinese Banking at the Present Stage" 現段階之中國金融業, *Chingchi-hsüeh Chik'an*, Vol. VII, No. 4 (Feb., 1937).

———, "Chinese Banking Displayed" 中國金融業之陣容, *Shenpao Yüehk'an*, Vol. IV, No. 8 (Aug., 1935).

Wang Wen-pin 王文彬, *The Supervision of Liquid Funds in Industrial Enterprises* 工業企業流動資金管理, Peking, Financial and Economic Publishing Company, 1964.

Watanabe, Nagao 渡邊長雄, *On the Currency of New China* 新中國通貨論, Tokyo, Institute of World Economy, 1948.

Yang P'ei-hsin 楊培新, "On the Relation between Credit-Provision and Agriculture"

論金融和農業的關係, *P-TKP* (17 Dec., 1962).

Yeh Chin-t'ang 葉錦棠, "Centralize Financial Powers, Strengthen Supervision!" 集中財權加強管理, *P-TKP* (1 Dec., 1961).

Yen Fang-wen 嚴方文, "How Should Bank Credit Work Support Agriculture?" 銀行信貸工作如何支援農業, *P-TKP* (5 May, 1961).

———, "On the Problems of Strengthening the Supervision of Bank Credit" 論加強銀行信貸監督問題, *P-TKP* (7 March, 1962).

———, "On the Problems of the Supervision of the Fixed-Sum Funds in the Liquid Funds of the Enterprises" 論企業流動資金的定額管理問題, *P-TKP* (25 Aug., 1961).

Yoshikawa, Shigezō 吉川重藏, *A Guide to Chinese Communism* 中共總覽, Tokyo, Jijitsūshin-sha, 1950.

Yung Sheng 永生, "An Essay on the Functions of Rural Credit Co-operatives under a Socialist System" 試論農村信用合作社在社會主義制度下的作用, *T-TKP* (7 Apr., 1957).

Yü Chieh-ch'iung 余捷琼, "The Monetary Crisis Connected with the Concentration of Silver in Wuhan in the 16th Year of the Chinese Republic" 民國十六年武漢的集中現金風潮, *Shehui K'ohsüeh Tsachih*, Vol. VI, No. 4 (Dec., 1936).

EDITORIALS

"Activize Rural Finance!" 活躍農村金融, *T-TKP* (28 June, 1956).

"A New Direction for Banking" 銀錢業的新方向, *Jenmin Jihpao* (24 Aug., 1950).

"An Important Measure for Strengthening the Supervision of Liquid Funds in the Enterprises" 加強企業流動資金管理的一項重要措施, *P-TKP* (30 June, 1961).

"An Important Measure for the Support of Agriculture" 支援農業的重要措施, *P-TKP* (30 Apr., 1961).

"A Thorough Stock-taking in the Commercial Warehouses" 認眞清理商業倉庫, *P-TKP* (5 Sept., 1961).

"Carry Out a Thorough Tidying up of the Rural Credit Co-operatives" 認眞對農村信用社進行一次整頓, *P-TKP* (23 Oct., 1963).

"Develop Positively Rural Credit Co-operatives!" 積極發展農村信用合作社, *Jenmin Jihpao* (12 Sept., 1954).

"Disburse Agricultural Loans and Support Autumn Agricultural Production" 發放農業貸款支援秋季農業生産, *P-TKP* (15 Aug., 1962).

"Help Poor Peasants and Peasants of the Lower-Middle Stratum to Improve Their Economic Position by Giving Them Financial Assistance" 從資金上帮助貧農下中農改善經濟地位, *P-TKP* (12 Sept., 1963).

"How the State May Support the Development of Funds for Agriculture" 管好用好國家支援農業資金的發展, *Jenmin Jihpao* (28 Jan., 1964).

"Improving the Settlement of Payments for Purchases of the Products of Agriculture and Agricultural By-products" 做好收購農產品的結算工作, *P-TKP* (24 Nov., 1962).

"Improving the Supply of Funds for the Purchase of Agricultural Produce and the Settlement of Payments" 做好農產品收購的資金供應和結算工作, *P-TKP* (19 Oct., 1961).

"Make Positive Efforts to Develop the Credit Co-operation!" 積極發展農村信用合作, *Jenmin Jihpao* (23 Nov., 1954).

" Make Positive Improvements in the Supply of Funds for the Purchases of the Products of Agriculture and Agricultural By-products " 積極做好收購農副產品的資金供應工作, *P-TKP* (22 Sept., 1962).

" On the Strained Balance " 論緊張的平衡, *P-TKP* (5 Feb., 1957).

" Protect the Newly Issued People's Currency ! " 擁護發行新的人民幣, *Jenmin Jihpao* (21 Feb., 1955).

" Pursue the Agricultural Loan Work in 1962 Successfully " 做好一九六二年農業貸款工作, *P-TKP* (22 Feb., 1962).

" See to It that Production Funds for Agriculture Are Well Supplied and Well Used " 切實把農業生產資金安排好使用好, *P-TKP* (27 June, 1962).

" Strengthen the Work of the Specialist Financial Supervisory Personnel and Bank Credit Personnel " 加強財政專管員和銀行信貸員的工作, *P-TKP* (22 Apr., 1962).

" Supply Production Funds for Spring Cultivation Successfully " 做好春耕生產資金供應工作, *P-TKP* (2 March, 1961).

" The Prospects since the Movement for Strengthening Supervision of State Financial Administration and Credit " 加強財政信貸管理以後, *P-TKP* (27 May, 1962).

" The Route by which the Banks Can Give Support to Agricultural Production " 銀行支援農業生產的途徑, *P-TKP* (25 Apr., 1961).

STAFF COMMENTATOR'S ARTICLES

" Disburse Agricultural Loans Accurately and in Time " 及時正確地發放農業貸款, *P-TKP* (9 July, 1962).

" How May the Credit Personnel Be Caused to Perform Their Duties to the Best Advantage ? " 怎樣當好信貸員, *P-TKP* (25 May-1 June, 1962).

" Let the Bank Credit Personnel Perform Their Functions to the Full ! " 充分發揮銀行信貸員的作用, *Jenmin Jihpao* (25 Aug., 1962).

" New Measures for the Supervision of Liquid Funds in Commerce " 商業流動資金管理中的新措施, *P-TKP* (3 Aug., 1962).

" The Credit Co-operatives Should Give First Priority to the Service of Their Members " 信用社首先要為社員服務, *P-TKP* (12 May, 1963).

NEWSPAPER ACCOUNTS

" Great Achievements in Rural Financial Work in the Last Ten Years " 農村金融工作十年來成就巨大, *P-TKP* (26 Sept., 1959).

" How Should We Arrange Credit Departments and Credit Sub-Departments in the People's Communes ? " 怎樣辦好人民公社信用部和信用分部, *P-TKP* (12 Oct.-16 Nov., 1959).

" Rules for the Effecting of Dicision of Work in the Joint State-Private Banks of Shanghai " 上海公私營銀行實行業務分工辦法, *H-TKP* (9 Fed., 1953).

INDEX

270